Garlic and Friends

Also by Penny Woodward

An Australian Herbal (Hyland House, 1986)

GARLIC
and
Friends

The History, Growth and Use of Edible Alliums

PENNY WOODWARD

HYLAND HOUSE

First published in Australia in 1996 by
Hyland House Publishing Pty Ltd
Hyland House
387–389 Clarendon Street
South Melbourne
Victoria 3205

US edition distributed by
Seven Hills Book Distributors
49 Central Avenue
Cincinnati
OH 45202, USA

National Library of Australia
Cataloguing-in-publication data:

Woodward, Penny.
    Garlic and friends: the history, growth and use of edible alliums.

    Bibliography.
    Includes index.
    ISBN 1 875657 62 2.
    ISBN 1 86447 009 7 (U.S.A.)

    1. Garlic. I. Title.

641.3526

Illustrated by Fran Gilbert
Typeset in Australia by Solo Typesetting, South Australia
Printed in Singapore by SNP Printing Pty Ltd

Foreword

He came up the garden swinging some sort of onion by its stem. 'I enjoyed the dish so much,' he said, 'that I asked the chef what he had put in it. "Argentine garlic" was the reply. So, knowing that you were interested in onions, I asked him to give me a bulb. And here it is.'

That bulb has multiplied like the sands of the shore, and has given us much gustatory pleasure. But it was not Argentine garlic. What it was you can learn from this fascinating and astonishly comprehensive book, which covers almost every conceivable aspect of the edible members of the genus *Allium*.

Those who have used Penny Woodward's earlier book *An Australian Herbal* will know how thorough she can be. Welsh Onions, Potato Onions, Leeks, Elephant Garlic, ordinary garlic (of which Australia imports enormous quantities instead of growing it for itself)—all these and many more—species, cultivars, and varieties—are covered with their taxonomy, their history, their cultivation, their suppliers and their uses in medicine and, of course, gastronomy, with an unostentatious scholarship and lightness of touch exemplified by the title. Who would have thought that garlic had so many friends? We hear mostly about those who shy away from it!

Just think what cooks would do without onions!

I very much doubt whether any comparable book about a single group of vegetables has been written anywhere in the world. Chefs, nurserymen, ordinary gardeners and those who make their own pickles, salves and spices will find it a quite invaluable reference book.

T. R. GARNETT
July 1995

To
Lois Woodward
and
Joyce Nicholson,

two remarkable women who by their example, and in different ways,
have made it easier for women of my generation to achieve their goals.

Contents

List of Illustrations

Colour Photographs

Line Drawings

Acknowledgements

There are many people who have helped me with this book, but I particularly want to thank Fran Gilbert for her enthusiasm, dedication and the beautiful drawings she has created; Yoshi and Kazuko Kamikura for their help with the chapter on rakkyo and some of the photographs; Edythe Anderson, Graham George, Bill Hankin, Rosemary Holmes, Rose Marie Lacherez, Mazza, David Nicholson, Howard Nicholson, Dave Pomare, Liz and Barry Potifex and Liz Souter for sharing their knowledge and their plants. Also all the people too numerous to mention who answered my letters and responded to my enquiries. Thank you also to Chris Bayly, Helen Cohn, Sarah Joyce, Gina Reed, Dad and Mum who helped with things as diverse as research, proof-reading, advice, encouragement and baby-sitting, and Tony who helped with all of these at different times. To my publishers and especially my editor, Rose Kitching—thank you too. Finally to Ellen and Dan, who didn't really understand what I was doing but tolerated my absences and the many kilometres we covered with pungent alliums as our constant companions, thank you.

Introduction

Garlic and Friends was written firstly to provide the person who is just beginning to develop an interest in garlic, onions, leeks and other related plants with the basic information needed to grow and to use them, and secondly to give the person who already grows and uses these plants an added dimension to their interest, whether it be the derivation of a name, the history of a plant, how it is used in another part of the world or simply a new recipe. This book is also an attempt to collect together in one place, information about a group of plants which has suffered from huge gaps in readily available knowledge, as well as a long history of confusing nomenclature and associated myths and misconceptions.

The plants described are known collectively as alliums. Edible alliums, and garlic in particular, are currently achieving prominence because of their contribution to good health. Most alliums can be used medicinally and there is a section on the medicinal uses, past and present, of each main group. In the chapter on garlic this section is comprehensive and includes simple home remedies as well as up-to-date information on its usefulness in preventing some cancers and in treating heart disease, chest infections and many more ailments. The medical sections of *Garlic and Friends* were probably the most difficult to write—attempting to understand and put into simple terms the results of recent research. Although I have a scientific background it is not in the medical field, so I have had to rely heavily on the conclusions of the researchers involved and in most cases have simply summarised their findings. Any reader who wants to know more should consult the references at the back of the book.

An important starting point for the medicinal or culinary use of a plant is its correct identification. So every major species discussed has a detailed botanical description and drawing. There is also an Easy Identification Chart (Appendix 2) listing distinguishing features of the main species (and some varieties). Ornamental alliums as a group are beyond the scope of this book, although some have been included because they are also eaten.

Nearly all alliums have a variety of botanical and common names. I have chosen to use the botanical and common names which I believe are the most accurate and least confusing. The rules of botanical nomenclature say that the botanical name given to a plant when it is described for the first time is the correct one to use. Where possible I have also listed others which have been used. A further explanation of botanical nomenclature is included in A Botanical Explanation (Appendix 1). Cultivar names are particularly confusing but I have tried to use the cultivar names most commonly accepted and have listed alternative names where possible.

Obviously I have not grown all the cultivars or even all the species described—it would be a lifetime's work. I have, however, grown representatives of all the major species. For the rest, I have relied on the advice and wisdom of keen gardeners, both amateur and professional, and seed suppliers who answered my requests for information from all over Australia, Britain and the United States.

We are probably most familiar with alliums as ingredients in our food. All alliums are edible (none are poisonous) but some are rank and pungent in flavour and are not worth collecting or growing for this purpose. Some cultures have made more use of alliums than others; garlic has been used almost everywhere, but in very different ways, while rakkyo, an allium with which many readers will be unfamiliar, is very popular in Japan and China. I have collected recipes from all over the world to show the multitude of ways in which each plant has been and can be used. We should be grateful for the accident of nature which gave us these pungent bulbs. What would life be if there were no onions to add spice to our curries, leek soups to warm us on winter days, no garlic in our pasta sauces, or chives or onion greens to add to salads or countless other dishes? Much of life's piquancy and relish would be missing.

Alliums, especially garlic, leeks and onions, were also an essential part of the diet of early civilisations. Their rich history reflects this and the history of each plant is discussed in the book. One of the earliest references comes from Egypt in about 2500 BC during the building of the Great Pyramid of Cheops at Gizeh. According to a memorial plaque placed on the pyramid and translated for the Greek historian Herodotus, 1600 talents of silver were spent on radishes, onions and garlic to feed the workers. Some historians suggest, though, that Herodotus' guide was not capable of translating the inscription and made it up. The plaque no longer exists but other records show that all three of the vegetables mentioned were in use in Egypt at about this time, so it is fair to suppose that they were also eaten by the workers.

Onions, leeks and garlic were also widely available during biblical times. In the account of the exodus of the Israelites from Egypt (1500 BC), the Children of Israel complain that they 'remember the fish we used to eat in Egypt, the cucumbers, the melons, the leeks, the onions and the garlic . . .'.

By the 1st century AD both wild and cultivated species of alliums could be found on every continent except Australia and Antarctica and in nearly every country in the northern hemisphere. Charlemagne, king of the Franks and Roman Emperor (AD 742–814), mentioned chives, onions, leeks, shallots and garlic in a list of plants to be included in his famous *Capitulare de Villis* (Decree Concerning Towns). The list was probably a selection of the most desirable plants that could or should be grown within the Carolingian Empire. A bit later (about 1080) and not far away, the Arab botanist Ibn Bassal was writing his *Book of Agriculture*. Among the root vegetables he discusses are leeks, garlic and spring onions.

Onions, leeks, chives and garlic are all listed by the English herbalist John Gerard in *The Herbal or General History of Plants* (1597), along with more than 30 salad herbs in general use in England in the 1500s.

Alliums have appeared again and again in the writings of all cultures, right up to the present day. The recurrent theme is that edible alliums are indispensable in cooking and medicine, but the smell presents everyone who consumes them with something of a social dilemma.

Xenophon, the Athenian gentleman and soldier, exemplified the mixed feelings that existed towards onions and garlic even as long ago as 400 BC. In his *Memoirs of Socrates and The Symposium* Charmides says, 'Niceratus is set on going home smelling of onions, so as to convince his wife that nobody would even have thought of kissing him'. Socrates argues 'Onion does really seem to be a kind of relish, because it adds pleasure not only to food, but to drink too', but Callias retorts, 'It's all right for a soldier going into action to munch an onion first, just as some people feed their cocks on garlic before they set them on to fight; but we are presumably planning to give somebody a kiss, not to start a battle.'

Much later, in his poem *The Canterbury Tales* (1390s) Geoffrey Chaucer described the Somonour (a constable of the ecclesiastical court) in very unflattering terms:

> Wel loved he garleek, oynons, and eek lekes,
> And for to drinken strong wyn, reed as blood

William Shakespeare confirmed this attitude in the 1500s. In *A Midsummer Night's Dream*, Bottom advises:

> And, most dear actors, eat no onions nor garlic,
> for we are to utter sweet breath;

Also from around this time, a popular jingle of unknown origin suggests an unusual solution to the problem of the smell:

> If leeks you like but do their smell disleek
> Eate onyons and you shall not smelle the leeke.
> If you of onyons would the scent expelle,
> Eate garlicke, that shalle drowne the onyon's smelle.

While the Irish author Jonathan Swift, writing in the early 1700s proposed a more practical solution:

> But lest your kissing should be spoil'd
> Your onions must be thorough boil'd

The research for *Garlic and Friends* has not only involved extensive reading of botanical texts, but has also found me immersed in historical, sociological and anthropological books, journals and scientific papers. Discovering the part that alliums have played in the history, religion and folklore of many cultures has been a fascinating search and is a large part of their attraction. Now as I kneel in the garden pulling out the odd weed near the garlic, I think of Alexander the Great and his armies marching to victory on a diet which included garlic and onions, the Egyptians deifying the humble onion and the German miners wearing bulbs of victory root (*A. victorialis*) to protect them from the evil spirits found underground.

1. Garlic

Derivation of Names

THE GENERIC NAME *ALLIUM* WAS THE ORIGINAL LATIN NAME FOR GARLIC. BY THE time the Swedish botanist, Carolus Linnaeus, established his classification of plants (1753), the term *allium* was being used as the botanical name, derived from the vernacular of the time—the same source can be seen for the common names in French, Italian and Spanish. The specific name, *sativum*, is also derived from Latin and means cultivated, pointing to the very early domestication of this plant.

The common name, garlic, comes from the Anglo-Saxon *gar*, a lance, and *leac*, a pot herb, and refers to the spear-shaped leaves. The name treacle, as in churl's treacle and poor man's treacle, is derived from *theriac*, meaning cure-all or antidote.

Top-setting garlic is a form of garlic about which botanists disagree. Some believe that it should be classified as a different sub-species from the softneck garlics—others see them all as the same species. This book treats them all as cultivars of the one species, *Allium sativum*. Top-setting garlic is widely grown and used and has a number of common names in different languages.

Rocambole is the name often applied to forms of top-setting garlic with a coiled flower stem. This name probably comes from the Danish *rochen*, or rock, and *bolle*, or bulb. An alternative botanical name is also sometimes used for rocambole garlic—*Allium sativum* var. *ophioscorodon*. This name sets rocambole apart as a different variety. *Ophis* is Greek for snake and *skorodon* Greek for garlic.

Other common names refer to either its snake-like scape or the countries where it is grown. The common names rocambole and serpent's garlic have also been used in the past for *Allium scorodoprasum*. This is no longer considered to be correct (see Ch. 11).

Allium sativum

Other Common Names

Aglio—Italian
Ail commun—French
Ajo—Spanish
Bawang puteh or Bawang putih—Indonesian and Malaysian
Churl's treacle or Clown's treacle—Old English
Chyet-thon-phew—Burmese
Knoblauch—German
Knoflook—Dutch
Krathiem—Thai
Lashuna, Lasan, Lassoon or Luson—Indian
Mahoushouda—Sanskrit
Ninniku—Japanese
Poor man's treacle
Sarimsak—Turkish
Schoum or Shumim—Hebrew
Seer—Afghan
Sekhdor—Armenian
Sir—Iranian
Skortho—Greek
Suan or Suen tau—Chinese
Sudulunu—Sinhalese
Thoum, Toom or Tum—Arabic
Toi—Vietnamese
Vellaypoondoo—Tamil

Top-setting Garlic

Aglio d'India, Aglio di Spagna, Aglio romana—Italian
Echalote d'Espagne—French
Ophio garlic
Rocambola—Italian
Rocambole—French
Rochenbolle—Danish
Schlangenknoblauch—German
Serpent's garlic
Spanish garlic
Viper's garlicke

1

Distribution

Garlic has been in cultivation for so long that it is difficult to trace its ancestors. One possibility is *Allium longicuspis*, which is a native of the mountainous regions of central Asia. There is no doubt that garlic's ancestor came from the deep gullies of this remote region, but there is no certainty about the exact ancestor. A recently developed technique which 'paints' plant DNA may help to trace this, as well as the ancestors of other crop plants.

Garlic was carried along ancient trade routes, spreading east through China, and west to Egypt and the rest of northern Africa. Eventually it found its way to Europe, and from there it was taken to other more remote corners of the globe by colonists and seafarers. It is now cultivated in most countries, either in the home garden or commercially.

History

The earliest indications of the use of garlic have been found in Egyptian cemeteries. They are clay models of what seem to be garlic bulbs—the clay in the models has been dated to as early as 3750 BC. During the time of the Pharaohs (starting about 2500 BC), garlic was fed to the labourers who built the pyramids to maintain their strength. A compilation of Egyptian medical texts known as the *Codex Ebers* (about 1550 BC) includes 20 or so garlic-based remedies for ailments ranging from headaches to throat tumors. And when Tutankhamen's tomb was discovered in 1922, among the artefacts rescued were six cloves of dried but perfect garlic, dating from 1500 BC. Although ancient Egyptians used garlic in food, medicine and religious ceremonies, it was never represented in tomb paintings. This is possibly because—unlike onions—it was not regarded as worthy of worship. It seems that even 2500 years ago garlic generated mixed reactions.

Garlic was also used in Ancient China. It is mentioned in the *Calendar of the Hsia*, parts of which date back to 2000 BC. The Chinese word for garlic, *suan*, is written with a single character, indicating its use in the formative days of the Chinese language and suggesting a very early introduction. It has been used in China as both medicine and food ever since.

In the Indian medical treatise, *Caraka-Samihita* (about the 1st century AD), garlic is listed as a remedy for numerous ailments, including being good for the eyes, the heart (as a stimulant) and the joints and muscles (as an anti-rheumatic). Another manuscript, from AD 350, describes Indian medical traditions dating back to the 1st century—the first part of this deals entirely with garlic.

Ancient Greeks were also well aware of the many ways in which garlic could be used. It was praised by some and despised by others, who saw it as a sign of vulgarity. The comic dramatist Aristophanes (about 400 BC) made humorous references to it in his plays. Aristotle, the great physician and scientist (384–322 BC), described it as a tonic. Pedanius Dioscorides, the physician and pharmacologist, and author of the much quoted and copied *De Materia Medica* (AD 40–90), called garlic *skorodon hemeron* and believed it to be the cure for all manner of ailments. Galen, the Greek physician who practised mainly in Rome (AD 129–199) and whose patients included emperors of the time, prescribed garlic frequently and called it 'heal all'. On the other hand, people who had eaten garlic were refused entry to the temples of the ancient Greek and Asian goddess Cybele.

Garlic has been cultivated and naturalised since these times and is still used in both cooking and medicine in Greece and Italy. However, like the Greeks, the Italians had mixed reactions to this infamous allium. Aristocratic Romans refrained from eating garlic, detesting its strong odour. But they did feed it to their soldiers, labourers and game-cocks, believing it imparted strength, stamina and courage. Carbonised flattened cloves of garlic were found in the remains of Pompeii, an Italian city which was destroyed in AD 79 by the volcanic eruption of Vesuvius.

Probably the most extreme reaction to garlic comes in 'The Purveyor's Story' from *The Thousand and One Nights*:

> A young man partook of a dish containing garlic; when he went to his bride,
> she ordered him to be bound, and cut off his two thumbs and two great toes. . .
> Ever after this he washed his hands 120 times with alkali and soap after
> partaking of garlic in a ragout.

Alfonso XI of Castile and Leon (1311–1350), also known as Alfonso the Just, disliked garlic intensely and founded an order of chivalry whose members were forbidden the consumption of garlic. A later Spanish ruler, Isabella the Catholic (1451–1504), also reviled garlic to the extent that she refused to consume plants that had been grown near it.

Garlic was often carried to give the wearer protection against infectious diseases and was used widely during the Great Plague of 1665. Doctor Felix Bremand, writing in the 1500s, noted that certain people, especially doctors, 'condemned themselves to constant carrying of several cloves of garlic in their pockets to protect themselves, and their patients, from the bad air of epidemic diseases'. It was also grown in medieval gardens and often used to mask the flavour of rotten meat.

The Romans were probably responsible for introducing garlic to Britain. In 1609, Sir John Harrington encapsulated popular opinion in his *The Englishman's Doctor*:

> Garlic then have power to save from death
> Bear with it though it makes unsavoury breath,
> And scorn not garlic like some that think
> It only maketh men wink and drink and stink.

According to Margaret Visser in *Much Depends on Dinner* (1986), the Finns, Icelanders, Irish, Norse and Scots used to flavour butter heavily with garlic,

A rocambole plant just beginning to show the distinctive twist in the flower stem.

pack it into wooden barrels and bury it in peat bogs. This was not only to preserve it for later use—because the cool, anaerobic acidic qualities of the bog prevented putrification, as did the antiseptic garlic—but also because butter was a precious commodity and burying it protected it from robbers or enemies. Barrels which were buried in the 1600s and 1700s are still being dug up today and the butter is well preserved—although more like cheese and grey in colour.

By Elizabethan times (1558–1603) the term 'garlic-eater' denoted low social status, later becoming a derogatory expression used by the English for foreigners. British astrologer and physician, Nicholas Culpeper (1600s), listed the uses of garlic:

> It helpeth the bitings of mad dogs; killeth worms in children; purgeth the head; easeth pain in the ears and is a remedy for any plague, sore, or foul ulcer.

But warned that:

> Its heat is very vehement . . . it will attenuate the humours, and send up strong fancies, and as many strange visions to the head: therefore let it be taken inwardly with great moderation: outwardly you may make more bold with it.

Garlic was widely used in Britain up until the late 1700s. It experienced a lull in popularity in the 1800s—despite Louis Pasteur's discovery that it killed bacteria, documented in 1858. Mrs Beeton, well-known author of the *Book of Household Management* (1861), thought the flavour of garlic alien to the English palate. And in 1870 the medical publication, *The Practitioner*, described it as one of several remedies 'now obsolete amongst physicians'. However, its usefulness was soon recognised again, this time when its antiseptic properties came to the fore—on the battle fields of World War I. The raw juice of garlic was diluted with water and applied with sterile sphagnum moss as a bandage. In Britain garlic was still seen mainly as a food of Mediterranean countries. During World War II, Charles Fraser-Smith—the civil servant who made gadgets to help escaping prisoners and agents working behind enemy lines—persuaded a British chocolate manufacturer to add garlic to their product so that agents dropped into France or Spain could eat the chocolate and acquire the appropriate odour.

Garlic was taken to the Americas by the Spanish, Portuguese and French. Cortez was recorded as having eaten it in Mexico and the Spanish Jesuit missionary José de Acosta (1539–1600) described the Peruvian Indians as 'esteeming garlike above all the roots of Europe'.

Two 'Garlick' plants, along with fruit trees and other herbs, landed in Australia with the first fleet. There is no record of whether these particular plants survived, but certainly garlic was described in nursery catalogues in the 1850s.

Whole garlic bulb.

The popularity of garlic in Australia, the British Isles, New Zealand and the United States has increased with immigration, and the increased consumption of Mediterranean and Asian-style foods in the last 20 years, but it is still most popular in southern Europe and Asia. In the British Isles, the main garlic growing region is the Isle of Wight. The original bulbs grown here were selected from wild strains found in the mountainous regions of France. However, the bulk of the garlic comsumed in the British Isles today is imported—mainly from Argentina, France, Spain and the United States.

Diagrammatic cross-section of (*top*) the leaf and (*bottom*) the scape.

American production of garlic at the end of the 1980s was estimated by the United Nations Food and Agriculture Organisation to be in excess of 2,315,000 tonnes. Much of this is exported, but the popularity of garlic inside the United States is definitely increasing. In 1993 more than 5000 people attended the Hudson Valley Garlic Festival (one of several held each year). Garlic flavoured food at this festival ranged from simple roasted cloves to garlic flavoured ice-cream. Australians consume around 3000 tonnes of garlic a year, about two-thirds of which is imported—mostly from China and the United States.

It can be seen from this brief account that garlic has a long and colourful history. Its mixed reception continues today. The great French chef, Louis Diat, who first created Vichyssoise soup for the Ritz-Carlton in New York, said that garlic 'is as important to our existence as earth, air, fire and water'. He went on to say that without garlic life would no longer be tolerable. In contrast, until fairly recently in parts of Indiana, it was illegal to travel on public transport within four hours of having eaten garlic!

Botanical Description

Garlic is a perennial which is usually grown as an annual. A typical garlic plant consists of a compound bulb made up of smaller cloves. They are called cloves from the word *cleave*, which means both to cling together and to divide along natural lines. Individual cloves are made up of two leaves, one of which forms the protective papery outer skin. The other, which is a storage leaf, thickens to form the storage structure and accounts for nearly all of its bulk. The number, flavour, colour, shape and arrangement of these cloves vary enormously among the different cultivars.

The leaves are flat, linear, grey-green and longitudinally folded, with a keel on the lower surface. Six to twelve of them grow from a central stalk and are widely spaced. The ultimate height of the plant varies from 25–120 cm (10 in–4 ft) depending on whether the plant produces a flower stalk or not. Leaves of top-setting cultivars are often more blue-green than the softneck cultivars.

The bulb develops very little in the first few months—all the growth is in the root system and leaves. But as day lengths begin to increase and temperatures rise, the plant will put most of its energy into the developing bulb.

As the weather warms, the bulbs begin to mature and ripen, and the leaves wither and yellow—they are now ready to harvest. If the bulbs are left in the ground, the cloves will begin to shoot and produce new plants the following season.

If the garlic cloves are planted too late, if they are too small, or if the weather is too damp, then instead of a bulb consisting of numerous cloves being produced, a single small solid clove—usually called a 'round'—will be produced. These rounds are much smaller than those produced by elephant garlic, *A. ampeloprasum* (Ampeloprasum Group). If rounds are replanted, they should produce the usual composite bulb with cloves the

A rocambole flower head showing the distinctive coil in the stem.

Softneck garlic, *Allium sativum*, about two weeks before it is ready to harvest.

0 1 2 3 4 5

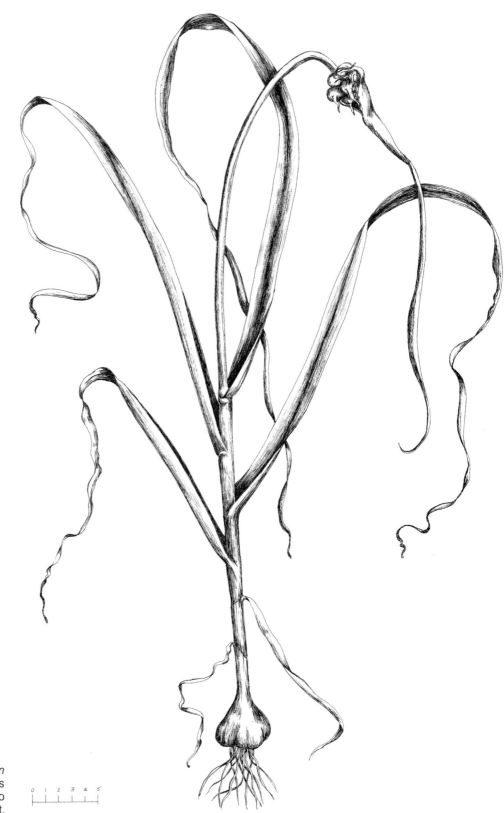

Top-setting garlic, *Allium sativum*, about two weeks before it is ready to harvest.

0 1 2 3 4 5

following year. If the bulbils from the flower head are planted, these too will usually produce a round in the first year, and bulbs with cloves in the following season.

Some garlic plants do not produce distinct flower stalks and flower heads but swell near the base of the stem.

Explanation of Softneck, Hardneck and Top-setting

Some forms of garlic produce no flower stems or flowers—the leaves simply die back when the bulb is mature. These forms are usually called 'softneck'. Other forms produce a flower stem in early summer, which is smooth, round and solid for its entire length—the flower can be imbedded in the stem or occur at the top. These forms are usually called 'hardneck' or top-setting garlic. Rocambole is a form of top-setting garlic where the flower stem produces a distinctive twist (see p. 6).

Top: Bulb and cloves of top-setting garlic, showing the base of the flower stem. *Bottom:* Bulb and cloves of softneck garlic, with no flower stem.

Flowers and Seeds

If flower heads are produced, they occur in late spring or early summer, but sometimes the bulbils simply form a swelling in the stem a short distance above the bulb. Mostly, the flower head occurs at the top of the solid stem, which may be coiled in the early stages. The papery spathe that covers the flower head has a long beak and splits on one side to reveal the umbel. The spathe remains attached to the umbel base. The umbel consists of many bulbils that can vary enormously in size, and the greenish-white, purple or pink flowers vary in number or may be absent altogether. The flowers rarely open, usually wither as buds and seldom produce seeds. If seeds are produced, they are black and are contained in a small capsule, but are infertile.

A top-setting cultivar.

Cultivars, Varieties and Closely Related Species
See also Appendixes 3.1 and 4 at the back of the book.

There are now probably more than 300 cultivars and varieties of garlic grown world-wide. They vary in colour, size, pungency and flavour. Many have resulted from vegetative mutations during the thousands of years of garlic cultivation. Often cultivars are named after their place of origin. Today more cultivars are being produced to improve commercial production. These cultivars vary greatly—not only in the bulbs and cloves as already mentioned, but also in yield, plant size, times of maturity, length of storage, and the presence or absence of flowering stalks and flowers. Top-setting cultivars generally have fewer, larger cloves in each bulb than softneck cultivars (see p. 9 for explanation of top-setting and softneck).

0 1 2 3 4 5

Three stages of bud
development in top-setting
garlic. In this example the
bulbils have sprouted in the
flower head.

Most countries that produce garlic have many of their own distinct cultivars which match climatic conditions and the demands of the market (see Appendix 3.1).

In many seed lists for home gardeners, garlic is not given the name of any particular cultivar but simply sold as 'garlic'. Garlic sold as 'Elephant', 'Great-headed' or 'Russian' garlic is usually not garlic, but a relative of the leek (see Ch. 3).

Propagation

Choosing the Cloves

Garlic is always grown vegetatively from cloves, as plants do not often flower and never set fertile seed. Plant only healthy bulbs obtained from a reliable source—this will prevent the spread of disease. Also, choose only cultivars suited to the local climate. As a general rule, the larger the clove the larger the resultant bulb will be. If possible, purchase bulbs from local growers to start the garlic crop and then save enough good bulbs to replant the following year. Many bulbs are now being treated with sprout inhibitors to stop them from sprouting during storage. Unfortunately this also makes the cloves unsuitable for propagation.

Sprouting, and the subsequent growth of cloves, is influenced by the temperature at which cloves are stored. Storage at temperatures between 0°

and 10°C (32°–50°F) will hasten bulbing in spring. Cloves stored at temperatures greater than 25°C (77°F) may not sprout at all. In warmer regions, garlic should be refrigerated at about 10°C (50°F) for two or three weeks before planting to increase the chances of sprouting and bulb formation.

Preparing the Cloves

Bulbs should only be separated into cloves just before planting, as whole bulbs store better than individual cloves. The papery covering over each clove should not be removed, but all cloves should be separated from one another, or double plants will be produced. With softneck cultivars use only the larger, outside cloves—the smaller ones can be eaten or grown for garlic sprouts (see p. 16).

A crop of the softneck cultivar 'California Early' which was planted late is almost ready for harvest. *Ellisfield Farm, Red Hill, Victoria.*

A crop of the softneck cultivar 'Italian White' planted at the same time as the 'California Early'—it is slightly more advanced and is now ready for harvest. *Ellisfield Farm, Red Hill, Victoria.*

When to Plant

Warm temperatures and long days encourage bulb development. Cloves need to be planted early enough to allow the roots and leaves to develop during the cooler, shorter days. In mild temperate regions, where the winter is not too cold and the summer not too hot, the best time to plant is late autumn to early winter. If it is really hot bulbs should not be planted until mid-winter. At the other climatic extreme, in regions which experience snowfall, plants need to be well established and mulched before it gets really cold, so they too need to be planted in autumn. In these areas cloves are often replanted soon after they are harvested.

If you are in a cold area with heavy rainfall or heavy soil, your bulbs may rot during winter. So, delay planting until spring. This delay can result in small bulbs, so an alternative is to plant cloves in deep pots in autumn ready to be carefully planted out in spring.

Cloves should be spaced about 10 cm (4 in) apart, in rows about 40 cm (1 ft 4 in) apart. Place them so that the thicker or root end is pointing down, with the neck just below the surface of the soil. Loosen the surface layer of the soil with a trowel so that you don't have to force the clove in, as this can damage its base and result in poor root growth. Then firm down the soil around the clove, or the developing roots may push it out of the soil. Water immediately to encourage growth, because the sooner cloves sprout the less chance there is of decay.

Plants that flower produce bulbils, or top-sets, in the flower head and these can also be used for propagation. If the bulbils are a similar size to the cloves they will produce useful bulbs in the first year. Smaller bulbils may take two seasons of growth before the bulbs are large enough to use. Plant them in the same way as the cloves.

Planting Bulbils

Cultivation

Garlic does best in light soils with good drainage, although heavier soils can be used if the cloves are planted in soil ridges to improve the drainage. Soil should be enriched with well-rotted manure or fish meal before planting. Very sandy soils may be low in phosphorus, so add this at the time of planting. Top-dressing with blood and bone, or a similar slow-release fertiliser, during winter and early spring is beneficial, but once the bulbs start to enlarge fertilisers have little effect. The area for planting should be changed each year, on a three-year cycle to prevent build-up in the soil of fungal spores and other potential pests (see Ch. 13).

Soil

Keep the plants free from weeds because the bulbs have only shallow roots and weeds create considerable competition for available water and nutrients. Garlic is capable of growing through quite thick mulch, so this is a simple way of reducing weed growth. Mulch will also protect the bulbs from extreme weather conditions, such as severe frosts and snow, but don't let mulch allow the soil to become sodden as the bulbs may rot. In very wet winters, pull the mulch away from the developing plants. Freshly cut grass, straw and chopped leaves all make good mulch.

Weeds and Mulch

Full sun and regular water during the months when the bulbs are growing is essential. Most commercial crops are grown under irrigation to ensure a

Sunlight and Water

reliable water supply—the best yields are obtained if the plants are never allowed to dry out during bulb formation. Stop watering when the tops begin to turn brown, as the bulbs are now almost mature and continued irrigation can cause rotting. With top-setting garlic, once the seed stalk is obvious, begin withholding water as this will stress the plant, causing it to form tight layers of protective skin.

Daylight Hours and Temperature

Garlic forms bulbs in response to increasing daylight hours in spring and matures faster if temperatures are high. It grows best in temperate regions which get plenty of rain in spring and are warm in summer. Some more recent cultivars are day-length neutral, which means that they can be grown in more tropical regions with fewer hours of daylight. It is the combination of climate, in particular temperature and rainfall, and soil type that determine which cultivar is most suited to a particular region. So anyone starting to grow garlic should trial several cultivars over a number of years before concentrating on the most successful one.

The distinctive flower heads of *Allium sativum* 'New Zealand Purple'.

Garlic is also influenced by the temperatures to which the just planted cloves and young plants are exposed before the bulb starts to develop. If they are exposed to temperatures between 5° and 10°C (41°–50°F) for one to two months—as is typical of temperate climates—then bulbs will form quickly. If they are never exposed to temperatures below 20°C (68°F) then, even if day-length criteria are met, bulbs may still not form. Also, too much exposure to cold—long periods below 5°C (41°F)—can be harmful, resulting in a roughened appearance to the bulb.

Some growers advocate the removal of the flower stems before the flower heads are formed, so that the plant's resources are directed entirely towards the developing bulb. Others disagree, maintaining that top-setting garlics store better if the tops are not removed. Also, the bulbils formed in the flower head can be used to produce new plants.

Remove Flower Heads?

Harvest and Storage

Bulbs are ready to harvest in summer about eight months after they have been planted. The outward signs are the green leaves, which will begin to turn brown, and the stems, if present, which will begin to soften—although staying green. Don't leave harvesting until the leaves have died back completely, as with onions—by this time the bulbs will have started to split. Rocambole cultivars are ready to harvest when the coil in the stem begins to straighten.

Remove the bulbs by inserting a fork deeply under them and carefully lifting the whole plant. Shake or brush off any excess dirt. The bulbs should never be banged against anything as they will be bruised and this will render them useless for storage.

In dry areas, some growers place the freshly dug bulbs in groups on top of the soil so they can dry out and cure. They are arranged so that the green leaves from one bulb protect the next bulb from the sun. However, even then bulbs can get sunburnt and the dramatic rise and fall in temperature from day to night can harm them. If an appropriate space is available they are better cured under cover, where temperatures fluctuate less. Plants should be left intact and hung in bunches or spread on racks for two to three weeks. If the leaves show any sign of going mouldy, remove them immediately because this mould will spread to the bulb.

Curing is particularly important if the bulbs are not quite mature, as they will continue to absorb moisture from the stem and leaves after harvest. Top-setting garlics should be harvested and dried with the flower head and stem still attached. An old window screen, resting on sawhorses or something similar, makes a good drying tray. This can be placed under a tree, but must be moved under cover when rain threatens. Bulbs with the leaves attached can also be plaited into strings and hung in a dry airy position.

Curing

Storage for Use

Once the bulbs are cured, the skins will be papery and dry and the bulbs should feel firm and tightly packed. Check for any damaged or bruised bulbs and remove them. Unless the bulbs are to be plaited or hung in bunches, cut off the leaves, stems and roots just above the bulb. Do not try to wash off dirt or separate the individual cloves as either of these actions will radically shorten their storage life. Bulbs can be stored in shallow cardboard boxes, in slatted wooden boxes, on trays, in net slings, in stockings, or in plaits—in fact in any way that allows air circulation around each bulb. The room where they are stored must be dry, airy and not too cold. Check the bulbs occasionally and remove any diseased ones. Properly stored, some cultivars will last for 12 months.

The optimum temperature for the storage of commercial crops is 0°C (32°F). These bulbs are not suitable for planting, as cloves kept at very low temperatures tend to produce rough bulbs, bulbs that produce side-shoots as they mature, or bulbs that mature too early.

Storage for Replanting

To allow for replanting, 10 to 15 per cent of the crop needs to be retained. The optimum storage temperature for bulbs to be replanted is 10°C (50°F), with limits of 5° (41°F) and 18°C (64°F).

Versatile Garlic

Garlic Sprouts

Small cloves, or those that sprout before they can be used in the kitchen, should not be thrown away but grown as garlic sprouts. Place them in a pot in any reasonable potting mix, or in the ground, spacing the cloves about 2 cm (1 in) apart just below the surface of the soil.

In China garlic sprouts provide a tasty and nutritious addition to the diet in the middle of cold winters. Here the most tender sprouts are grown in heated greenhouses—often under darkened tents to blanch them, but perfectly edible sprouts can be grown on a sunny windowsill, or warm corner in the garden, in any reasonable soil or potting mix (see p. 23).

Sprouts are usually harvested whole with the roots attached, although only the green tops are used. It is also possible to make two cuts, removing just the green tops the first time and leaving the bulbs to reshoot. The leaves are used fresh.

Green Garlic Shoots (or Garlic Leeks)

Green garlic shoots are grown under the same conditions as garlic bulbs, but the plants are harvested before the bulbs are mature and the whole plant is used, not just the bulb. Garlic grown for the stem can be planted more closely than those grown for the bulb. Cloves are usually placed 6–8 cm (2½–3 in) apart. A plot planted with this spacing can all be used for stems, or if every second plant is harvested for the stem, the others can be left to develop bulbs. Harvest between four and five months, just as the new bulb is forming. The whole plant is used fresh.

In China, crops are planted in raised beds, top-dressed with fertiliser when they are about 8 cm (3 in) high, and harvested about four months after

Garlic bulbs just after harvest. The bulb on the right is beginning to split as it was left in the ground a little too long.

planting. If they are to be blanched, they are planted in flat-bottomed furrows which are gradually filled in as the plant grows.

Flowering Stems

In China, the flower stems are regarded as a delicacy. These are harvested in summer while they are still green and before the spathe has split to reveal the bulbils. The stem is delicately prised from the bulb, leaving the latter to continue growing. The flower stems are used fresh, or dried for winter use by hanging in bunches. They can also be frozen and tinned.

Dehydrated Garlic

To dehydrate garlic, the bulbs are dried and cured in the field, the tops are removed and the bulbs are split into cloves. The skins and other debris are removed and discarded. Cloves are washed, thinly sliced and placed on drying trays. When dry, they can be powdered or left whole and stored in airtight containers away from direct light. To produce 1 kilogram (2 lb 3 oz) of dried product requires 3–4 kilograms (6½ lb–8lb 12 oz) of fresh garlic bulbs.

Useful Garlic

Garlic does not take up much space and can be usefully interplanted with other crops—perhaps in perennial flower beds or among roses, where it will help to protect these plants from insect attack. If garlic is not harvested, it will gradually form very dense clumps with very small bulbs. The young leaves and stems can be picked when needed, or they can just be left to continue multiplying.

Pests and Diseases
See also Chapter 13.

Garlic is subject to a range of pests and diseases. The most serious ones for the home grower are black mould, downy mildew, mites, onion thrips, soot and white rot. However, if the bulbs are carefully selected from a reliable source and only the healthiest cloves planted in a disease-free site, then pests and diseases should not be a problem.

Companion planting. A clove of garlic planted at the base of a young rose has grown into a dense clump. The garlic seems to keep the plant healthier and less prone to insect attack.

Unfortunately, garlic virus, which causes yellow streaking of leaves and reduced yields, is nearly endemic in some areas. There are some varieties of *Allium longicuspis*—the possible ancestor of garlic—that show no yellow streaking and seem to be immune to the garlic virus. It is possible that if these varieties can be crossed with *Allium sativum*, virus-resistant hybrids may eventually be produced. This simple case emphasises the importance of preserving old species and varieties.

The Chemistry of Garlic

A typical raw compound bulb is made up of:

> water (61.3%)
> carbohydrates (30.8%)
> proteins (6.2%)
> fats (0.2%)
> other (1.5%)

It also contains:

> 10 different sugars (in small amounts)
> cellulose, mucilage, pectin and peptides
> minerals including copper, germanium, iron, manganese, potassium, selenium and sodium
> vitamins A, B1, B2 and C—more specifically, every 100 grams (3½ oz) of garlic contains:
>> 0.25 milligrams thiamine
>> 0.08 milligrams riboflavin
>> 0.5 milligrams niacin
>> 15 milligrams ascorbic acid

Garlic bulbs also contain numerous sulphur compounds. One of these compounds is **alliin**, which is colourless, odourless and water-soluble. It is present in uninjured garlic cloves and accounts for about 0.24 per cent of the weight of a typical garlic bulb. When cloves are bruised, cut or crushed, an enzyme called **alliinase**, contained in the plant's cells, is released and comes into contact with alliin. The alliin breaks down in the presence of alliinase into numerous constituents, including up to 10 volatile sulphur compounds, the predominant one being another sulphur-containing compound called **allicin**. Allicin produces the typical odour of fresh garlic and is the source of some of its anti-bacterial properties.

However, allicin is itself unstable and, if heat is applied, it breaks down into compounds made up principally of **diallyl disulphide** and lesser amounts of several other organic sulphur compounds, including **ajoene**, which is formed from allicin molecules which combine. Diallyl disulphide is the main compound found in garlic oil which has a very strong pungent odour and flavour.

The constituents of garlic oil vary markedly depending on the method of extraction. If garlic oil is prepared by steam distillation of ground garlic cloves, according to Dausch and Nixon in their paper *Garlic: Its Role in Cancer Prevention*, the relative proportions of the sulphur components are:

diallyl disulphide (60%)
diallyl sulphide (14%)
allyl propyl disulphide (6%)
allyl methyl trisulphide (4–10%)

The proportions vary depending on the method of analysis. Ajoene cannot be detected in oil prepared by steam distillation.

If garlic cloves are quickly frozen without being cut or crushed, dried while still frozen and then ground, the dry powder has little or no odour because the alliin has not broken down. This is the way many odourless garlic tablets are produced (*see also* Garlic Products, p. 24).

More detailed chemistry is beyond the scope of this book. Readers who want to know more should consult the references at the end of the book, especially the definitive work by Eric Block, *The Chemistry of Garlic and Onions*.

Garlic Breath and Body Odour

Garlic breath has caused embarassment and consternation for hundreds of years. Some people are more affected than others and different forms of preparation will cause more of the flavour and odour to be present. As a rule, the stronger the garlic flavour, the stronger the effect on breath and body odour. So, raw chopped garlic will produce stronger odours than boiled whole garlic, but freshly prepared garlic never leaves as much odour as commercially prepared garlic pastes.

Early antidotes were raw beans, parsley and baked beetroot—chewed vigorously. Today the list is longer and suggestions include angelica water, cardamon or fenugreek seeds, celery, chervil, cloves, coffee beans, fennel, ginger, milk, parsley, peppermint, spinach and various proprietary brands of mouthwash.

Early experiments showed that the source of some of the breath odour is small particles of garlic retained in the mouth, and if this is the case then it is possible that the above suggestions will alleviate or mask the odour. However, odour and flavour constituents also enter the bloodstream. Several days after eating garlic, perspiration can still be odorous. Cows that have been eating alliums will produce contaminated milk very soon after-wards, and the only means of this contamination is through the bloodstream. For the same reason, breastfeeding mothers are often advised not to eat garlic or onion if their babies are colicky. Once garlic is in the bloodstream the air leaving the lungs will also be affected. The major odour components isolated from human breath are allyl mercaptan and diallyl disulphide.

There seems to be no total solution to breath and body odour. A long bath in very warm water is supposed to cause the garlic to be exuded from the body more quickly. Regular intake of small amounts of garlic seems eventually to lead to the smell becoming less noticeable. As both the flavour and the medicinal efficacy of garlic depend on the presence of the chemicals that produce the odour, then it is best to view garlic in the same way as the people of China, Greece, Italy and many other countries, who eat it on a daily basis—if everyone eats garlic, no one will be offended by the smell.

Myth, Magic and Medicinal Miracles

Garlic has been recorded as a cure for almost every disease and disaster known to the human race. It was the main ingredient in Four Thieves Vinegar, a mixture used by thieves in Marseille who plundered the bodies of plague victims in 1722 and, reputedly, never caught the plague themselves. The thieves washed in it, doused their clothes in it and sprinkled it around their houses.

It has been used for things as unrelated as removing corns and an ingredient in glue. Aristotle believed that it could cure rabies, Mohammed apparently used it to treat scorpion stings, and the Greek physician, Hippocrates, recommended it for those who intended to drink excessive amounts of alcohol—or for those already inebriated.

Chopped garlic in a linen cloth was supposed to cure smallpox if applied to the soles of the feet and to revive an hysterical sufferer if sniffed into the nostrils. Indian children once had strands of garlic leaves wound around their wrists to protect them from whooping cough. In Africa bulbs were regarded as being capable of repelling mosquitoes and crocodiles.

Garlic is also believed to be an aphrodisiac and in the Middle East the bridegroom would pin a garlic clove to his lapel to ensure a happy wedding night. Conversely, a story from the American north-west says that to rid yourself of an unwanted lover you can place a piece of garlic with two crossed pins in the middle of two roads which intersect. The lover is asked to walk over the clove and will immediately lose interest. One writer has suggested that if garlic were marinated in red wine vinegar and left to mature in the sunshine it could be used as a toilet water!

Belief in the strength and power of garlic is typified by the suggestion that, if a garlic clove is rubbed on the soles of the feet, a few minutes later the breath will smell. In the Middle Ages, garlic was carried in the pocket to protect the bearer against witchcraft and vampires. Also, when plaited into braids, it was used to decorate cradles to stop the fairies from stealing the sleeping baby. In some cultures it is still traditional for the grandmother to present a newborn baby with a bulb of garlic to ward off evil spirits.

A legend from the East—which emphasises the very mixed responses to garlic—says that after the fall of man, when Satan left the garden of Eden, from his right footprint onions grew, and from his left garlic.

Other strange suggestions and uses include that of Pliny the Elder, who recommended that garlic should be planted 'when the moon is below the horizon' and gathered 'when it is in conjunction' to ensure no objectionable smell. In biblical times garlic was considered able to neutralise the venom of an asp and capable of purifying penitent criminals and absolving them of guilt. Punters in Hungary encouraged the practice of tying a clove to a horse's harness—the theory being that the smell would cause the other horses to drop back. In the same vein, Spanish matadors carried garlic to stop the bulls from attacking.

Medicinal Uses

Garlic has been used medicinally for as long as it has been known to the human race. It has been used both as a protective agent and as curative agent for countless ailments and is still widely prescribed all over the world as a home remedy. Indigenous and introduced medicinal plants form the basic core of medicines for 70 per cent of the world's population, and garlic features prominently in most countries.

Garlic is increasingly being regarded as a mainstream medicine. Recent rigorous scientific studies have confirmed the efficacy of some traditional remedies. Many of the medicinal uses of garlic reflect the antiseptic qualities of this plant. This, and several other of the supposed properties of garlic, have been the subject of more than 1000 scientific studies, most of which show benefits from taking garlic.

The potency of garlic depends very much on the form in which it is taken, and the effectiveness is dependent on the dose and the length of time for which it is taken.

The two main constituents of garlic which have so far been shown to have most medicinal value are **allicin** and **ajoene**. Allicin is produced by the enzyme, alliinase, when the bulb is cut or bruised. Ajoene is formed from allicin by the application of heat (*see* The Chemistry of Garlic).

The most medicinally effective way to take garlic is raw and sliced. However, for many people this has the major drawback of the strong odour. It is also very difficult to quantify the potency of raw garlic, which can vary from bulb to bulb. The odour is lessened to some extent by gentle cooking—but heat over 60°C (140°F) can also cause the medicinal properties of garlic to be lost.

Despite the need for care in some areas, there is overwhelming evidence to suggest that regular intake of garlic is beneficial to health. Population studies comparing societies where garlic is a daily part of the diet, with those where it is not, suggest that regular intake can prolong life by reducing the incidence of some diseases.

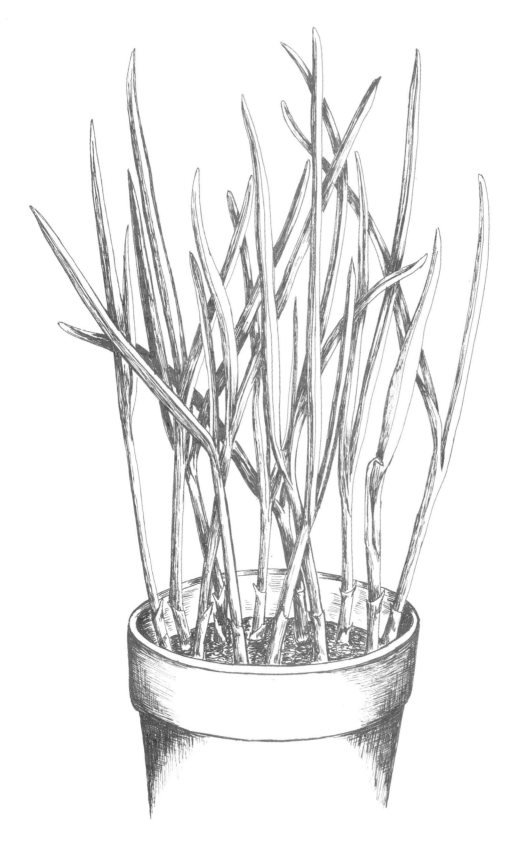

A pot of garlic sprouts.

The following is a summary of the results of recent scientific research. Any reader who wants to know more should consult the references at the back of this book.

Garlic Products

Garlic can be processed to produce tablets that contain the medicinally important components of garlic—allicin, and sometimes diallyl disulphide and ajoene—but their potency depends on the level of alliin present. In garlic tablets and other garlic extracts, what is termed the 'allicin releasing potency' is affected by

    (1) the level of alliin that is present in untouched bulbs,

    (2) the activity of the enzyme alliinase and

    (3) the way the garlic is processed.

Most tablets and powders are produced by the gentle grinding of carefully sliced dried cloves. With these products it is possible to quantify the level of alliin, and thus the potency of the tablet or powder. Other tablets are made out of gel capsules which enclose small amounts of garlic oil. This oil will be medicinally active as long the oil has been extracted using the correct techniques.

Two kinds of odourless garlic tablets are produced—one that is free of odour because the active constituents are enclosed within a covering which is not broken down until the tablet comes in contact with the gastric juices, and another that contains alliin which has no smell until it is converted to allicin, again when it reaches the stomach. Both of these products produce some odour once the ingredients are active. Only those preparations with no active ingredients have no smell at any stage. However, it seems likely that they also have little medical benefit.

Possible Harmful Side-effects

There are no recorded harmful medical effects from the consumption of garlic, as long as it is only used in moderate doses. However, garlic oil and concentrated extracts may irritate the stomach's mucous membranes. Some people are very sensitive and even small doses may cause problems. Also anyone with a blood clotting disorder should seek medical advice before taking garlic supplements.

Garlic extracts and garlic oil should never be given to babies or small children and should not be used by breastfeeding mothers. Large doses of preparations containing garlic oil have resulted in poisoning and even the death of young children.

People who regularly work with garlic may develop contact dermatitis. Housewives, cooks, farmers and greengrocers are all at risk. According to Lembo, et al. (1991), it is the diallyl disulphide in the garlic which acts as a sensitiser, causing the onset of dermatitis. The cure is to stop handling garlic.

Antiseptic Properties

In recent years, there has been a worrying increase in antibiotic-resistant organisms, so more attention is being paid to plants such as garlic, which are anti-bacterial. A report by K. S. Farbman, et al. in the *Paediatric Infectious*

Diseases Journal (1993) said that laboratory analyses 'confirmed the anti-microbial efficacy of fresh aqueous garlic extract against current laboratory and clinical strains of bacteria, including antibiotic-resistant organisms'. The bacteria tested included forms of *Haemophilus* (which can cause meningitis in children), *Staphylococcus* (which includes golden staph) and *Streptococcus*.

As an antiseptic, garlic acts in two ways, killing both bacteria and fungi. This means that it is useful in treating mild intestinal infections such as diarrhoea as well as lung infections such as bronchitis, and seems to act as a protective agent against these infections if taken regularly. It has also been popularly used to prevent and treat dysentery (inflamation and ulceration of the bowels) and its potency against this infection has recently been confirmed.

Fungi and moulds that may also be adversely affected by garlic include those which cause athlete's foot and ringworm. The yeast which causes thrush (*Candida albicans*) has been shown in the laboratory to be inhibited by garlic preparations. However, similar results have not been seen from simply eating garlic, and a more direct application may be necessary.

Asthma

Some writers have suggested that garlic can be used to treat asthmatics, but there is also evidence that hyper-sensitive people may develop occupational asthma as a result of exposure to garlic powder in food processing. Caution would be needed by sensitive individuals.

Cancer

Experiments in the laboratory, animal investigations and population studies all support the premise that garlic may interfere with tumour activity. Cancers of the stomach, colon and skin seem to be the most likely to be affected. The exact mechanism is unclear and probably consists of several different actions, but both fresh garlic and diallyl disulphide (*see* The Chemistry of Garlic) have shown promising results.

An epidemiological study done in China compared a population with high garlic intake with one where garlic consumption was low. They found that the mortality rate from gastric cancer was significantly lower in the population whose garlic consumption was high (see J. G. Dausch, *Garlic: A Review of Its Relationship to Malignant Disease*). Two trace elements usually found in garlic—germanium and selenium—may also be important in anti-oxidant and anti-tumour activity.

The World Cancer Research Fund stated in 1990 that recent research justified the idea that regular intake of garlic may have beneficial effects on the development and progression of some cancers.

Cardiovascular Disease

The regular medicinal intake of garlic has been shown by numerous scientists to decrease the risk of heart disease. Garlic seems to be effective against several factors which influence a person's potential to have a heart attack. The four main areas in which garlic is effective are: (1) on cholesterol levels, (2) on platelet formation, (3) by acting as a fibrinolytic agent and (4) in lowering blood pressure.

Bulbs of 'California Early' plaited and spread out to dry.

(1) CHOLESTEROL LEVELS

Cholesterol is made up of low density lipoprotein (LDL) cholesterol and high density lipoprotein (HDL) cholesterol. It is the LDL cholesterol which through oxidation can be deposited on artery walls, leading to a narrowing of the arteries. This condition, known as atherosclerosis, can lead to heart disease.

In 1993, an international research team issued a report on the study of garlic as an anti-oxidant and its effect on the cardiovascular system (M. Fogarty, *Garlic's Potential Role in Reducing Heart Disease*, Conference Review, 1993). Several studies had previously shown that garlic can prevent the build-up of cholesterol on artery walls but the process by which this was achieved had not been understood. Recent research by this team shows that garlic has anti-oxidant properties and these properties inhibit the formation of free radicals. It seems to be these free radicals that modify LDL cholesterol and increase the likelihood of it being deposited in the arteries. Garlic has also been found to increase the level of HDL cholesterol and to protect it from decomposition. A higher level of HDL cholesterol is thought to decrease the risk of heart disease.

(2) PLATELET FORMATION

There is not as much evidence for garlic's anti-platelet activity. Platelets are involved in the blood clotting process, but they can also contribute to heart disease. They will adhere to injury sites in arteries and to other platelets, thus leading to the development of thrombi or blood clots that restrict the blood flow and can cause heart disease. Two experiments conducted in the early and mid-1980s (Apitz-Castro, R., et al.) showed that several components of garlic demonstrated anti-platelet activity in the laboratory. The most potent of these was ajoene, which is formed in small quantities when garlic is heated (*see* The Chemistry of Garlic). Ajoene was also shown to increase the activity of other anti-platelet drugs.

(3) FIBRINOLYSIS

Fibrin, like platelets, is involved in the thickening and hardening of arteries in atherosclerosis. Fibrinolysis is the dissolving of fibrin—so anything that shows fibrinolytic activity may be beneficial in treating heart disease caused by atherosclerosis. Two studies by Bordia, et al. showed that garlic oil and raw and fried garlic all increased fibrinolytic activity in the people tested, and the majority of other studies support this theory to some degree.

(4) BLOOD PRESSURE

Some animal studies and a limited number of tests on people have shown that garlic may lower blood pressure.

SUMMARY

McElnay and Li Wan in *The Pharmaceutical Journal* (1991) conclude that 'the claim that regular intake of garlic may help to prevent the development of this condition [coronary heart disease] appears defensible.' They go on to qualify this slightly by saying that results from short-term clinical trials cannot necessarily be extrapolated into long-term effects and that much more work needs to be done on the standardisation of prepared garlic products. They also comment that little work has been done on the effects of regular dietary intake of garlic as opposed to medicinal intake.

Contraception

Chinese researchers have found that allitridum, a constituent of garlic, has spermatocidal properties indicating a possible contraceptive role for garlic. Again more investigations need to be carried out to determine, among other things, if there is any practical way in which it could be used.

Diabetes

There is some evidence to show that garlic may be useful in the treatment of late onset diabetes, but much more work needs to be done in this area.

Folk Remedies

This is a brief summary of some of the ways garlic is used medicinally around the world, followed by a few recipes for simple ailments. The folk remedies mentioned have not specifically been the subject of any scientific research.

In Nepal, oil from the crushed bulb is used to treat coughs and pneumonia. Further south, in India, extracts of the bulbs combined with honey are given for bronchitis. In Oman (on the Arabian peninsula), crushed cloves are rubbed into the scalp for dandruff; eaten daily for colic and diarrhoea, as well as diabetes; and boiled in water and inhaled to treat tuberculosis. Mexicans believe that eating the bulb will speed birth and that, used as a poultice, it will relieve rheumatism. The Chinese use garlic to treat bites, boils, colds, dysentery, gastroenteritis, lead poisoning, nose bleeding and whooping cough.

A tincture made by steeping garlic bulbs in alcohol and taken daily for a month is described in a medical brochure from Venezuela. This brochure lists its effects as: reducing arterial tension; slowing heart palpitations; stimulating the liver; curing haemorrhoids and varicose veins; overcoming constipation and intestinal catarrh; reducing uric acid and so relieving rheumatism and gout; counteracting chronic fatigue, headache, neuralgia, melancholy, hysteria and insomnia; acting as a tonic for women during menopause; expelling worms; improving kidney and bladder complaints; curing eczema and helping diabetes and asthma!

In developing countries, garlic is often prescribed for bacterial and viral diseases, such as cholera, dysentry, enteritis and typhus. In Africa, it has been commonly used to treat amoebic dysentery.

Green garlic shoot harvested just as the bulb begins to swell but before the cloves are formed. The whole plant is used.

Garlic Syrup

Garlic is prescribed in many countries as an expectorant for colds and fevers. It is supposed to make the body sweat and expel fluids, being both diaphoretic and diuretic. For coughs, colds and sore throats, garlic syrup—a tablespoon taken every few hours—is a common home remedy all over the world. There are numerous recipes but one of the simplest follows.

Combine the water and the sugar. Bring slowly to the boil, stirring until the sugar dissolves. Then boil rapidly for about 5 minutes. Pour this mixture over the crushed garlic bulb, cover and leave to stand overnight. Strain—the mixture may need to be heated to strain properly—and pour into small bottles. Seal the bottles. To reduce the smell, fennel seed can be boiled in a little vinegar for a few minutes. Cool, strain and add the vinegar to the syrup before bottling.

1 cup water
1 cup sugar
1 whole bulb of garlic, peeled and crushed

Garlic Ointment

Garlic has also been used as a remedy for rheumatism and whooping cough. In cases of rheumatism, the affected joint is rubbed with the raw garlic clove, or garlic ointment can be used.

Combine the garlic and lard (or oil) in a saucepan, bring to the boil and simmer for 15 minutes. Strain through a fine sieve and pour into small pots. This will keep in the refrigerator for several weeks. For whooping cough, the treatment is to macerate the garlic together with lard (or oil) and rub it into the chest and back of the sufferer.

Both these remedies are very smelly and not suitable for someone with sensitive skin or a tendency to dermatitis.

6 cloves garlic, roughly crushed
1 cup pure lard (or thick vegetable oil)

Worms can be treated by boiling garlic in milk and then drinking the milk. Garlic, because of its antiseptic properties, is also useful for the treatment of pimples. It is added to vinegar and cotton wool dipped in the mixture is dabbed on the affected skin (see the recipe for Simple Garlic Vinegar, p. 44).

Other Uses

For Animals

For almost as long as people have eaten garlic, they have also fed it to their animals. When garlic is added to chicken feed, the hens are healthier and lay more eggs.

Dogs dosed regularly with garlic are also healthier and worms are less of a problem. One whole clove of garlic a day for an average-sized dog is the recommended dose.

As an Insect Repellent

Oil containing garlic is sprayed on breeding ponds in Africa to destroy mosquito larvae. In China, the expressed juice from the whole plant is used to protect crops from a range of pests and diseases and, in many Western countries, garlic spray is used to deter insect pests such as ants, aphids, spiders and, among others, the cabbage and tomato caterpillar.

GARLIC SPRAY
There are numerous recipes for garlic spray but a simple effective one is as follows:
(1) Finely chop or macerate 80 grams (3 oz) of garlic cloves, just cover with paraffin oil, cover the vessel and soak for one or two days.
(2) Dissolve 10 grams (⅓ oz) of an oil-based toilet soap in 4 cups of water, slowly add this to the garlic mixture and mix well.
(3) Strain the liquid through fine muslin and store in a glass bottle.
This mixture should be diluted with water at a ratio of about 1:50. The tougher the insect, the stronger the spray should be.

If garlic is planted in a circle around fruit trees it is supposed to keep borers away. It will also deter weevils from stored grain. Planted near tomatoes, garlic is supposed to guard against red spider mite and, near roses, to reduce the number of aphids and keep the plants generally healthier. The leaves and other debris left after harvesting the garlic bulbs can be used as a mulch to protect nearby plants.

As a Fungicide

Recent field trials by the International Crops Research Institute for the Semi-Arid Tropics have shown that a simple crushed garlic-and-water mixture is almost 100 per cent effective in protecting sorghum crops from infection by ergot (caused by the fungus *Claviceps sorghi*). Plant breeders have been unable to produce a strain of sorghum that is resistant to this fungus, which can wipe out entire crops. As almost 58 million tonnes of sorghum are grown world-wide every year, this could be a very important discovery. The main drawback is that the spray is washed off by rain, but scientists are working on ways to increase its 'stickability' and are also testing garlic on other crops.

Garlic cloves mixed in with stored fruit will delay the onset of rot. And on the Island of Mauritius (off the east coast of Africa), garlic is planted in a circle about 1 metre (3 ft) from the trunks of peaches and apricots to prevent leaf curl.

Garlic oils produced by steam distillation are used to flavour manufactured foods.

Culinary Uses

Garlic cloves are used in cooking all over the world, but they are an everyday ingredient in Africa, China, southern Europe, Mexico, the Middle and Far East, South America and the West Indies. Garlic combines well with an enormous range of foods, enhancing the flavour of the food with which it is mixed, as well as adding its own flavour.

A convenient way of storing garlic bulbs is in a terracotta pot with holes in the side. This allows fresh air in but keeps out bright light which decreases storage life.

For the best flavour, only good quality garlic should be used. The cloves should be plump and firm and not shrunk away from the papery sheath. The base needs to be very hard, and there should be no discoloured spots. Discoloured garlic has a rank taste, as does garlic that is harvested too early or which has started to shoot. This can spoil the flavour of a dish. If there is no alternative to using discoloured garlic, then carefully cut out all the spots before use.

Selecting Bulbs for Flavour

The flavour of garlic varies depending on the cultivar and the climate in which it was grown. As a general rule, the softneck cultivars are stronger and more pungent, while the top-setting cultivars are usually milder, sweeter and more nutty. The best garlic comes from temperate areas with hot, dry summers. Garlic grown where the summers are cool or wet can

A garlic sprout—usually only the stem and leaf are used.

develop rank flavours. Much of the garlic available in supermarkets is imported and/or has already been stored for long periods, so it often does not keep for long. The flavour is never as good as fresh garlic. If possible, purchase only locally grown garlic—or grow it at home.

Preparation and Flavour

Garlic can be used whole—with the skin on or off—and the cloves left in the food or removed before serving. It can also be sliced, bruised, chopped or crushed and eaten raw, blanched, stewed, roasted or fried. The way it is prepared determines the strength of the flavour, and the way it is cooked determines the nature of the flavour imparted to the dish. Allicin—the chemical that gives raw garlic its characteristic scent and flavour—is only produced when the clove is damaged by cutting, bruising, chopping or crushing. Cooking transforms the allicin into other complex organic sulphur compounds, which impart a set of aromas and flavours quite different from that of raw garlic. The flavours and aromas can be varied by changing the duration and temperature of cooking. For more information on the chemistry of garlic, see page 19.

The garlic recipes that follow include a traditional French one in which a chicken is cooked with 40 cloves of garlic. This may sound alarming but, since it uses only whole cloves, the result is sweet and delicious. If the garlic were to be chopped, however, the result would be overwhelming. To sum up: for a mild flavour leave the clove whole; for the most powerful flavour, cloves should be raw and sliced or crushed. For warm pungency cook the garlic—if it is finely chopped the flavour will be stronger than if it is left whole. Fried garlic should not be browned too much as the flavour can become acrid.

Fresh garlic is always better than preserved garlic. Most methods of preserving garlic accentuate the pungency of the oil but lose most of the flavour of the freshly cut cloves.

Since the way garlic affects a dish depends on so many factors, it is recommended that, to understand its influence, you experiment in the kitchen. This effort will be repaid with the ability to produce a wide range of sophisticated dishes.

Removing the Skin

The easiest way to remove the papery sheath that covers the clove is to place the clove with the concave side down on a cutting board, and press down firmly with your hand or the side of a broad-bladed knife. The clove will snap loose from the papery case. Once the skin has been removed the garlic can be further bruised, cut or crushed.

Bruising

To bruise garlic just press the clove gently with the side of a knife, enough to release the flavour, but not enough to crush. The skin can be removed at the same time. Garlic prepared in this way can be easily taken out of the dish before serving.

Slicing

Hold the clove at one end and cut with a sharp knife into thin slices. This is the best way of preparing garlic if it is to be cooked for some time.

Chopping

First slice the garlic as above, then turn the clove around and slice in the other direction. For a quicker but rougher result, place the cloves on a board and hold the tip of a broad-bladed knife onto the board, then hold the handle with the other hand and chop the knife up and down in a semi-circle over the board. This is a quick way of chopping several cloves at once.

Crushing

Crushing is best done by placing the clove on a pinch of salt on a board, and pressing down firmly with the side of a broad-bladed knife. A garlic crusher can also be used, but it is not as easy to clean as a knife and board, and any stale residue may taint the food next time the crusher is used. This is not such a problem if the crusher is used regularly and cleaned carefully. One benefit of using a crusher is that the clove does not have to be peeled. The flesh is forced through the holes and the skin remains behind.

Lingering Odours

A chopping board—or at least one side of a board—should be reserved specifically for preparing alliums, as the flavour tends to linger and will taint other foods prepared on the same board. Any odour on the hands is removed more easily by first rubbing with salt and lemon and then washing with cold water rather than hot.

Raw Garlic

Raw garlic should be used carefully because it is strong and pungent and not everyone likes its flavour. If you are unused to using garlic, start with a salad bowl rubbed with a garlic clove, or a whole uncut clove added to a salad dressing a couple of hours before it is to be used. This imparts a very subtle flavour. Garlic vinegar and garlic oil can be made and used in salad dressings, to cook food, or to marinate meat (see recipes). Finely chopped garlic mashed into butter is delicious with meat or in garlic bread. Famous garlic sauces, such as Aioli from the south of France and Spain and Skordalia from Greece also use raw garlic; and finely chopped raw garlic is often mixed through cooked greens in Middle Eastern cookery.

Cooked Garlic

Cooked garlic is used as the basis for many dishes and sauces. It can be used whole, sliced, chopped or crushed in varying quantities and with varying types and degrees of cooking to flavour soups, stews, vegetables, curries, sauces, meat and fish dishes. It is also delicious on its own—usually whole—roasted, steamed, or stir-fried, with or without other vegetables.

Garlic Sprouts and Fresh Green Leaves

The green tops are used fresh in salads as a garnish, or in stir-fry dishes. Their flavour is milder and sweeter than that of the cloves.

Green Garlic Shoots (Garlic Leeks)

The green shoots taste sweeter and more subtle than the bulbs. In Tuscany, garlic harvested just as the bulbs begin to form is known as *aglio fresco*, or fresh garlic. At this stage it looks rather like a cross between a spring onion and a small leek. Both the green and white parts are used, usually sliced in the same way as leeks—in fact they can be used instead of leeks in many of the recipes listed in Chapter 5. In France, green garlic is often used in soups.

Flower Stems

Young, sliced flower stems can be fried on their own in oil and soy sauce. They also mix well with other ingredients, particularly in stir-fry dishes, where they retain their dark-green colour. Slightly older flower stems can be peeled before use.

Botulism

Two serious outbreaks of botulism occurred in Canada and the United States in the 1980s. These were shown to be caused by garlic preserved in oil products which relied only on refrigeration to preserve the garlic. While botulism (caused by the bacteria *Clostridium botulinum*) is relatively rare, it causes infection and often results in death. Laws were subsequently passed in the United States, Canada and Australia to ensure that herbs, spices and vegetables preserved in oil have a pH no greater than 4.6. Foods with a pH below 4.6 will not usually support the growth of bacteria which cause food poisoning. To achieve a low pH, acid is added to the food. The most readily available source of acid is vinegar which is usually 4 per cent acetic acid. So to preserve garlic in oil the following steps must be followed:

(1) To 300 grams (10½ oz) of garlic add 100 grams (3½ oz) of vinegar, so that the ratio is 3:1 garlic to vinegar.

(2) Leave the garlic to stand in the vinegar for about an hour and then add the garlic and the vinegar to the oil.

This should ensure that food poisoning will not occur, but refrigeration is still needed to stop the product from spoiling.

Blue-green Garlic

One drawback of the acidification of garlic-in-oil products is that sometimes the cloves turn a blue-green colour. While still perfectly edible it can be off-putting. The colour change occurs only in certain cultivars which contain a higher than usual proportion of one amino acid. This colour change can be prevented by storing the bulbs at temperatures above 23°C (73°F) for a month before preservation.

Recipes

Garlic and Olives

Add a little extra flavour to ordinary bottled olives.

Crush the cloves of garlic and add to the olive oil. Drain the liquid from the olives, prick the olives with a fork, return them to the jar and pour the oil and garlic over the top. Keep in the refrigerator and allow to stand for a few days before using. If the olives are to be kept for more than a week, add 2 tablespoons of vinegar to the crushed garlic before adding it to the oil.

Bruschetta

This is Italian garlic bread made with olive oil instead of butter. It is traditionally eaten at the time of the olive harvest, when the oil is fresh and sweet.

Cut the bread into thick slices and toast both sides until golden-brown on the outside but still soft in the middle. Cut the garlic cloves in half and rub on both sides of the toasted bread. Spread the slices over a big plate and drizzle the warmed oil over the top. Sprinkle with salt and serve immediately. This is the simplest form. You can also squeeze juicy fresh tomatoes over the top of the slices, and/or sprinkle finely chopped basil over them.

Garlic Dip

Add the garlic cloves to the milk and slowly bring to the boil. Allow to simmer for 5 minutes. Beat the egg yolks with the warm cream and add a little of the hot milk—beating vigorously to avoid lumps. Add the egg yolks and cream to the simmering mixture, continuing to stir rapidly. Remove from the heat and force through a sieve to cream the garlic. Season with salt and pepper. Allow to cool and serve with crisp toast fingers to dip into the mixture.

Appetisers and Light Meals

2 cloves garlic
1 cup olive oil
1 jar plain olives

1 breadstick
4 cloves garlic
virgin olive oil, warmed
salt

5 peeled garlic cloves
1 cup milk
2 egg yolks
¼ cup warm cream
salt and freshly ground black pepper

Taramasalata

3 slices white bread, crusts
    removed
½ cup milk
120 grams (4 oz) cod's roe
    (available from
    continental delicatessens)
4 cloves garlic, peeled and
    crushed
juice of one lemon
3 tablespoons olive oil
freshly ground black
    pepper

Soak the bread in the milk. Meanwhile, pound the roe in a mortar until it is creamy. Squeeze the extra milk from the bread and add the bread, with the garlic, to the roe. Mix well and pound some more. When the consistency is really smooth, add the lemon juice, oil and pepper to taste. Continue to mix until it is creamy. Serve with crisp toast or pitta bread and a bowl of black olives.

Albanian Cucumber Dip

2 cloves garlic
½ cup walnuts
2 medium cucumbers
pinch of salt
1 teaspoon vinegar
¼ cup water
¼ cup olive oil

Grind the garlic and the walnuts to a fine paste using a pestle and mortar or food processor. Peel the cucumbers and chop finely. Mix with the salt, vinegar, water and olive oil. Slowly add the garlic and nut paste and mix thoroughly. Serve as an appetiser with crusty bread.

Green Garlic Potato Cakes

500 grams (1 lb 1½ oz)
    potatoes
2 tablespoons green garlic
    shoots, finely chopped
1 tablespoon parsley, finely
    chopped
salt and freshly ground
    black pepper
olive oil for frying

This dish can be served as an accompaniment to a main dish, or as a meal on its own.

Peel the potatoes and grate them into a large bowl. Add the green garlic, parsley, salt and pepper to taste. Put in enough oil to cover the bottom of a heavy-based frying pan. Heat until it is very hot. Put several separate tablespoons of the mixture into the pan so that there are several flat heaps. Fry until golden on one side, then turn over and repeat. Drain well and serve very hot. Alternatively, the whole mixture can be placed in the pan, turned once and cut into wedges to serve.

Serves two as a main course or four as an accompaniment.

Garlic Soup 1

Soups

Peel the garlic cloves and fry gently in the olive oil for a few minutes. Remove from the heat and mash the garlic into the oil. Add this mixture to the stock and season with salt and pepper. Simmer for 45 minutes. Place the slices of bread in the bottom of a soup tureen and pour the very hot soup over the top. Alternatively, place a slice of bread in each bowl and pour the very hot soup over the top.

Serves six.

12 cloves garlic
1 tablespoon olive oil
8 cups stock
salt and freshly ground black pepper
8 thin slices of bread, buttered

Garlic Soup 2

Plunge the garlic into boiling water for 30 seconds. Remove, run under cold water and drain thoroughly. Peel and roughly chop the cloves.

Heat the oil in a heavy saucepan and add the onions and capsicum. Fry gently until the onions are golden and the capsicum soft—about 10 minutes. Add the garlic, and a few minutes later the tomatoes. Cover and continue to simmer on a low heat for about 30 minutes. Add the stock and bring to the boil.

Tear up the bread and add it to the soup. The bread should disintegrate and in the process thicken the soup. Add more bread for greater thickness. Serve with grated cheese and salt and pepper to taste.

Serves four.

20 cloves garlic
3 tablespoons olive oil
2 medium onions, sliced
1 large capsicum, thinly sliced
3 cups tomatoes, peeled, seeded and chopped
3 cups stock
3 or 4 slices of dark bread, crusts removed
strong cheese, grated
salt and freshly ground black pepper

Garlic Soup 3

This is a very old European recipe for a soup traditionally served to invalids. It is nourishing, easy to digest and the antiseptic properties are supposed to hasten recovery.

Put the water, salt and garlic in a large saucepan. Bring slowly to the boil and simmer for about 30 minutes. While the soup is cooking, place the slices of bread on a flat tray in the bottom of a moderate oven until they are dry and crunchy. Strain the liquid to remove the garlic, return the liquid to the heat and continue to simmer. Break the eggs, one by one, into the gently simmering liquid. Cook for about 2 minutes—the whites should be solid but the yolk still runny. Put each crisp slice of bread into a shallow soup bowl. Remove the eggs with a slotted spoon and place one egg on each slice of bread. Pour the soup over the egg and bread. Sprinkle with parsley and freshly ground black pepper.

Serves four.

4 cups water
1 teaspoon salt
20 cloves garlic
4 thick slices of crusty bread
4 eggs
1 tablespoon parsley, finely chopped
black pepper, freshly ground

Vegetables

Garlic cloves
Olive oil

Roasted Garlic

This has a lovely sweet, nutty flavour and can be eaten with roasted meat, used in purées, sauces and soups, or simply spread on crusty bread as a snack.

Place the unpeeled cloves in the bottom of a shallow dish. Sprinkle the olive oil over the top and stir the cloves in the oil so they are well coated. Roast in a moderate oven for about 15 minutes. Whole bulbs can also be roasted in a small terracotta oven, inside a conventional oven.

Roasted Garlic and Potatoes

500 grams (1 lb 1½ oz)
   potatoes
4 tablespoons olive oil
10 cloves garlic, unpeeled
1 teaspoon fresh lemon
   thyme, finely chopped
salt and freshly ground
   black pepper

Potatoes cooked in this way make an excellent appetiser on a cold winter's day—or they can accompany other dishes. The garlic is sweet and can be eaten by squeezing the flesh from the skins.

Pre-heat the oven until very hot—220°C (425°F). Drop the potatoes in boiling water, bring back to the boil and simmer for about 5 minutes. Remove from the heat, drain and allow to cool. Peel and cut into chunky pieces. Place the potatoes in a large roasting pan, pour the oil over the top and stir the potatoes until they are coated in the oil. Place in the oven and cook for 15 minutes, add the garlic cloves and cook for another 15 minutes. Sprinkle the thyme over the top and return to the oven for a few minutes. Remove from the oven and arrange the garlic and potatoes in a heated serving dish. Sprinkle with salt and pepper and serve very hot.

Salads

A very delicate garlic flavour can be achieved by using the following method. Cut a thick crust of bread about 6 cm (2½ in) square. Sprinkle salt on each side and rub with a peeled garlic clove. Then place the crust at the bottom of the bowl and the salad on top. After tossing, remove the bread. Garlic chapons are an extension of this idea.

Bulbs of garlic are delicious baked in a terracotta oven placed inside a conventional oven. The tops are trimmed and the bulbs basted with olive oil and cooked at 160°C (300°F) for about an hour. The sweet baked flesh is spread on bread or toast.

Endive with Garlic Chapons

Cut the breadstick into slices and rub each slice all over with the garlic clove. Sprinkle with the olive oil and vinegar, salt and pepper. Put the slices on a tray in the oven on a low heat for 15 minutes, until they are crisp. Leave to cool, cut in half and add to the broken up and washed endive. Toss and serve.

1 small French breadstick
1 clove raw garlic
olive oil
vinegar
salt and freshly ground
**   black pepper**
1 bunch endive

Garlic and Cumin Vinaigrette

This vinaigrette is particularly good with chickpea or bean salads.

Mix all the ingredients together using a whisk. Pour over the salad and leave to stand for about 30 minutes. Serve at room temperature.

6 tablespoons good olive
**   oil**
4 garlic cloves, crushed
1 hot red pepper, minced
3 tablespoons fresh mixed
**   herbs, finely chopped —**
**   coriander, mint, plain-**
**   leaf parsley, tarragon and**
**   thyme are all suitable**
2 tablespoons red wine
**   vinegar**
1 teaspoon cumin seeds,
**   roughly crushed**
salt and freshly ground
**   black pepper**

Turkish Roasted Red Capsicums with Garlic

6 sweet red capsicums
1 tablespoon garlic, minced
¾ cup red wine vinegar
salt and freshly ground
    black pepper
1 dessertspoon fresh thyme
    leaves, chopped

Garlic is used abundantly in Turkish cooking. It is usually peeled and then pounded with a little salt, using a pestle and mortar, until it is reduced to a paste.

Roast the capsicum directly over a gas flame or under a grill, turning frequently until charred all over. Transfer to a covered plastic container or plastic bag to steam for about 8 minutes—this helps to remove the skin of the capsicum. Scrape the charred skins off, remove the stems and seeds and cut lengthways into 5 or 6 pieces. Put the capsicums and any juice into a bowl. Combine the garlic, vinegar, salt and pepper in another small bowl, mix and pour over the capsicums. Sprinkle thyme leaves on top and refrigerate for several hours. Arrange on a flat dish and serve at room temperature.

Sauces and Relishes

Garlic Butter

2 cloves garlic
1 tablespoon lemon juice
10 tablespoons butter
salt and freshly ground
    black pepper

Peel the garlic cloves and blanch briefly in boiling water. Remove and dry. Crush in a mortar or bowl, add the lemon juice, butter, salt and pepper and pound with a pestle or fork until creamy. Shape into a long thin roll and chill. Slice the butter and serve with steak, lamb chops, strong flavoured fish, potatoes or bread. This butter will keep, securely wrapped in the refrigerator, for about 2 weeks. It can also be frozen.

Aioli

10 cloves garlic, peeled
3 egg yolks
¼ teaspoon salt
2 cups olive oil
1 tablespoon lemon juice

This classic sauce is essentially garlic added to mayonnaise and originates in the Mediterranean region. Aioli is traditionally served with poached or boiled fish, but it is also delicious with grilled lamb, eggs, vegetables, leafy salads and even as a dip.

Crush the garlic cloves in a mortar or food processor until they are pulp. Add the egg yolk and salt and mix well. On a very slow speed, add half the olive oil, drop by drop. Blend in between each drop to avoid curdling. This should result in a very thick mixture. Now add the rest of the oil in a steady, slow stream, still blending all the time. Finally add the lemon juice.

Pesto

This Italian sauce can be eaten with any pasta or gnocchi, or added to vegetable soups. It is similar to Pistou, usually varying only in the relative amounts of the ingredients and in the addition of parsley.

Place all the ingredients—except the olive oil and pepper—into a large mortar or food processor. Pound or grind to a fine consistency. Slowly add the oil, whisking all the time. The sauce should be thick and smooth. Season with pepper.

Pesto will keep for a couple of weeks in the refrigerator, if stored in a glass jar with some olive oil poured over the top.

3 cloves garlic, peeled
4 tablespoons fresh basil, roughly chopped
4 tablespoons fresh parsley, roughly chopped
1 tablespoon pine nuts
2 tablespoons parmesan cheese, finely grated
1 cup olive oil
freshly ground black pepper

Persillade

Serve this with fish or chicken. It is particularly good if spooned over the hot food just before serving.

Peel the garlic and remove the coarser stalks from the parsley. Place both on the chopping board and chop together very finely. Place in a small bowl, add the lemon juice and a teaspoon of finely grated zest, then stir in the olive oil. Cover and leave to stand for a couple of hours.

3 cloves garlic
1 bunch parsley
juice and zest of one lemon
2 tablespoons olive oil

Pistou

Pistou is actually the name used in Provence for basil, reflecting the ingredients in this classic French sauce. It usually consists simply of garlic, basil and olive oil—but pine nuts and/or breadcrumbs can be added for more body, and finely grated parmesan cheese gives it a different flavour. In its simplest form it makes a delicious addition to any vegetable soup. With the pine nuts and breadcrumbs it can be used to stuff chicken breasts or barbecued fish.

Place the garlic and basil leaves into a large mortar or a food processor, and pound or process until well crushed and mixed. Gradually add the oil to make a thick pourable sauce.

5 cloves garlic, peeled
2 handfuls basil leaves, roughly chopped
4 tablespoons olive oil

Rouille

1 red chilli pepper, fresh or
   dried
1 red capsicum
3 cloves garlic
100 grams (3½ oz) white
   bread
8 tablespoons olive oil
1 teaspoon tomato paste

This fiery garlic sauce is traditionally served with fish soup in the Mediterranean, but it is also delicious with pasta.

Halve and seed the red chilli. If it is dried, then soak it in warm water for a few minutes first. Skin, core and seed the red capsicum. Finely chop both the red chilli and the capsicum and place them with the peeled garlic into a mortar or food processor. Pound or process the pepper, capsicum and garlic together. Soak the bread in cold water, squeeze gently and add this to the mixture. Blend a little longer. Slowly add the olive oil, blending until it is a smooth thick paste. Finally, stir in the tomato paste. Serve cold.

Garlic and Mint Sauce

1 small bunch fresh
   spearmint
½ cup rice vinegar
1 garlic clove, crushed
1 pinch sweet paprika

Finely chop the mint and mix with the vinegar, garlic and paprika. Leave to stand for at least 1 hour. Use with lamb—for example the Grilled Garlic Lamb Chops.

This sauce will keep in a glass jar in the refrigerator for several weeks.

Skordalia

This classic Greek sauce, known as Skorthalia or Skordalia has many variations:

(1) Greek Garlic Sauce

6 cloves garlic
½ teaspoon salt
1 cup cold mashed potatoes
2 slices of stale white
   bread, crusts removed
⅓ cup olive oil
1 tablespoon lemon juice
1 tablespoon vinegar
black pepper, freshly
   ground

This garlic sauce is served with fried or boiled vegetables and hot or cold seafood. It is particularly delicious with fresh boiled and sliced beetroot, and with fried eggplant (aubergine).

In a mortar or bowl mash the garlic with salt. Add the potato and continue to mash. Pour cold water over the bread, remove and squeeze dry. Add the moistened bread to the garlic and potatoes and continue to mash and stir until smooth. Add the olive oil very gradually, stirring all the time. Then add the lemon juice and vinegar a few drops at a time. Continue stirring until the mixture is smooth. Add some freshly ground black pepper to taste. Cover and chill before serving.

(2) Greek Garlic Salad Dressing

Serve with boiled fish, fried oysters or fried eggplant (aubergine).

Mix the garlic and nuts to form a thick paste. Soak the bread in a little water for 10 minutes, then squeeze dry. Add the bread to the paste. Then add the oil, vinegar and salt and pepper. Stir slowly with a wooden spoon until the mixture is smooth.

Store in a cool place until ready to use.

5 cloves garlic, crushed.
½ cup pine nuts or almonds, crushed
2 slices bread
1 cup olive oil
1 tablespoon vinegar
salt and freshly ground black pepper

Tabil

This spicy condiment is used in Tunisia, added to soups and stews.

Peel the garlic. Halve, seed and chop the capsicum. Combine all the ingredients, except the oil, in a mortar or food processor, and pound or process until it forms a smooth paste. Slowly add the olive oil.

4 cloves garlic
1 sweet red capsicum
2 small dried chillies
½ teaspoon caraway seeds
1 small bunch fresh coriander leaves
1 tablespoon olive oil

Taklia

Taklia is popular in Middle Eastern, especially Egyptian, cookery. It is a fragrant mixture of ground coriander seeds and crushed garlic in roughly equal proportions. They are fried together in a little oil and added at the end of cooking to meat, bean and green vegetable dishes.

Green Garlic Frittata

Main Courses

Clean and trim the garlic shoots and slice into rounds. In a heavy-based frypan, heat the olive oil and add the sliced garlic shoots. ·Cook slowly on a low heat until the shoots are soft and a pale-straw colour. While the garlic is cooking, break the eggs into a bowl, season with salt and freshly ground black pepper and beat. Increase the heat under the pan, arrange the garlic shoots evenly over the pan and pour the egg-mixture over the shoots. Once the eggs have set over the bottom, turn the heat right down and allow the eggs to cook for a few minutes to set the bottom into a crust. When cooked through, slide the frittata onto a hot plate, reheat

2 green garlic shoots
3 tablespoons olive oil
4 eggs
salt and freshly ground black pepper

the pan and replace the frittata, uncooked side down. Once the eggs have set on the bottom, remove the frittata and serve very hot, cut into wedges.

Serves two.

Grilled Garlic Lamb Chops

5 peeled garlic cloves
½ teaspoon salt
1 tablespoon soy sauce
**black pepper, freshly
   ground**
8 loin lamb chops

Mash the garlic and salt together to form a thick paste. This is best done with a fork on a flat surface. Scrape the paste into a bowl and add the soy sauce and ground pepper. Mix together and spread onto both sides of the lamb chops. Leave to stand for about an hour. Grill the chops for about 3 minutes on each side, until they are brown on the outside but still pink in the middle. Serve with Garlic and Mint Sauce (see p. 42).

Serves four.

Baked Chicken with Forty Garlic Cloves

1 large fresh chicken
**salt and freshly ground
   black pepper**
**small bunch of herbs —
   lemon thyme, parsley,
   bay leaf, sage and
   tarragon**
40 unpeeled cloves garlic
½ cup olive oil
**1 cup flour mixed to a thick
   paste with ¼ cup water**
crusty fresh bread

A traditional recipe from the south of France.

Remove the giblets, neck and any excess fat from the chicken. Rub the salt and pepper on the inside and outside. Place the small bunch of herbs and 4 garlic cloves inside the chicken. Into a casserole dish just big enough to hold the chicken, pour the oil and spread the rest of the garlic cloves evenly over the bottom. Gently heat the oil and then put the chicken into the dish, turning it so that it is coated with oil. Put the lid on the dish and seal it to the base with the flour and water mixture.

Place in a pre-heated, moderate oven and cook for 1½ hours. Remove from the oven and open the dish by breaking the crust. Carve the chicken and serve with the juices, the baked cloves of garlic and some crusty bread. The soft meat of the garlic cloves can be simply eaten by squeezing out the flesh. It has a delicious nutty flavour and can be spread on the crusty bread.

Serves four.

Preserves

Simple Garlic Vinegar

8 cloves garlic
pinch of salt
2 cups vinegar

Pound the garlic with the salt—it doesn't need to be peeled. Place the mixture in the bottom of a large glass jar, bring the vinegar to the boil and pour over the garlic. Leave to cool, seal and leave to stand for a couple of weeks. Strain and pour into warmed, sterile bottles. For a stronger mixture, the process can be repeated with a fresh batch of garlic before bottling.

Garlic and Herb Vinegar

This vinegar can be used in salad dressings, drizzled over vegetables or added to other dishes. It also makes an attractive gift.

Pour the vinegar into a saucepan and add several sprigs of the fresh herbs. Reserve enough sprigs to place one in each jar. Bring the vinegar and herbs slowly to the boil and then boil rapidly for 1 minute. Remove from the heat, cover and leave to stand for a few hours. Carefully peel the cloves of garlic and place 2 or 3 into each warm, sterile jar (the number depends on the size of the jar). Strain the vinegar into a jug and pour into the jars. Add a fresh sprig of the herb previously used to each jar. Seal and store in a cool dark place for at least 2 weeks before use.

4 cups white wine vinegar
bunch fresh parsley,
**   tarragon or rosemary**
garlic cloves—2 or 3 to
**   each small jar**

Simple Garlic Oil

Peel and bruise the garlic cloves and cover with the vinegar in a very small bowl. Leave to stand for 1 hour and then add them to the olive oil in a clear glass bottle. Leave the bottle in a warm place for about 5 days. Strain into a clean bottle and use as required for cooking, in salads or drizzled over hot vegetables.

2 cloves garlic
2 tablespoons vinegar
2 cups virgin olive oil

Spicy Garlic Oil

Place the garlic cloves in a small bowl and cover with the vinegar. Leave to stand for one hour. Place the garlic and vinegar and all the other ingredients in a glass jar or bottle with a tight-fitting lid. Seal and shake well to mix. Leave in a cool dry place for at least 2 weeks before using, shaking occasionally. Store for up to 3 months. Use in salad dressings or for cooking.

**Botulism has been associated with low-acid, garlic-in-oil products, so acidifying agents must be added, the most common being vinegar (see p. 34 for more detail).

3 garlic cloves, peeled and
**   bruised**
2 tablespoons vinegar**
bunch of fresh basil, mint,
**   rosemary or tarragon**
2 bay leaves
6 whole black peppercorns
4 juniper berries
½ teaspoon of saffron
**   strands (optional)**
4 cups olive oil
⅔ cup walnut oil

Iranian Pickled Garlic

**500 grams (2 lb 1½ oz)
   garlic cloves
3 fresh beetroot, washed,
   dried and chopped into
   small squares
4 cups vinegar
2 tablespoons salt**

Peel the garlic and prepare the beetroot. Sterilise the bottling jars in boiling water and dry thoroughly. Fill the jars nearly to the top with alternate layers of garlic and beetroot. Sprinkle salt into the tops of the jars and fill to the brim with vinegar. Seal the jars and keep in a cool place for at least 6 weeks before using.

Japanese Garlic with Soy Sauce

**garlic cloves
Japanese soy sauce (shoyu)**

Garlic prepared in this way is not too strong and is often served as an appetiser or a side dish with meat dishes.

Skin the garlic cloves. Place in a clean sterile jar and pour soy sauce over the top until the cloves are covered. Leave to stand for 3 weeks before use.

Garlic plaits are not only a good way of storing garlic, but they can also be very decorative and make wonderful gifts.

2. Chives

Derivation of Names

THE BOTANICAL NAME, *SCHOENOPRASUM*, IS DERIVED FROM TWO GREEK WORDS— *schoinos* meaning rush and *prason* meaning leek—and refers to its rush-like leaves. Chive, or cive, as it was known until the late 1800s, comes from the Latin *cepa*, meaning onion, and used to be applied to any small onion plant. Most of this plant's other names are derived from similar sources. Both the wild and garden forms of chives are extremely varied. As well as the range of common names listed above, there have been more than 13 botanical names used to describe this versatile plant at different times in history. Most of these were the result of botanists thinking they had found a new species, when it was actually only a variant of one already identified.

Distribution

Chives are naturally more widely distributed than any other edible allium. They grow wild in the cooler regions of the British Isles, China, Europe, India, Iran, Japan, Siberia and the United States (as far north as Alaska). Their preferred habitats are grassy alpine slopes and rock crevices up to very high altitudes. They are also cultivated in gardens in most temperate regions of the world.

History

Chives have been collected in the wild and cultivated in gardens since very early times. One of the earliest records of their cultivation is in the list of plants grown in the gardens of Charlemagne's Empire (about AD 800).

From the 1500s, chives were frequently mentioned in literature. John Gerard, in *The Herbal or General History of Plants* (1597), describes them as 'A pleasant Sawce and a Good Pot-Herb'. His other remarks, however, are not so complimentary: 'Cives attenuate or make thinne, open, provoke urine, ingender hot and grosse vapours, and are hurtfull to the eyes and braine. They cause troublesome dreams.'

Allium schoenoprasum

Other Common Names

Aglio di serpe—Italian
Ail civitte—French
Bieslook—Dutch
Ceboletta—Spanish
Cebolinho—Portuguese
Ciboulette—French
Ciethe—Scottish
Cives, Civette—French
Common chives
Erba cipollina—Italian
Garden chives
Infant onion
Onion chives
Petit poureau—French
Rush-leek
Schnittlauch—German
Syes—Scottish
Wild onion

Diagrammatic cross-section of (*above*) the leaf and (*below*) the scape of chives.

Romanian gypsies used chives in their fortune-telling ceremonies in the 1600s. Also around this time, the more subtle flavour of chives was being recognised and they began to appear regularly in recipes from England and Europe—before this they were thought to have the same culinary attributes as spring and welsh onions and were used interchangeably.

Chives formed an important part of the diet in some very cold places where people were more reliant on food collected from the wild. In Siberia they were salted for winter use, and in Alaska the Inuits kept the plants for long periods in airtight sealskin bags. In the Yukon, north-west Canada, chives were known as wild onions and were cooked and used as a flavouring.

Chives have been grown in gardens in the United States since colonisation and were included in a list of American garden vegetables in 1806. However, by the turn of the century Sturtevant (Hendrik, 1919) describes them as 'grown in but few American gardens'. Today chives are grown commercially in several American states, including California, where much of the crop is snap frozen and added to dairy products such as cottage cheese.

When the first fleet landed in Australia, 'Sives' were listed among the cargo of the supply ship *Sutro*. Another supply ship, the *Guardian* which departed three years later to relieve the acute shortages of the infant settlement, carried two chives plants but these died before the ship reached Cape Town.

Chives are still widely used in Australia, the British Isles, northern Europe, New Zealand and North America. They are less common in warmer countries such as Egypt and Spain—probably because they do not do as well in hot climates and because a wealth of other onion and garlic plants are easy to grow and readily available in these countries.

Botanical Description

Chives are perennial. They grow as a dense clump from numerous slender bottle-to-cone shaped bulbs, which cluster on a short rhizome. When the older portions of this rhizome die, the bulbs become disconnected. One or two leaves grow from each bulb to a height of about 30 cm (1 ft). The leaves are hollow, cylindrical, blue-green and 2–4 mm (⅛ in) wide. They sheathe the scape (flowering stem), which is also hollow and grows to about the same height.

The plant is usually dormant in winter. The leaves die back completely in late autumn and re-emerge in late winter or early spring.

A single chive flower with pedicel.

Flowers and Seeds

Chive flowers occur in spring, gradually reducing in number through summer and autumn. The short spathe splits to reveal a flower head up to 5 cm (2 in) in diameter, with as many as 30 upright flowers on short pedicels (stalks). These flowers open first at the top and then progressively towards the base—the only other commonly eaten onion where this happens is the

Chives, *Allium schoenoprasum*, in spring with flower buds and and flowers.

welsh onion (*Allium fistulosum*). Flowers are usually pink-mauve but flowers of cultivars may be dark-red, purple, blue and sometimes white. The spathe remains attached to the base of the flower head.

The fruit is a small capsule which contains the seeds. These seeds are small, hard and black. They are usually prolific and self-sow readily. Seed will last up to two years, but in hot, humid areas it should be used in the first year. Chives will not cross-pollinate with any other species of cultivated allium.

Cultivars, Varieties and Closely Related Species

Chives can vary markedly depending on their source, but in seed catalogues world-wide they are usually listed simply as chives (*Allium schoenoprasum*). Variation occurs in height, flower size and colour and the height of the flower in relation to the leaves. There are also some forms which do not die back in winter. Only a few cultivars have been named, probably because chives are a plant of the home garden and of little commercial importance. These cultivars, which occasionally appear in seed lists include the following:

Allium schoenoprasum 'Forescate'
Deep rose-pink heads on stems 40–45 cm (1 ft 4 in–1½ ft) tall.
Seed does not usually produce plants true to colour.

Allium schoenoprasum 'Grolau'
Bred in Switzerland for intensive indoor cultivation.
Very small, growing to 25 cm (10 in). Thick, dark-green foliage.
Does best if cut regularly.

Allium schoenoprasum 'Shepherd's Crook'
Grows to about 40 cm (1 ft 4 in) with contorted leaves.

Allium schoenoprasum 'Schnittlauch'
A dwarf German cultivar which grows to 20 cm (8 in).

Varieties of chives still found growing in the wild include the following:

Allium schoenoprasum var. laurentianum
Found in the United States and Canada from Washington in the south to Alaska and Newfoundland in the north.

Allium schoenoprasum var. sibericum or sometimes A. sibericum
A larger flowered form with the flower heads taller than the leaves.
Found in the mountainous regions of Asia, northern Europe and Russia— also in the Arctic.
Commonly grown in gardens in the United States; rarer in Australia.

Chives, *Allium schoenoprasum*, larger variety.

Propagation

All chives can be grown from seed sown in spring, summer and autumn. Either sow straight into the ground, or into pots and transplant when they are about 5 cm (2 in) high. Seed is best used fresh but will keep for up to two years. It takes about 10 days to germinate.

Chives can also be propagated by dividing clumps of bulbs in early spring or autumn. Place groups of 8 to 10 bulbs about 20 cm (8 in) apart.

For large plantings or commercial crops it is better to use seed, partly because of the number of plants to be grown, but more importantly to minimise the spread of diseases such as rust.

Cultivation

Chives do best in a fertile, humus-rich, well-drained soil. To increase leaf growth add compost and manure and empty any coffee grounds or tea leaves around the plants. In areas where the summers are dry, make sure the chives are kept moist for prolific growth—heavy mulching will help to achieve this. They are hardy plants and will survive long dry periods, although they may not grow as well.

Chives are cool-climate plants and will tolerate light shade, frost, snow and a damper position than most other edible alliums—but they do not like their roots constantly wet. They do not do well in the tropics, but will survive if grown in a raised bed where the drainage is very good—even then they seldom flower. Chives make excellent borders around vegetable plots and rose beds because they are neat, attractive and help to keep insect predators away. A dense border can be quickly established by placing groups of 8 to 10 plants about 10 cm (4 in) apart.

Every few years, no matter where they are grown, clumps should be lifted, divided and replanted. Small clumps should have the flower heads removed to encourage leaf growth, but once clumps are established they can be allowed to flower freely without inhibiting leaf growth. If you want masses of flowers—the flower heads are both very attractive and edible—then don't fertilise too heavily, as this encourages leaf growth at the expense of flowers.

Chives can also be grown inside on a sunny window sill. They will do better if moved outside occasionally during the day, and spring growth will be stronger if the pot is left outside for a few weeks when they are dormant in winter. Ideally, either seeds or transplanted bulbs can be planted into several pots and these pots can be alternated. This allows the plants from which the chives have been cut to rest and regrow outside.

Chives are easy to grow and will thrive in any odd corner of the garden.

Harvest and Storage

Hand-pick the leaves one by one from a small clump—but leave the smaller, newer leaves to continue growing. From larger, well-established clumps, part or all of the leaves can be cut just above ground level. The leaves are then left to regrow and this process can be repeated several times during the growing season. Flowers can be harvested as buds or when they are fully open. Chives are best used as fresh as possible, so only cut those needed for immediate use.

Most chives die back and are dormant in winter, but can be preserved for use during this period by cutting and drying in a microwave. Microwave-dried chives retain a good colour and reasonable flavour:

Microwave Drying

(1) Cut a good handful of chives into small pieces and spread over a plate.
(2) Process on 'High' for 2 minutes, remove and redistribute the chives.
(3) Process for a further 2 minutes.
(4) When cool, store in an airtight glass jar out of direct light. Dried chives should not be kept for more than one year.

Chives dried by hanging in bunches lose their colour and flavour and are not worth the effort.

Hanging in Bunches

Chive plants with their delicate foliage and attractive flowers do not have to be confined to the herb garden. They make a cheerful addition to a dull corner or can be used to edge a flower bed.

Freezing

Another way of preserving chives for winter use is to freeze them:
(1) Take freshly harvested leaves with flower stalks removed and cool them in the fridge.
(2) Then, cut them into short lengths and place into small containers.
(3) Freeze as quickly as possible.

Chives which have been frozen can look limp and discoloured in salads, but are fine added to butter and cottage cheese or as a garnish or flavouring in any cooked dish.

Dried Flowers

Flowers can be dried for use in cooking or in dried flower arrangements by hanging them upside-down in bunches out of direct light, in a dry airy position.

Pests and Diseases
See also Chapter 13.

The main home garden pest of chives is the onion thrip, which sucks the juice from the leaves. If left uncontrolled it may eventually kill the plant. In the early stages, thrip can be easily removed by running the fingers along individual leaves and squashing them. Alternatively, a strong jet of water will kill many of them. Larger infestations can be killed by washing with soapy water or spraying with pyrethrum.

Rust is another disease which occasionally affects chives.

Medicinal Uses

Chives have many of the attributes of onion and garlic, but they are much milder so are not often used medicinally. They will stimulate the appetite and promote digestion—especially of fatty foods—and are mildly antibiotic. They also contain vitamins A, B1, B2 and C, and sulphur and iron, which makes them a useful addition to a healthy diet.

In parts of Alaska, where other edible alliums are rare, juice extracted from the leaves is used as a cold remedy. In Holland they are listed in Steinmetz's *Materia Medica Vegetabilis* (1954) as a blood purifier and diuretic.

Other Uses

To Protect Other Plants

Planted as borders or in rows between vegetables or other tender plants, chives will act as a general insect repellent. If planted near apple trees they seem to reduce the incidence of apple scab. A tea made from chives can be sprayed or sprinkled over cucumbers and other cucurbits to reduce fungal problems such as mildew.

For Animals

Young poultry will benefit from chopped chives being added to their mash. J. C. Loudon in *The Encyclopedia of Gardening* (1853), said that

No cottage garden ought to be without the Chive; it forms one of the most wholesome herbs for chopping up and mixing among the food for young chickens, ducks and turkeys—making them thrive wonderfully, and preventing that pest the gripes.

Chive flowers are attractive, profuse and maintain a good colour when dried, so they are useful in dried-flower arrangements.

Flower Arrangements

Culinary Uses

Unlike most other edible onions, chive bulbs are not eaten—but the leaves, flower stem, buds and flowers are. The leaves have a mild onion flavour and this, combined with their fresh bright-green colour makes them suitable as a garnish and to add flavour to a wide range of dishes. They have the advantage over other alliums of leaving almost no trace of onion on the breath.

The flavour of chives has its greatest affinity with eggs and cream, but it also combines well with tomatoes, boiled and baked potatoes, and cottage and cream cheeses. Chives can be used successfully as a garnish with most salads, sandwiches, soups, stews and sauces, as well as with other vegetables such as peas, carrots, beetroot and cabbage.

To minimise bruising and flavour loss, it is best to cut chives with sharp scissors. They should only be added near the end of the cooking process and, preferably, once the pot has been removed from the stove—the volatile oils which impart the flavour are quickly destroyed by heat; similarly, the oils are mostly lost when chives are dried, so dried chives have little of the flavour of fresh chives.

The flower heads, both whole or broken into individual flowers, make an attractive garnish and have a mild sweet onion flavour. The flower buds can also be used and are particularly good in stir-fry dishes.

A clump of chives about to burst into flower. The buds can be added to a range of dishes.

Chives

Recipes

Fines Herbes

This traditional French mixture combines four herbs with subtle flavours that blend together beautifully. The mixture can be added to egg dishes, simple chicken and fish dishes and green salads. Simply collect equal amounts of chervil, chives, parsley leaves and tarragon, chop finely and sprinkle over the dish. These herbs should always be added fresh and towards the end of cooking. See the omelette recipe below.

Appetisers and Light Meals

1 tablespoon butter
5 eggs
1 tablespoon each of chervil, chives, parsley and tarragon, all finely chopped
salt and freshly ground black pepper

Fines Herbes Omelette

Heat the butter in a heavy-based frying pan. Lightly beat the eggs and pour into the very hot pan — cook quickly for a few minutes. Add most of the herbs and salt and pepper to taste. Lift the edges of the omelette and allow the uncooked eggs to run underneath. When nearly cooked, but still soft in the middle, fold in half and sprinkle the remaining herbs over the top.

Serves two.

1½ cups cottage cheese
2 tablespoons mayonnaise
1 clove garlic, crushed
2 tablespoons chives, chopped
salt and freshly ground black pepper

Chive and Cottage Cheese Dip

Mix all the ingredients together in a bowl and season with salt and pepper. Cover and chill for an hour before serving. Garnish with chive flowers and serve with crusty toast or vegetable pieces for dipping.

Avocado Dip

Coarsely chop the avocado and blend with the yoghurt, chives, lemon juice and chilli powder. Sprinkle the chive flowers over the top and serve with dry biscuits or corn chips.

1 ripe avocado
2 tablespoons plain yoghurt
1 tablespoon chives, chopped
1 tablespoon lemon juice
a pinch of chilli powder
chive flower head, broken into individual flowers

Tomato, Onion and Chive Soup

Add the finely chopped onion to the butter in a saucepan. Cook gently until the onions are clear.

Plunge the tomatoes into boiling water, remove the skin, cut and remove the seeds. Chop roughly and add to the onions—mix well and cook gently for a few minutes. Pour in the stock, add the sugar and season with salt and pepper. Bring to the boil and simmer for 15 minutes, or longer for a thicker soup.

Cool, then purée in a blender and add the chives. Chill thoroughly and serve with a dollop of fresh yoghurt in each bowl and crusty bread.

1 large, strong flavoured onion, peeled and finely chopped
4 tablespoons butter
750 grams (1 lb 10 oz) ripe whole tomatoes
1¼ cups chicken or vegetable stock
1 teaspoon sugar
salt and black pepper to taste
2 heaped tablespoons chives, finely chopped
yoghurt

Chives with Baked Potatoes

Vegetables

Potatoes baked in their jackets can be served with yoghurt or sour cream, which has had a handful of chives stirred into it about an hour before serving. Season with salt and freshly ground black pepper.

Cherry Tomatoes and Chives

2 whole garlic cloves,
   peeled
1 tablespoon olive oil
300 grams (10½ oz) cherry
   tomatoes
2 tablespoons of chives,
   finely chopped
black pepper, freshly
   ground

Gently sauté the garlic cloves in the olive oil for a few minutes. Add the cherry tomatoes and continue to cook for a few more minutes. Sprinkle the chives over the cherry tomatoes and mix. Remove from the heat, season with the pepper and remove the garlic cloves. Serve hot as an accompaniment to meat or fish dishes.

Snow Peas with Chives

250 grams (9 oz) snow peas
3 tablespoons unsalted
   butter
½ teaspoon sugar
salt and freshly ground
   black pepper
½ small lettuce, sliced
1 tablespoon chives, finely
   chopped
2 spring onions, finely
   sliced
chive flower heads, broken
   into individual flowers

Trim the peas and melt all but a heaped teaspoon of butter in a frying pan. Stir in the peas with the sugar and salt and pepper to taste. Cover the pan and simmer gently for 5 minutes.

Add the lettuce, chives and spring onions, stirring and tossing gently until the lettuce has wilted.

Add the final teaspoon of butter and serve with a garnish of chive flowers as soon as the butter has melted.

Salads

Cucumber, Tomato and Fetta Salad

1 medium cucumber,
   peeled and chopped into
   chunks
2 large tomatoes, chopped
   into chunks
200 grams (7 oz) fetta cheese
2 tablespoons chives, finely
   chopped
1 tablespoon olive oil
1 tablespoon white wine
   vinegar

Combine the cucumber, tomatoes and fetta cheese. Sprinkle the chives over the top and mix well. Add oil and vinegar and mix again. Refrigerate for 1 hour before serving.

Potato Salad

Peel and cut the potatoes into chunky pieces. Cook until firm but tender. Drain and allow to cool until warm. Add the yoghurt, chives and basil or mint and mix well. Season with pepper to taste and refrigerate for about 1 hour before serving.

500 grams (1 lb 1½ oz) potatoes
3 tablespoons full cream plain yoghurt
2 tablespoons chives, coarsely chopped
1 tablespoon fresh basil or mint
black pepper, freshly ground

Blue Chive Dressing

Combine all the ingredients in a small bowl and whisk together. Serve with leafy salads and/or tomatoes.

Sauces, Dressings and Relishes

100 grams (3½ oz) soft blue cheese
2 tablespoons chives, finely chopped
½ cup olive oil
¼ cup white wine vinegar

Chive Butter

Serve with any grilled meat or fish—also eggs, carrots and cauliflower.

Slowly mash the butter and lemon juice together with a fork. Add the chives and continue to mash. Add salt and pepper to taste. To store, shape into a roll and chill. Then cut into slices, wrap, label and store in the refrigerator for up to 3 weeks, or freeze for up to 3 months.

This butter is at its best when the chives are young and juicy in the spring. An alternative is to combine the butter, lemon juice, salt and pepper. Shape the butter into balls and roll through freshly cut chives to form a coating over the outside.

8 tablespoons unsalted butter
1 tablespoon lemon juice
2 tablespoons fresh chives, very finely chopped
salt and freshly ground black pepper

Ravigote Butter

This butter is made in the same way as Chive Butter but uses chervil, parsley, tarragon and shallots as well as chives. See French Ravigote Butter, page 152.

Chive and Apple Jelly

**1 kilogram (2 lb 3 oz)
  apples
water
sugar
juice of 1 lemon
2 or 3 handfuls fresh chives,
  chopped**

This jelly is delicious with meat—especially poultry. For a slight variation, chive flower heads, broken into individual flowers, can be added with the leaves.

Place the apples (these can be windfalls or even apple peel) into a large pan and cover with cold water. Bring to the boil and allow to simmer for about 1 hour, occasionally stirring and mashing the mixture. Leave to cool a little then pour the contents of the pan into a jelly cloth suspended over a large bowl. The jelly cloth can be a piece of muslin or cheesecloth—or even a bit of old, clean sheet. Tie the cloth firmly and leave to drain for several hours, or overnight. Do not squeeze the cloth or the jelly will be cloudy. Discard the contents of the cloth and measure the drained liquid into a large pan. For every 2 cups of liquid, add 1½ cups of sugar. Stir over a low heat until the sugar dissolves, then increase the heat and bring to the boil.

Cook until the setting point is reached—this can be tested by placing a teaspoon of the mixture onto a saucer. If it wrinkles when cool then it is ready. Alternatively, the setting point can be judged using a thermometer. When the mixture reaches 105°C (220°F) the jelly will set.

Once the setting point has been reached, remove the mixture from the heat, add the lemon juice and chives and stir. Pour the jelly into hot, dry jars, seal and label.

Chive and apple jelly mixture
suspended over a bowl to drain.

3. Garlic Chives

Allium tuberosum

Other Common Names

Chinese chives
Chinese flowering leeks
Chinese leeks
Cuchay chives
Gau choy, Jiu cai, Kau, Kiu
or Kiu ts'ai—Chinese
Ku cai—Malaysian
La he—Vietnamese
Nira—Japanese
Tareh—Iranian
Tsoi

Derivation of Names

THE BOTANICAL NAME, *TUBEROSUM*, MEANS TUBER-BEARING, SWOLLEN OR ENLARGED, and refers to the well-developed rhizomous roots. At different times this plant has been wrongly named *Allium ramosum* and *Allium odorum*.

Garlic refers to the garlic-onion flavour of the leaves and these plants were called chives because, like common chives, only the leaves and flowers are eaten—not the tuberous roots. The name Chinese chives indicates their probable place of origin, and the other names highlight their wide use in China, Japan and other east Asian countries.

Distribution

Garlic chives are native to eastern Asia and still grow wild in much of this area—although, because they have been cultivated for centuries, it is possible that in some regions they are actually garden escapes. They range from China, Mongolia and Japan in the north, to the Philippines in the south, and west through Thailand to India. They are also grown commercially in most of these countries. Garlic chives were introduced to Western countries by Asian immigrants, and are now much more widely grown and used throughout the world.

History

Garlic chives have been used for centuries as a salad crop in China and Japan. In the Chinese *Book of Poems*, which is made up of poems from 1000 to 500 BC, *kiu* (garlic chives) is mentioned as being offered in sacrifice with lamb. It is likely that *kiu* was regarded as a precious or holy vegetable at that time. The Mandarin name for garlic chives, *kiu ts'ai*, is listed in a dictionary of the Han period (206 BC−AD 220). In Japan, garlic chives are called *nira* and are believed to have been originally introduced from China. Records exist of their culture in Japan as early as AD 928.

Young garlic chive plants make an attractive border to the herb garden. *Heronswood, Dromana, Victoria.*

In China, garlic chives are traditionally grown in large fields, intercropped in broad bands with spinach, lettuce or pak choi, or in raised beds where they are blanched. A fascinating book, *Vegetables as Medicines* by C. Chang, et al., describes the traditional uses of vegetables in southern China. It lists several alternative common Chinese names for these chives, which demonstrate their wide use. These are *bian cai* (flat vegetable), *zhuang yang cao* (robust male grass), *qi yang cao* (rising sun grass) and *chang sheng jiu* (long life chives).

Despite their long history in eastern Asia, garlic chives were only recently introduced to Western gardens, where they have been readily available for the last 10 to 15 years.

Botanical Description

Garlic chives are vigorous perennials. They grow in dense clumps from conical bulbs on short branched rhizomes with cord-like roots. Four to nine leaves grow from each bulb, sheathing the central stem to one-eighth of its length. The bright-green leaves are solid and flat with a keeled undersurface. The solid flower stems are angular and erect, and reach a height of about 60 cm (2 ft). Garlic chives do not die back in winter in mild climates—but they will become dormant during severe winter cold. The whole plant has a mild garlic-onion smell when crushed.

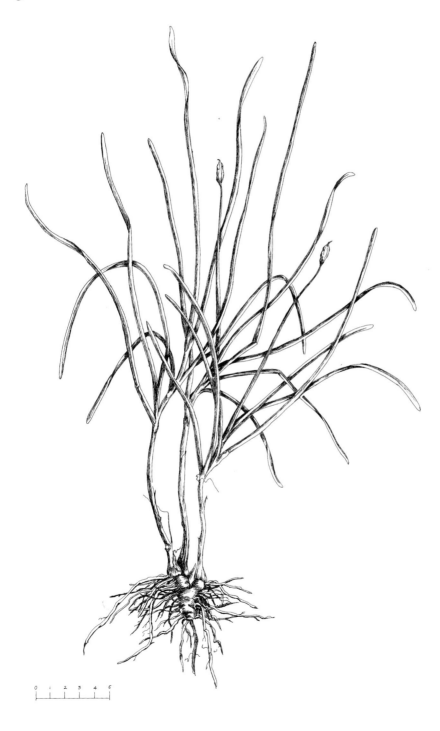

Garlic chives, *Allium tuberosum*, showing the well-developed rhizomous root system and the flower buds just starting to grow.

Diagrammatic cross-section of (*left*) the leaf and (*right*) the scape.

Flowers and Seeds

Flowers occur in hemispherical umbels from mid-summer to mid-autumn and are white, sweetly scented and star-like. They open irregularly over the flower head, and the short spathe is persistent at the base. Each perianth segment (petal) is white with a faint green or brown line on the undersurface.

The seeds are black, numerous and larger than the common onion. They can be harvested as the seed heads begin to turn brown and the seeds become visible. The heads should be randomly bent and shaken into paper bags over a number of days. Seed viability falls off rapidly so it is best not to use seed that is more than a year old.

A single garlic chive flower with pedicel.

Garlic chive flower heads opening to reveal the star-like flowers.

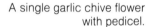

Cultivars, Varieties and Closely Related Species

In several countries there are two varieties of garlic chives: one grown for its big or broad leaves, either fresh or blanched, and the other a flowering type grown mainly for the flower stem and flower. In Japan there is a variety of garlic chives known as tender pole, which is grown for its succulent flower stalks. In Taiwan the big-leafed type is called *taai ip*, while the flowering type is known as *nin fa*. In China there are six or more distinct varieties and cultivars, including one with exceptionally fleshy roots which are pickled, and another grown for both its flowers and leaves. The latter is probably the predominant form grown and available in Western countries where the plants are sold simply as *Allium tuberosum* and no cultivars are listed.

A. tuberosum (garlic chives) is often confused with *A. ramosum*, a native of Siberia — which is also sometimes sold as Siberian chives. And *A. ramosum* should not be confused with yet another plant, *A. schoenoprasum* var. *sibericum*, also sold as Siberian chives (see p. 50). The following chart makes it possible to distinguish between *A. tuberosum* and *A. ramosum* (for more information on *A. ramosum* see Chapter 11).

Allium tuberosum	Allium ramosum
Cross-section of the leaf is keeled and solid	Cross-section of the leaf is semi-circular and hollow
Leaves sheathe stem to ⅛ of its length	Leaves sheathe stem to ⅓ of its length
Hemispherical umbel	Funnel-shaped umbel
Flowers star-shaped, white with a faint green line underneath	Flowers bell-shaped, white with a red stripe

Propagation

Garlic chives can be grown in spring, summer or autumn from seed or by root division. Sow seed directly into the ground and cover with a layer of fine soil or plant the seed in pots and then transplant the seedlings when big enough to handle. Seed must be fresh and will normally germinate in 10 days. Plants will often self-sow.

Alternatively, new clumps can be generated by dividing old ones. Lift the whole clump, pull the rhizomes apart and replant about 30 cm (1 ft) apart in groups of four or five. Water well.

Cultivation

Garlic chives grow best in sub-tropical climates. They will survive well in tropical regions if grown at higher altitudes. They are one of the hardiest of the edible alliums and will tolerate a wide range of climatic conditions. They are resistant to both heat and cold—the underground rhizomes have been known to survive −40°C (−40°F).

Garlic chives will tolerate a wide range of soils also. They do best in a well-drained, fertile soil which is rich in organic matter. Full sun and plenty of water during hot summers will produce maximum growth—but they will survive in semi-shade and during long dry spells.

They grow well in pots, making them an excellent plant for small gardens or flats with balconies. They can be planted and left untouched for many years, but for optimum production need to be divided and replanted every two to three years.

They also make useful borders for vegetable gardens and rose beds, and here can be planted more closely. Groups of three to four bulbs 15–20 cm (6–8 in) apart. In mild climates, garlic chives will grow right through the winter. In very cold regions they will die back and you may need to protect the rhizomes with mulch.

A border of garlic chives coming into flower.

Garlic Chives in China

Garlic chives are widely grown in China, with seeds either sown directly into 8-cm-deep (3-in) trenches or into seedbeds and then transplanted. They are grown in clumps of about 20 seedlings, placed 12 cm (4½ in) apart in rows 50 cm (1 ft 8 in) apart. The plants are kept weed-free and only watered when absolutely necessary—this encourages deep root growth. When the leaves are about 30 cm (1 ft) long they are harvested, by cutting just above the rhizome, and allowed to regrow. A well-grown clump can yield over 4 kilograms (9 lb) of chives a year and a clump lasts four to five years, after which it needs to be replaced. In the second and following years in some cultivars the final cut will be of flower stems.

To ensure that the clumps last as long as possible, as soon as the roots begin growing in spring they are raked over to stimulate root growth and remove old dead roots. They are then top-dressed with sandy soil and fed regularly with liquid manure, before or just after the leaves are cut.

Often garlic chives are blanched or softened. This is achieved by excluding all light once the plants have started to grow. One method is to plant in trenches and fill in with earth as the chives grow. In heated greenhouses or hot beds light is excluded by bamboo or straw mats. In the open, straw mats can be hung from overhead bamboo poles, or straw tents are built over rows. When crops are grown for alternate green and blanched crops, after the green chives are cut the stumps are covered with clay chimney pots. Each pot has a lid and the cracks are sealed with clay. It takes only three to four weeks for the blanched, yellow chives to grow and be ready to harvest.

In warmer regions garlic chives can be harvested up to nine times. A typical combination is four green, four blanched and one in the early autumn when the tender flower stalks are cut and used as well as the leaves. In colder regions only three or four cuts are possible.

Garlic Chives in Japan

Garlic chives are also grown in Japan for their leaves and flowers. When grown for flowers they are sown in seedbeds in spring and the seedlings transplanted after about three months, in clumps of two to three seedlings 25 cm (10 in) apart each way. In the first season the flower stalks are removed to encourage denser growth. The flowers are then harvested from the second season for the next five years. After this the clumps need to be replaced.

Harvest and Storage

Leaves for use in the home are best picked just before they are needed. Take only a few leaves at a time, cutting just above the sheath. They are much more flavoursome if used fresh and, after washing and drying, will keep for two or three days in the crisper of the refrigerator.

However, it is also possible to dry them, and the best results are obtained in the microwave. A handful of chopped leaves takes about 3 minutes and they can be stored in dry jars out of direct light.

Flowers for use in Chinese cooking are harvested with their long tubular stems when the flowers are still tightly enclosed within the spathe.

Pests and Diseases
See also Chapter 13.

Garlic chives are relatively disease-free but can be attacked by onion thrip which suck the juice from the leaves. These can be controlled by hand (by squashing) or by spraying with soapy water or pyrethrum solution.

Medicinal Uses

Garlic chives are rich in vitamin A and fibre and also contain lesser amounts of vitamins B1, B2 and C, and iron and sulphur.

They stimulate the appetite and in China the bulbs and leaves are used as a tonic. They are anti-bacterial and are used in the treatment of amoebic and bacterial dysentery. They are also used to treat tuberculosis, whooping cough and externally for skin complaints such as dermatitis and tinea.

The oil extracted from the seeds is used medicinally. *Vegetables as Medicines* by C. Chang, et al. describes a treatment for impotence which involves crushing some garlic chive seeds and adding them to rice wine in the

Garlic chive flowers make a delightful addition to any garden, and can also be eaten or added to flower arrangements.

proportion of 1:5. They are left to soak for a week and 1 spoonful of the wine should be taken three times a day after meals.

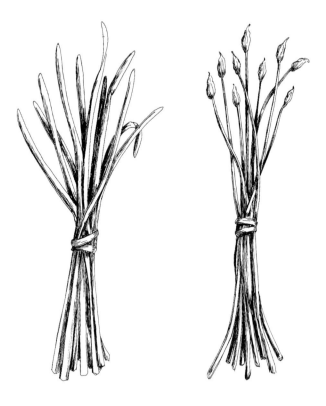

Left: A bunch of garlic chive leaves. *Right:* A bunch of garlic chive flower buds and stems.

Other Uses

In China, where garlic chives are plentiful, the diluted, pressed juice of the whole plant is sprayed over crops to protect them from aphids, spider mites and some plant diseases.

The dried flower heads make a useful addition to flower arrangements. The plants are decorative and the flowers sweetly scented, so they can be grown among other perennials.

Culinary Uses

In Western cooking, garlic chives are used in much the same way as common chives (see Ch. 2)—as a garnish where the mild onion-garlic flavour enhances the flavour of the dish. The leaves are more tender if cooked only briefly but long cooking does not completely destroy the flavour as it does with common chives. The flower buds, flower stems and flowers can also be used.

The green leaves can be chopped and fried in oil before other ingredients are added. They can be used in omelettes, with soft cheeses, to make garlic bread, in salads and as a garnish.

They are also used in numerous ways in Asia—in spring rolls, dumplings, omelettes, dressed with salt and sesame oil as a salad, mixed with mushrooms or with bean curds and noodles.

The tender yellow blanched leaves are used in Asian cookery. They are regarded as a delicacy and eaten in small quantities. They are more tender than the green leaves and need to be used very fresh, served chopped with noodles, in soup or fried. They can also be used in the same ways as green leaves. Garlic chives are also used extensively in Iranian cooking.

Tender flower stems and buds have a mild onion flavour and maintain their green colour well when cooked. These too can be used as a chives substitute in the same way as the leaves. In Java, small bunches are deep fried in rice batter. The flower stems are delicious stir-fried with bean sprouts and can be added fresh to salads. The Chinese also stir-fry the flowers, either on their own or to be used as a side dish with beef or beancurd.

The star-shaped flowers make a decorative addition to salads and in China they are dried for use as a garnish or flavouring and are often used as a spice.

If a stronger, more garlicky flavour is desired, garlic chives can be used instead of common chives in all the recipes in Chapter 2. The following recipes are examples of dishes where garlic chives are particularly appropriate.

Garlic chive flowers beginning to open. Flower stems and buds for cooking need to be harvested when still very young or else the stem will be tough.

Recipes

*Appetisers and
Light Meals*

Green Salad with Creamy Chive and Tarragon Dressing

This can simply be served with common lettuce, but is better if a variety of leaves is used.

Break up the lettuce and rinse all the salad leaves under cold water. Pat dry and pile the leaves in the bowl, roughly tearing the larger leaves. Separate the egg yolks from the whites, chop the whites and sprinkle over the top of the leaves.

Make the sauce by mashing the egg yolks with the cream and then stirring in the oil. Slowly stir in the vinegar, add the garlic chives and tarragon and season with salt and pepper. Pour the dressing over the salad just before serving. Mix well.

1 small red lettuce
1 small handful each of
    corn salad, endive, land
    cress, mizuna and rocket
    leaves
Dressing:
2 eggs, hard-boiled
2 tablespoons thick cream
2 tablespoons olive oil
2 teaspoons white wine
    vinegar
1 tablespoon garlic chives,
    finely chopped
½ tablespoon French
    tarragon, finely chopped
salt and freshly ground
    black pepper

Green Anchovy Dressing

This dressing is salty because of the anchovies. For a less salty dressing reduce the number of anchovies. Serve with any seafood dish, especially seafood salads.

Add the herbs to the mayonnaise, then stir in the anchovies and finally the vinegar. Chill for 2 hours before serving.

4 tablespoons garlic chives,
    finely chopped
6 tablespoons plain-leaf
    parsley, chopped
1 tablespoon French
    tarragon, finely chopped
1¼ cups mayonnaise
10 anchovy fillets, finely
    chopped
2 tablespoons white wine
    vinegar

Main Courses

Garlic Chive Omelette — Chinese Style

4–5 eggs
sesame oil
soy sauce
2 tablespoons vegetable
stock (or water)
2 tablespoons garlic chives,
roughly chopped
salt and freshly ground
black pepper

Beat the eggs. Add a couple of drops of sesame oil, a splash of light soy sauce, the vegetable stock (or water) and whisk. Mix in chives and salt and pepper to taste. Make four small omelettes by frying one-quarter of the mixture at a time in sesame oil, until set and golden brown underneath. Fold into a semicircle and cook a moment longer. Serve immediately.

Serves two.

Poached Chicken with Garlic Chive Sauce

1 large chicken
1 sprig each of lovage,
parsley and thyme
1 onion, cut in half
1 carrot
2 bay leaves
10 black peppercorns

Sauce:
2 tablespoons butter
2 tablespoons flour
2 tablespoons garlic chives,
roughly chopped
½ cup thick cream
salt and freshly ground
black pepper

Place the chicken in a saucepan which is just large enough to hold it. Cover with water and add the herbs, onion, carrot, bay leaves and peppercorns. Bring to the boil and simmer gently for 1 hour. Remove the chicken and cut into serving-size pieces. Keep warm. Boil the stock to reduce the liquid to 1¼ cups, skimming the fat from the top, then strain.

In a small pan, melt the butter and stir in the flour — cook for 1 minute. Add the stock and garlic chives and cook for a further 4 minutes. Finally add the cream and salt and pepper to taste. Pour the sauce over the chicken pieces and serve with rice or baked potatoes.

Serves four.

4. Elephant Garlic

Allium ampeloprasum
(**Ampeloprasum
Group**)

Other Common Names

Ail d'orient—French
Giant garlic
Great-headed garlic
Levant garlic
Perennial sweet leek
Pferdknoblauch—German
Russian garlic
Yorktown onion

Derivation of Names

THE SPECIFIC NAME, *AMPELOPRASUM*, IS DERIVED FROM THE GREEK WORDS *AMPELOS* and *prason*, which mean a vine and leek respectively. The common names refer to the size of the bulbs and flower heads or to the plant's place of origin.

Distribution

Elephant garlic is not cultivated commercially, but is found in gardens in many countries. Its parent plant, *A. ampeloprasum*, wild leek is native to northern Africa, Asia, southern Europe and parts of Russia, where it grows on dry, rocky or sandy ground and near cultivated land. In Australia, the British Isles and the United States, elephant garlic is often found as a garden escape and is naturalised in some areas.

History

There is little written about the history of elephant garlic because it has rarely been grown as a commercial crop, but bulbs have been collected from the wild, grown in gardens and eaten for many centuries.

One variety that grows wild in England, *A. ampeloprasum* var. *babingtonii*, is often found in places associated with early Christian sites and may have been cultivated by the monks who lived there. Another form, which was called great-headed garlic and commonly cultivated in the Mediterranean, is recorded as having been grown by John Tradescant the Younger (1608–62), botanist and gardener to Charles I of England. This plant is described as forming large garlic-like bulbs with numerous bulblets. It also had large flower heads, but set few seeds. It was probably the same as the elephant garlic seen today.

Botanical Description

The vegetative parts of elephant garlic look, superficially, like a very robust form of garlic but this plant is actually more closely related to the leek.

Large blue-green linear leaves, with a central dividing rib, sheathe the stem. In early or mid-summer, after about eight leaves have grown, a solid, cylindrical flower stalk grows up to 2 m (6½ ft) high. Large bulbs form under the soil, reaching 10 cm (4 in) in diameter and consisting of five or six large cloves. Surrounding these cloves, enclosed in the papery outer covering, are usually anything from 1 to 20 small bulblets, up to 1 cm (½ in) across, with one flat side.

Plants that do not flower often form one large, symmetrical clove, or round, rather than a bulb (see below). This round can be up to 4 cm (1½ in) in diameter, is terminal on the main stem and is solid—not made up of layers as in onions (*A. cepa*). Plants grown from rounds, or from very large cloves, frequently produce a large bulb with several cloves and a flower stalk. Plants grown from a smaller clove or from a bulblet frequently produce a round and no flower stalk. So elephant garlic tends to alternate between the production of cloves and the production of rounds, and goes to seed only every second year. A well-established clump will usually have a mixture of bulbs with cloves and rounds, so there will always be some flower heads.

As the elephant garlic bulb matures, the leaves will yellow and fade. Removal of the flower stalk will ensure larger bulbs, but as the bulbs are already very large this hardly seems necessary.

A fully grown elephant garlic bulb with cloves.

(a) An elephant garlic clove.
(b) An elephant garlic round.
(c) Bulblets which develop around elephant garlic bulbs.

A young elephant garlic plant with the bulb and cloves starting to form and the flower head beginning to grow.

Flowers and Seeds

In spring and summer, large flower heads form singly at the top of long flower stalks. The single long-beaked spathes split to reveal the flower heads, which are large, densely packed and up to 10 cm (4 in) in diameter. Flowers are pink or purple and open irregularly over the flower head. Stamens protrude slightly beyond the perianth segments (petals). Sometimes there are bulbils mixed in with the flowers but these are usually absent. The flowers are sometimes sterile, but will usually set some seed and even self-sow. If plants are left without water for long periods the flower head will droop, but later rain will cause them to start growing upwards again. This cycle can result in dramatically twisted scapes giving a sculptural appearance to the plant. This should not be confused with the rocambole form of top-setting garlic (*A. sativum*), where the scape loops vertically during early growth but straightens as the flower head develops.

A flower head where the flowers are finished and the stem shows the peculiar twists and turns which can result from irregular watering.

Cultivars, Varieties and Closely Related Species

A. ampeloprasum (Ampeloprasum Group) is a diverse group. There are a few cultivars and many varieties, both named and unnamed, found growing in different parts of the world. Elephant garlic and Pearlzwiebel are the most commonly available.

Allium ampeloprasum (Ampeloprasum Group) 'Pearlzwiebel'

Pearlzwiebel or pearl onion has been sold as multiplier leek, Argentine garlic and potato onion. To add to the confusion, its growth habit is similar to elephant garlic, except that it produces a cluster of solid spherical white bulbs or rounds, and never produces cloves. The bulbs can be distinguished from onion bulbs because they are solid, not layered.

A plant that produces a flower stem usually does not swell to form a bulb, but stays relatively straight. If the flower stem is removed then bulbs will grow. Flowers are often only produced every second year and closely resemble those of elephant garlic, except that they are a paler pink, smaller and do not usually produce seed, if they do produce seed it is not fertile.

Pearlzwiebel multiplies vegetatively by producing numerous small off-shoots surrounding the parent plant. Each of these has a rounded bulb at the base. The whole plant dies back after flowering, leaving a cluster of bulbs ranging in size from ½ to 6 cm (¼–2½ in) in diameter. If these are left in the ground they will all reshoot in late winter or spring, forming a dense clump.

Allium ampeloprasum var. babingtonii

British leek, Welsh leek
A wild variety found in the south of England and south-west Ireland.
Has flowers and bulbils in the umbel but otherwise resembles elephant garlic.

Allium ampeloprasum var. bulbiferum

Similar to var. *babingtonii* but has smaller bulbils.
Found in Guernsey and France.

Allium giganteum

This tall-growing allium is similar to elephant garlic but easily distinguised by the breadth of the leaf and the colour of the flower.
See Chapter 11 for more information.

Propagation

Elephant garlic is grown from cloves or rounds. In mild climates, they can be planted in autumn, winter and spring, but in cool climates, only autumn and

Young pearlzwiebel plant with the off-shoots growing and the round bulbs developing.

A dense planting of elephant garlic.

Elephant garlic provides a statuesque backdrop to the more diminutive chives. *Yuulong Lavender Estate, Mount Egerton, Victoria.*

A flower head where the spathe has split and the flowers are beginning to open.

An elephant garlic crop with the buds about to burst open. *Ellistield Farm, Red Hill, Victoria.*

spring. Plant them blunt or root ends down about 30 cm (1 ft) apart—the tops of the bulbs should be about 5 cm (2 in) below the soil surface. The small bulblets that form around the cloves can be saved and planted the following spring. Each bulblet should produce a round the first year, and the following year the round should produce a bulb with cloves.

Cultivation

Elephant garlic does best in rich, deeply cultivated, well-drained soil and likes full sun. It is very hardy, needs no special treatment and can in fact become a weed. In some gardens, elephant garlic may be difficult to control and remove because of the numerous bulblets that form around the cloves, each of which will grow into a new plant. When harvested regularly and/or confined to a definite bed, elephant garlic should not be a problem.

When plants are allowed to flower they will grow very tall, so plant them at the back of the bed. Mulch the beds after planting to keep the plants free from weeds—the strong leaves will push their way through quite a thick layer. If flower stems are removed before the flower heads are formed, the bulbs are usually larger. But the flower heads are dramatic and worth growing, so unless very large bulbs are essential the plants should be left to flower.

Elephant garlic is a useful home garden vegetable, especially in warmer, more humid climates where true garlic (*A. sativum*) is difficult to grow. It grows from the tropics to temperate regions and tends to grow taller in cooler regions.

Pearlzwiebel needs more water during hot weather than elephant garlic but otherwise its requirements are similar.

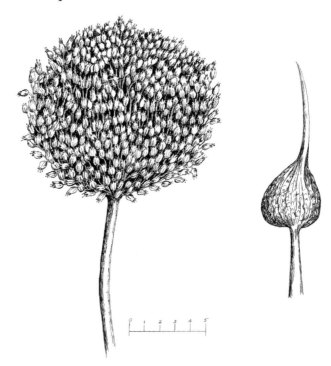

Flower bud and flower head of elephant garlic.

Harvest and Storage

Bulbs should be harvested when the leaves begin to die back if the flower heads have been removed, or when the flowers begin to dry out. Dig up the whole plant and hang the bulbs to dry, with part of the stem attached, in a shady but dry position. Flower heads with stalks should be hung in bunches in a similar position.

Bulbs can be eaten either straight from the ground or when dried, and they will keep for 10 months if stored in a dry airy position. If not harvested, bulbs will remain dormant in the ground until it is time to start growing again, usually early winter. Bulbs often turn green if left in the ground too long and they should not be eaten once this has happened.

Pearlzwiebel bulbs are harvested as the leaves die back. They store well and will keep for up to six months in a dry airy, well-ventilated position.

A flower head where the spathe has almost fallen off and more of the flowers have opened.

Medicinal Uses

Elephant garlic does not share the medicinal properties of garlic (*A. sativum*). It is more closely related to leeks, so is high in vitamins A, C and E and is a healthy addition to any diet.

Other Uses

Flowers, fresh or dried, make an interesting addition to flower arrangements, although the strong odour can be overpowering. Elephant garlic can also be planted at the back of rose borders or near climbing roses to help keep aphids and other pests at bay.

Culinary Uses

Elephant garlic has a mild sweet flavour that is somewhere between garlic and onion. Cloves are large, easy to peel and easy to grow, making them a very useful home garden vegetable. Bulbs do not have the pungency of garlic and so are not a good substitute in any dish that requires the true garlic flavour.

Cloves and rounds can be eaten raw, sliced into salads, or steamed or boiled as a vegetable with or without a sauce. They can also be cooked like onions in soups, stews or casseroles, or baked in the oven with roasts. Young leaves can be sliced and added to salads or used as a garnish.

Pearlzwiebel are usually pickled in the same way as onions, but they are sweeter and their texture is crisper.

Flower heads drying.

Elephant garlic which has been harvested drying on
a rack to allow air circulation around all the bulbs.

Pearlzwiebel flower buds are very similar to those of
elephant garlic.

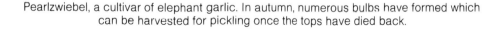

Pearlzwiebel, a cultivar of elephant garlic. In autumn, numerous bulbs have formed which
can be harvested for pickling once the tops have died back.

Elephant Garlic

Recipes

Yuulong Lavender Mustard

100 grams (3½ oz) whole
    yellow mustard seed
200 grams (7 oz) whole
    black mustard seed
10 whole cloves
1 tablespoon fresh tarragon,
    chopped
1 tablespoon fresh thyme,
    chopped
¾ cup parsley sprigs
3 large cloves elephant
    garlic
4 pieces stem ginger
4 dessertspoons honey
3 dessertspoons salt
1 cup white wine vinegar
½ cup dry white wine
1 cup olive oil
2 tablespoons English
    lavender flowers (strip
    the individual flowers
    from the flower head)

This recipe is from the Yuulong Lavender Estate, Victoria, Australia.

Combine mustard seeds and cloves in a blender, add tarragon, thyme, parsley, peeled elephant garlic, ginger, honey and salt. Process until the ingredients are finely chopped. Gradually add the vinegar, wine and oil while continuing to process. Cover. Stand overnight, then add lavender and stir in thoroughly with a wooden spoon. Smooth into sterile jars, seal and label. If a smoother mustard is required, process a second time.

Pickled Pearlzwiebel

1 kilogram (2 lb 3 oz)
    pearlzwiebel bulbs
160 grams (5½ oz) coarse
    salt
6 cups water
6 cups spiced vinegar (see
    p. 160)

Select bulbs of similar size, wash and trim. Dissolve the salt in the water, place the pearlzwiebel in a bowl and pour the salted water over the top. Leave to soak overnight, drain and rinse thoroughly. Pat the bulbs dry and pack them into sterile jars. Fill with cold, spiced vinegar and seal with lids which will not be affected by vinegar. Store in a cool dark place for at least 4 weeks before using.

5. Leeks

Allium ampeloprasum
(Porrum Group)

Other Common Names

Aga — Early Roman
Hazir — Hebrew
Lauch — German
Look — Dutch
Luk — Russian
Pirasa — Turkish
Poireau — French
Porro — Italian
Puerro — Spanish

THIS PLANT IS ALSO COMMONLY GIVEN THE BOTANICAL NAMES *ALLIUM AMPELOPRASUM* var. *porrum* and *Allium porrum*. Leeks are a cultivated plant unknown in the wild. They have numerous traits in common with *A. ampeloprasum*, so they are more accurately placed in the Porrum Group of *A. ampeloprasum*, rather than as a distinct species or variety. A leek cultivar such as 'Bleu Solaise' should be labelled: *Allium ampeloprasum* (Porrum Group) 'Bleu Solaise'. For more information see Appendix 1.

Derivation of Names

The Latin word for leek is *porrum*. This gave rise to the French, Italian and Spanish names. Leek comes from Saxon *leac* and means a spear or spear-shaped; most of the other common names are derived from this. *Aga* is an early Roman name and *Hazir* means green herb.

Distribution

Leeks are no longer found as a wild plant but they are cultivated in many countries. They are particularly popular in cooler climates as they will grow and produce right through late autumn, winter and early spring when other crops are scarce.

History

Leeks were one of the earliest agricultural crops. Records exist of their cultivation in Egypt as early as 3000 BC. In the 1st century, the Roman scholar and author, Pliny the Elder (AD 23–79), wrote that the best leeks still came from Egypt. At the same time the infamous Roman Emperor,

Nero, was rumoured to eat leeks regularly in an attempt to improve his speaking and singing voice. He was given the derisive nickname of *porrophagus*, or leek-eater.

By AD 800, leeks were included in Charlemagne's *Capitulare de Villis*. This document contained a list made up of those plants suitable for planting in the Carolingian Empire, which stretched from the North Sea to Italy. It is likely that the Romans distributed leeks to the countries they conquered and, although they are only mentioned a few times in early English literature, they were certainly cultivated by the monks in England during the Middle Ages.

Leeks are a national emblem of Wales, but the origin of this tradition is difficult to trace. The plant is associated with Saint David's day (1 March) and may commemorate a victory by the Welsh over the Saxons in the 6th century. Welsh soldiers apparently wore leeks to distinguish them from the Saxons. However, it is difficult to be sure which plants the early historians intended to describe, and it is possible that it was actually daffodils that the soldiers wore—the Welsh name for daffodil is *Cenin Pedr* (St Peter's Leek).

Leeks look dramatic when planted in the flower garden.

The English poet, Michael Drayton (1563–1631), had a different explanation for the leek's association with Saint David. In his work *Polyolbion* he says that the Saint

> . . . did so truely fast,
> As he did only drink what crystal Hodney yields,
> And fed upon the leeks he gathered in the fields.
> In memory of whom, in each revolving year,
> The Welshmen, on this day, that sacred herb do wear.

Whatever the truth of Wales's ancient association with leeks, it is certain that the regimental badge of the Welsh Regiment of Foot Guards, formed in 1915, is a leek.

Leeks are mentioned by Chaucer, and later by Shakespeare in *Henry V* (1599) where Captain Fluellen forces Pistol to eat the leek he was wearing in his cap.

Margaret Dods in her *The Cook and Housewife's Manual* (1826) notes that 'the leek is the badge of a high-spirited, honourable, and fiery nation—the Ancient Britons'. She goes on to say that in Scotland and Wales 'where a young man would now be styled the *flower*, he was called the *leek* of his family or tribe, an epithet of most savory meaning'.

The first leek seed landed in Australia in 1786 with the first fleet. According to Sir Joseph Banks' lists, the supply ships carried 20 bushells of 'London Leek' seed and 10 bushells of an unspecified cultivar.

Today leeks are mainly a crop of the British Isles, northern Europe and parts of Africa and Asia. They have never achieved the same popularity in Canada and the United States, although they were cultivated by Choctaw Indians before 1775 and three cultivars were listed in a seed catalogue three years later.

Botanical Description

Leeks are biennials. They grow from suprisingly large root systems and have flat, broad, linear leaves which are folded lengthways. The elongated foliage leaf bases encircle each other to form a cylindrical elongated bulb that is scarcely developed. It is this bulb, more often called the stalk, that is blanched and eaten. Above the bulb, the flat leaves sheathe the stout, solid flower stem, which can reach a height of 1½ metres (5 ft). Flowering occurs in the second year, after a period of vegetative winter growth. However, leeks are generally harvested in the first year because once the flower stem develops, the stems are too tough to eat. The time from sowing to harvest is about 150 days.

Diagrammatic cross-section of (*top*) the leaf and (*bottom*) the scape.

Flowers and Seeds

A single leaf flower
with pedicel.

Leek flower bud.

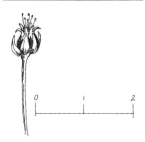

An open flower head.

Solid flower stalks grow to 1½ metres (5 ft). They are topped by a papery spathe which splits to reveal a globular umbel up to 9 cm (3½ in) diameter. The umbel is packed with hundreds of pink or white cup-shaped flowers which open irregularly over the flower head.

The seed is black and triangular or irregular and remains viable for two to three years. It should be collected when it is obvious in most of the flowers in the umbel. Cut the flower heads and carefully place them in a paper bag. When fully dry, rub the head to extract the seed and store in a dry place. Leeks will cross with other leek cultivars but not with other alliums.

Perennial or perpetual leeks (described below) flower later in the season than other leeks, and in warmer, more humid regions they may not flower at all, but will continue to produce new side-shoots. The seed of perennial leeks is usually fertile.

Cultivars, Varieties and Closely Related Species
See also Appendixes 3.2 and 4 at the back of the book.

Cultivars of leeks vary enormously, from giant leeks grown for competition to those which are smaller but tender and delicate. Variation occurs in the length and diameter of the sheath, the leaf spacing, the colour and the vigour of the plant, the risk of bolting and resistance to cold. Cultivars with blue-green leaves tend to be more cold-hardy.

Some cultivars produce bulblets around the base which can be replanted to produce new plants. These bulblets usually appear in the second year as the flower stem develops. If one of these cultivars produces a flower stem, this can be removed and often the bulblets will begin to grow around the base producing several smaller leek plants.

A leek cultivar which is a favourite in permaculture gardens is the perpetual or perennial leek. These leeks divide profusely at the base so that clumps of green tops are formed. One plant can produce up to 20 off-shoots in a season. Usually the stalks reach only finger thickness and they can be harvested at any time—they are always present and do not have to be regrown each year from seed. These leeks also produce very small bulbs or bulblets, usually flat on one side, which will grow new shoots. Perennial leeks are probably derived from old varieties of leek that were found growing wild in some regions of France and other European countries. They were probably garden escapes, able to survive because of their multiplying habit.

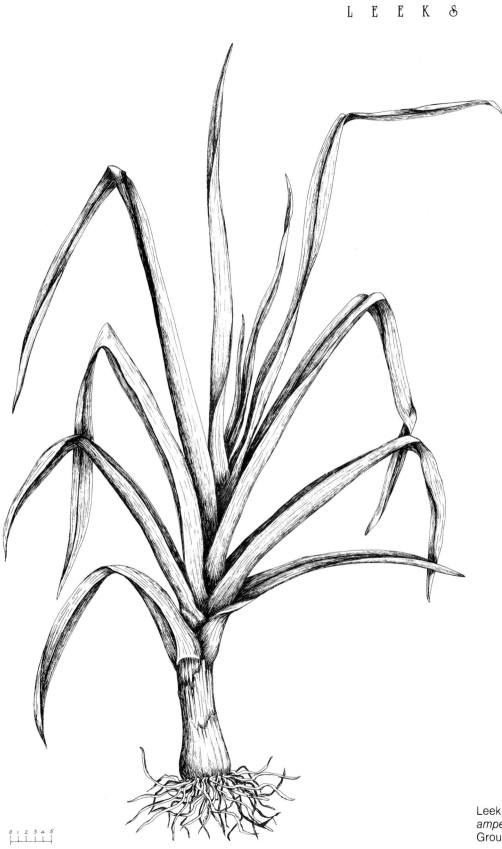

Leek, *Allium ampeloprasum* (Porrum Group), just after harvest.

0 1 2 3 4 5

Perennial leeks are sometimes sold as multiplier leeks, but this name is also used for a plant that looks similar to the leek: 'Pearlzwiebel'. This is a cultivar of elephant garlic and develops larger bulbs at the base than the leek (see p. 77).

Although there are many cultivars of leeks available today they were much more diverse in form 100 years ago. Perpetual leeks, those eaten for their green tops, and those grown for their bulblets or cloves are much more difficult to obtain today. As leeks are grown easily from seed and are generally not dependent on day length, seed obtained from other regions or countries can be sown in new regions.

Propagation

Leeks are usually grown from seed, which can be sown in autumn, spring or summer depending on the climate and the cultivar being grown. They need a long growing season and in cold climates should be planted as early in spring as possible. Early varieties can be sown indoors in late winter and transplanted when about 15 cm (6 in) high. Late varieties, and those that can be planted in autumn, should be sown in seed trays, or direct-seeded into friable soil, covered with a fine layer of soil and kept moist until they germinate.

A single leek plant with the flower head beginning to develop.

In some leek cultivars, bulbils grow around the base of the plant as the flower head develops. If the plant is cut off at the base each bulbil will grow into another small leek plant forming a dense clump. These can be harvested as needed.

Seed trays can be covered with plastic sheets after sowing to maintain moisture content—remove the plastic once the seeds sprout.

The optimum soil temperature for germination is 11°– 23°C (52°–73°F). Germination is drastically reduced at soil temperatures below 7°C (45°F) and above 27°C (81°F).

When seedlings reach 20 cm (8 in), which usually takes about 10 weeks, they can be transplanted into trenches or into individual holes. Space them about 15 cm (6 in) apart in rows, or up to 30 cm (1 ft) apart in a block. The larger the spacing, the larger the leek will be. Conversely, higher densities will give a similar yield of more slender leeks.

Perpetual leeks are most easily propagated by dividing the clumps at harvest. Replant the ones not used about 20 cm (8 in) apart. Some leeks, on going to seed, also produce bulblets around the base of the plant. These can be planted out and will produce robust seedlings more quickly than seed.

Cultivation

Leeks are generally extremely hardy and easy to grow. They will do best in a rich, well-drained soil in an open position, with plenty of moisture during the growing season. They grow in most regions, but very hot climates are not suitable and daytime temperatures greater than 25°C (77°F) may reduce

A good crop of 'Musselburgh' leeks. *The Garden of St Erth, Blackwood, Victoria.*

The blue-green leaves of the 'Bleu Solaise' cultivar combine well with flowers in the garden. *Heronswood, Dromana, Victoria.*

yields. The best temperature range for growth and production is 13°–24°C (55°–75°F).

Climate determines the planting time. If you live in a mild climate, start the leeks in summer and grow through winter. If you are in a cold region, start them in early spring and grow through summer for an autumn harvest. Cold temperatures will encourage some cultivars to bolt (flower and set seed). Those cultivars that grow happily through winter—often those with blue-green rather than green leaves—can simply have mulch spread thickly around them if temperatures go below freezing. Pull the mulch away as the weather warms up. Growth to maturity takes between 150 and 190 days, but plants can be used before they are fully mature.

To prepare the bed, dig in well-aged manure and some bone or fish meal to increase the phosphate levels. Just after planting, water in some manure solution to increase nitrogen levels.

Perennial leeks are very easy to grow. They like similar conditions to other leek cultivars, but will tolerate more shade and need plenty of water during dry seasons. If they are not being harvested on a regular basis, clumps will need to be dug and divided every few years or they will become overcrowded.

Two techniques which can be used to blanch leek stems.
Left: A trench.
Right: Individual holes.

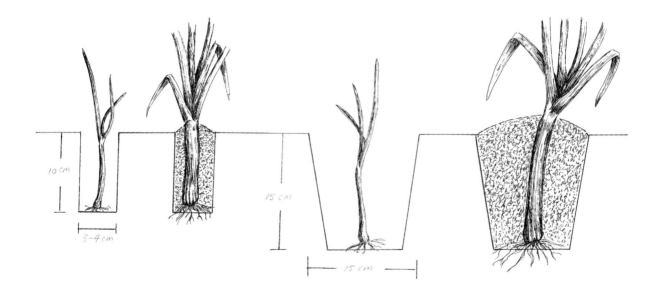

Blanching the Stems

To produce long white stalks, leeks need to be blanched. Leeks planted without attempting to blanch them are still perfectly edible, but the edible portion will not be as large or as tender. There are three main ways of blanching.

(1) Dig a trench 15 cm (6 in) deep and place the seedlings in this trench about 15 cm (6 in) apart. Firm into the soil and water carefully. Once the seedlings are about the width of a little finger, pull some dirt into the trench to cover the bottom of the leeks. Repeat this as the leeks grow

until the trench is full. The soil can then be mounded up, as long as it does not go above the point where the leaves diverge.

(2) Plant the leeks at the bottom of holes made by a thick pointed stick or dibber. These holes should be 10–15 cm (4–6 in) deep. Water the seedlings and then leave—rain and water gradually push dirt into the hole covering the stem. The soil around the hole should not be compressed as this may inhibit the swelling of the stem during growth.

(3) Leek stems can be blanched by tying paper around the stem. In fact anything that excludes light can be used—except plastic, as this can cause sweating and encourage rot and mould. This method can be combined with the first two to ensure a clean white stem.

Harvest and Storage

Unlike many other alliums, leeks do not enter a rest period but continue growing, so they can be harvested over a long period. This means that storage is generally unnecessary—simply leave the plants in the ground until they are needed. They can be harvested in the early stages of growth, even the larger thinnings can be tender and delicious. In Europe, the ideal size for harvest is when the diameter of the stem reaches about 2.5 cm (1 in). This is much smaller than the traditional size of leeks in Australia and the British Isles. In very cold regions with heavy snow, leeks can be harvested and stored in buckets or boxes filled with dry sand or soil in a cool room such as a cellar.

Leeks planted in early spring are ready to be harvested by late summer. Those planted later can be dug up in autumn, winter and even into the following spring. Simply dig up the plant, shake the soil loose and wash off the rest. Once leeks have gone to seed the stems are too tough to eat.

Pests and Diseases
See also Chapter 13.

Leeks are subject to some of the same diseases and pests as onions: downy mildew, nematodes, onion fly, pink root, smudge, smut, thrips, white rot and rust—rust is the most common disease. This seems a formidable list, but in reality leeks are one of the hardiest of the edible alliums and, if grown in good soil with good drainage and in an open position, there should be no problems. Most of the pests and diseases are the product of intensive monocultures and in an organic garden with a large variety of plants these problems are rarely apparent. In fact leeks are often planted beside other more tender plants to keep marauding insects away. If disease does strike, it is often in the final stages of growth—just before harvest. The affected plants can still be harvested and eaten. Just remove and destroy the outer leaves and eat the rest.

Medicinal Uses

Leeks do not have the medicinal reputation of garlic and onions but they are low in calories and high in vitamins A, C and E. They also have antiseptic properties.

In the past, a hot poultice made from the leaves was used to relieve the pain of haemorrhoids, and the roast stems were prescribed to remove bad phlegm from the lungs, to halt nose-bleeds and as an antidote for mushroom poisoning.

Other Uses

Leeks have also been used as an insect repellent. They can be planted between rows of other vegetables to protect them from insect pests. In Europe the leaves are infused and used as a fly repellent.

Culinary Uses

Leeks are a delicious vegetable. The stalks have a mellow flavour reminiscent of onion and garlic but sweeter and milder. Leek flavours tend to enhance other flavours rather than overpower. Reduced pungency also makes them more suitable for people who find the stronger alliums too powerful or indigestible.

Usually only the white part is used and all the green is discarded. However, there are some now very rare cultivars where the green tops are eaten. The best, most tender leeks have long white stalks and are not too thick. They must also be fresh, as stale leeks develop an acrid flavour. Perennial leeks are used in the same way as the other cultivars, although their flavour is generally milder.

Young, tender leeks have been added raw to salads since early Roman times. They can be steamed gently and served with butter, or a butter or cheese-based sauce, as an entrée or light lunch — in much the same way as asparagus is served. Leeks have been called 'poor man's asparagus'.

Leeks are the main flavour in classic soups such as Scotch broth, Pot-au-feu, Cock-a-leekie, Leek and potato and Potage bonne femme (and the American derivative Crème vichyssoise). These soups are usually served with cream, a little pepper and croutons of fried bread. Leeks are also added to a range of curries and stews and can feature in the bouquet for cooking pork and lamb. They are used to make a range of piquant sauces and are delicious when added to quiches. They combine particularly well with cheese, and both leeks and cheese combine successfully with white fish.

Leeks can also be substituted for onions in many dishes. They have half the carbohydrates of onions and so are low in calories. They are relatively high in vitamins A, C and E, and are a good source of iron and fibre.

On their own, leeks can be boiled, steamed, baked or fried and served with or without other vegetables and with or without sauces.

The blue-green leaves and tall flower spikes of leeks add an extra dimension in the garden. *Heronswood, Dromana, Victoria.*

Bulblets, sometimes formed underground when leeks go to seed, can also be cooked and eaten as a vegetable.

Cleaning

Remove the roots and most of the green leaves. Insert a knife into the white portion just below where the green leaves begin. Slit open upwards to where the leaves end. Fold back each leaf section and run under the tap, holding the plant upside down so that the water does not force the grains of dirt deeper into the white section.

Preparation

Like onions, leeks acquire a rank taste if exposed to the air for too long after cutting. They should only be cut just before use or, if they have to be prepared earlier, fried gently in butter until just clarified. Leeks can be kept like this for several hours. Browning, again like onions, alters the flavour of the leeks and so the flavour of the dish.

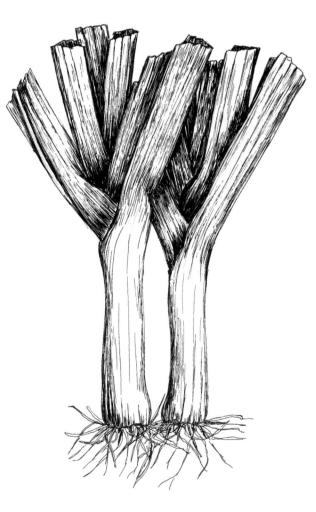

Leeks trimmed and ready to use.

Recipes

Leeks can be cooked in many ways. The following recipes from different countries show some of the possible variations.

Romanian Leeks and Oil

Trim and cut young leeks in half lengthways, wash carefully and simmer in salted water until tender. Drain carefully and cool. Cover with olive oil, season with salt and pepper and add a squeeze of lemon juice. Leave to stand for one hour before serving.

Light Meals and Appetisers

**2–3 young, succulent leeks
per person**
olive oil
**salt and freshly ground
black pepper**
lemon juice

Braised Leeks

Carefully wash and trim the leeks and cut them in half lengthways. Butter a fire-proof dish, arrange the leeks in it and season with salt and pepper. Pour the stock over the top. Dot the top with the remaining butter and cover tightly.

Bake in a hot oven at 200°C (400°F) for 20 minutes. Remove the lid and allow to brown slowly for a futher 5 minutes. Serve as an entrée or as a vegetable with the main course.

8 leeks (12 if small)
4 tablespoons butter
**salt and freshly ground
black pepper**
1 cup stock

Creamy Leeks

Wash and trim the leeks and cut into 5-cm (2-in) lengths. Place in a saucepan and just cover with water. Bring to the boil and simmer until tender. Drain and reserve the cooking water. Melt the butter in another saucepan and add the flour. Cook on a low heat for about 1 minute and then add a little of the leek cooking water. Pour in the cream and add the leeks. Cook gently until the sauce thickens. Sprinkle with grated nutmeg and serve hot.

500 grams (1 lb 1½ oz) leeks
4 tablespoons butter
1 level tablespoon flour
½ cup cream
**½ teaspoon nutmeg, freshly
grated**

Greek Leeks

6 large leeks
½ cup olive oil
1 cup white wine
1 cup water
2 tablespoons coriander
    seeds
3 bay leaves
salt and freshly ground
    black pepper

Wash and trim the leeks cutting them halfway through lengthways. Cut each leek into four and put them into a large frying pan. Pour over the olive oil, wine and water, add the coriander seeds, bay leaves, salt and pepper. Bring to the boil then reduce the heat to a simmer and cook without a lid, carefully stirring occasionally, until the leeks are cooked and the juice reduced. Strain off the juice, reserving a little to sprinkle over the leeks. Serve hot or cold.

Salads

10 small leeks (or 5 larger
    leeks cut in half)
3 tablespoons vinaigrette
    (preferably olive
    oil-based)
2 tablespoons parsley,
    chopped
1 tablespoon chives,
    chopped
1 spring onion, chopped
1 hard-boiled egg, finely
    chopped

Winter Salad

Carefully wash and trim the leeks, removing all the green leaves. Cut larger leeks in half vertically, almost to the base. Blanch in boiling salted water for about 10 minutes, drain quickly and cool under cold running water. Gently squeeze out the excess water.

Arrange the leeks side by side in the base of a shallow dish. Split any larger leeks completely in half and place them cut side down. Sprinkle over the vinaigrette, parsley, chives and spring onion. Just before serving add the crumbled hard-boiled egg. This salad can be served warm or cold.

Sauces

4 leeks
2 soft white bread rolls
3 hard-boiled eggs
1 cup mayonnaise
½ cup sour cream
juice ½ a lemon
1 tablespoon sugar
½ teaspoon of salt

Hungarian Leek Sauce

This sauce is served cold with fish, stuffed eggs and croquettes.

Wash and trim the leeks, chop finely and cook in a cup of water. While the leeks are cooking, soak the white rolls in lukewarm water for 5 minutes. Squeeze out most of the water from the rolls, place in a bowl with the hard-boiled egg yolks and mix to a creamy, smooth consistency. This can be done using a processor or blender, or by pushing through a sieve.

Drain and similarly purée the cooked leeks. Combine the two purées in a mixing bowl and add the mayonnaise, sour cream, lemon juice, sugar and salt. Mix well.

Quantities of salt, sugar and lemon juice can be adjusted to suit individual tastes.

Simple Leek Soup

Leeks lend themselves to rich, warm winter soups.

Carefully wash and trim the leeks and cut into thin slices. Melt the butter and gently cook the leeks in a covered frying pan until they are tender. Peel and cut the potatoes into small cubes and add these with the leeks to the stock. Season with salt and pepper and simmer for about half an hour until the potatoes are cooked. Sprinkle with finely chopped chives before serving.

Soups

1 kilogram (2 lb 3 oz) young leeks
2 tablespoons butter
3 medium potatoes
4 cups stock
salt and freshly ground black pepper
chives, finely chopped

Potage Bonne Femme

This simple French soup is delicious, warm winter fare.

Carefully wash the leeks and cut into thin slices. Melt half the butter in a saucepan with a heavy base, add the leeks and fry gently on a low heat until they are soft. Add the potatoes and the stock. Cover and simmer slowly for about 20 minutes, until the potato is soft. Add the hot milk and the rest of the butter. Season with salt and pepper. Serve hot, garnished with parsley.

Serves six.

2 medium leeks
4 tablespoons butter
2 potatoes, peeled and cubed
3 cups stock, chicken or vegetable
1 cup milk, hot
salt and freshly ground black pepper
parsley, finely chopped

Crème Vichyssoise

This classic American soup was invented by the famous French chef Louis Diat while working at the Ritz-Carlton in New York. It was derived from Potage Bonne Femme and is usually served cold.

Carefully wash the leeks and roughly chop them with the onions. Fry gently in the butter; do not allow to brown. When they are soft, peel and slice the potatoes into rounds and add them to the leeks and onions. Continue to cook gently, stirring constantly, for 5 minutes.

In a separate pan, heat the stock until it boils and add the leeks, onions and potatoes. Cover and cook until the potatoes are soft. Remove from the heat and allow to cool slightly. Liquidise in a food processor and then push through a sieve so that the liquid is completely smooth. Cool, add the cream and season with salt and pepper. Refrigerate. Serve with a few ice-blocks in each bowl and garnish generously with chives.

Serves six.

4 medium leeks
2 onions
2 tablespoons butter
5 medium potatoes
4 cups chicken or vegetable stock
2/3 cup of cream
salt and freshly ground black pepper
ice blocks
1/2 cup chives

Main Courses

4 large thick succulent leeks
150 grams (5 oz) lean meat
2 onions, finely chopped
1 clove garlic, finely
**   chopped**
2 teaspoons fresh parsley,
**   chopped**
2 teaspoons sugar
2 tablespoons plain flour
salt and freshly ground
**   black pepper**
1 egg, beaten with a little
**   water**
2 tablespoons olive oil
juice of ½ a lemon

Stuffed Leeks in Sweet and Sour Sauce

This recipe originates in Israel and is a good example of the way different alliums (in this case onions, garlic and leeks) can be combined to enhance the individual flavours.

Wash and trim the leeks carefully. Cut into pieces 8–10 cm (3–4 in) long and put into boiling, salted water—simmer for 5 minutes. Remove and drain. Slit one side and remove the centre leaving a hollow.

Finely chop the lean meat and mix with onions, garlic, parsley, half the sugar, flour, salt and pepper to taste. Finally, bind the mixture with the egg. Push the mixture into the hollows in the leeks and tie with cotton.

Fry in the oil until the leeks are light brown.

Put about 1 cm (½ in) of water in a pot and add the other half of the sugar and the lemon juice. Transfer the fried leeks to the pot, cover and cook slowly until the water has almost gone. Remove the cotton and serve hot.

Serves four, either as a light lunch or an entrée.

Leek Pie

5 tablespoons unsalted
**   butter and extra melted**
**   butter**
4 cups leeks, washed and
**   chopped**
2 cloves garlic, crushed
2 tablespoons fresh dill
**   leaves, chopped**
4 tomatoes, peeled, seeded
**   and chopped**
2 rashers bacon, crisply
**   cooked**
4 eggs
500 grams (1 lb 1½ oz)
**   ricotta cheese**
about 500 grams (1 lb 1½
**   oz) filo pastry**
salt and freshly ground
**   black pepper**

Melt the butter in a heavy-based frying pan over a medium heat. Add the leeks and cook until they are soft. Add the garlic, dill and tomatoes and simmer for about 10 minutes, until all the liquid evaporates. Remove from the heat and leave to cool. Stir in the crumbled bacon.

Beat the eggs in a bowl and mix in the ricotta cheese and the cooled leek mixture. Season with salt and pepper.

In a fairly deep pie dish (about 8 cm/3 in), lay about 10 sheets of filo pastry—brush each one with melted butter before adding the next. Pour the leek mixture over the pastry and distribute evenly in the dish. Cover with another layer of filo pastry slices to the same thickness as the base, brushing each with melted butter as before. Cover with a cloth and chill for 2 hours.

Place in an oven pre-heated to 190°C (375°F) and cook for 35 minutes until the surface is golden. Leave to sit for a few minutes and cut into squares. Serve warm.

Serves four.

Turkish Leek Fritters

Carefully wash and trim the leeks, drain well. Cut into quarters lengthways and chop finely. There should be about 4 cups of chopped leeks. Pour the olive oil into a heavy-based frying pan, add the leeks and a little salt and fry gently for a few minutes. Add the water, cover and simmer until the leeks are tender. If any liquid is left, boil rapidly until all the liquid has gone.

The leeks should now form a thick paste. Put this paste into a large bowl and leave to cool a little. Add the cheese and herbs and stir. Lightly beat the egg yolks and add these to the leeks, season with pepper. Stir in enough flour to make a thick batter. Beat the egg whites until they form firm peaks and gently fold these into the batter.

Clean the frying pan and add a little oil on a medium heat. Drop spoonfuls of the batter into the frying pan and cook until each fritter is golden on both sides but still moist in the middle. Serve immediately with a salad as a light meal.

Serves four.

4 medium-sized leeks
2 tablespoons olive oil
salt
⅓ cup water
1 cup fetta cheese, crumbled
2 tablespoons mixed fresh herbs — for example basil, dill, mint or plain-leaf parsley, finely chopped
4 eggs, separated
black pepper, freshly ground
4 tablespoons flour
olive oil for frying

Leeks with Cheese and Ham (a variation of a traditional English recipe)

Carefully wash and trim the leeks. Cut in half and blanch for about 10 minutes in boiling water until they are tender but not slimy. Drain thoroughly, reserving the water for stock. Spread each slice of ham with a thin scraping of mustard and wrap it around each leek stem. Butter a shallow baking dish and arrange the leeks in the bottom of the dish. Set the dish aside and make the mornay sauce as follows.

Mornay Sauce:
Melt the butter in a pan and sweat the onion until softened, cover and cook for 5 minutes. Slowly stir in the flour and gradually add the stock and the milk, stirring all the time. Cook down to a good thick consistency. Add the cheese and stir until it melts — do not allow to boil.

Pour the mornay sauce over the leeks and sprinkle with cheese and a little grated nutmeg, salt and pepper to taste. Bake for about 20 minutes at 200°C (400°F).

Serves two to four as an appetiser or light lunch.

6 medium-sized leeks
6 thin slices ham
mild mustard
butter
mornay sauce (see below)
1 tablespoon cheese, grated
grated nutmeg
salt and freshly ground black pepper

Mornay Sauce:
2 tablespoons butter
1 small onion, chopped
2 tablespoons flour
¾ cup leek stock (water left over from blanching the leeks)
¾ cup milk
2 tablespoons parmesan cheese, grated
2 tablespoons cheddar cheese, grated

6. Onions

(1) Common Onion

Besalim—Hebrew
Cebula—Polish
Cibule—Czech
Cebolla—Spanish
Cipolla—Italian
Küchen
   Zwiebel—German
Oignon—French
Sybo—Scottish
Ui—Dutch
Yang Cong—Chinese
Zwiebel—German

Derivation of Names

Caepa, or cepa, is the Latin name for onion and is probably the origin of the names *cebolla, cebula, cibule,* and *cipolla*. A less likely derivation is from the Celtic word *cep* meaning a head.

In about AD 42 the Roman soldier and farmer, Columella, wrote about the Marsicam, which he said the country people called *unionem*. The Latin word *unio* means to unite. The two alliums in use in early Roman times were garlic (made up of numerous cloves) and onions (made up of one single bulb) and the name *unionem* may originally have been used to distinguish onions from garlic. *Unio* also means a single large pearl and *unionem* may have been used specifically for white onions. The English name, onion, and the French *oignon* probably come from this early source.

Romans also called onions *bulbus*, which was probably borrowed from the Greek *bolbos* and means both an onion and a bulbous root. *Sybo* is the Scottish name for a young onion with its green top, while *yang cong* is a name used by the Chinese and means means foreign onion.

Distribution

Onions are grown thoughout the temperate and sub-tropical regions of the world, but are no longer known in the wild. Either the climate has changed and the onion's ancestor no longer exists, or the plant has changed so much under cultivation that the ancestor is no longer recognisable. Onions probably originated in an area which includes Iran, Turkestan, west Pakistan, Uzbekistan and as far north as the Atai region of Mongolia. From here they spread, with cultivation, to all continents (except Antarctica) and most countries. Even countries like China and Japan, which traditionally grow and use other allium species, now also grow the common onion.

An onion plant showing a flower stem with the typical bulge near the base and a flower bud with the short-beaked spathe.

Large red onions plaited into a rope for drying and storage.

History

Onions are one of the oldest cultivated plants and their cultivation could date back to 5000 BC. Evidence for this is that the names for onion in the basic ancient languages—Chinese, Greek, Hebrew and Sanskrit—are all quite distinct and different. Because there has been no borrowing between the languages, onions must have been present during the formative period of each language.

Egyptians used onions as early as 3200 BC and they were among the offerings at funerals near the beginning of the Pyramid Age (2780 BC−). They were placed on altars with other offerings to the gods and have been found with mummified human remains in the thorax and pelvic regions, against the ears and eyes, and attached to the soles of the feet. Both large peeled onions and bunches of slender immature onions can be seen on festive banquet tables illustrated in wall murals in tombs. Egyptian priests would refrain from eating onions during certain religious festivals because they were regarded as sacred. In about AD 127, Juvenal, the Roman satiric poet, mocked the Egyptians for endowing onions with souls. A rough translation of his *15th Satire* says: 'It is sacrilege to bite the leek or onion, Oh holy nation, in whose garden divinites spring up!'

Hippocrates, the Greek physician also known as the 'father of medicine' (about 460−377 BC), mentions onions in his writings, but the introduction of onions to Greece is attributed to Alexander the Great, the Macedonian king (356−323 BC) who brought them from Egypt. At this time onions were renowned among the Egyptians for their ability to impart strength and excite martial fervour and so became a regular addition to the diet of Alexander the Great's army.

The Greek philosopher, Theophrastus (about 372−287 BC), listed four local varieties of onions. The Roman scholar and author, Pliny the Elder (AD 23−79), lists the onion varieties used by the Greeks as 'Sardinian, Samothracian, Alsidenian, setonian, split, Ascalon and Tuscany onion'. Columella, a Roman soldier and farmer writing at about the same time, mentioned a variety of onion named for Pompeii, called Pompeian— carbonised bulbs of *A. cepa* which must date from AD 79 were found by archeologists in the ashes of Pompeii.

Also around the 1st century, onions were mentioned in the famous Indian medical treatise *Caraka-Samihita*. They were listed as being diuretic, beneficial to the digestive tract and the eyes, stimulating to the heart and anti-rheumatic. However, onions were also seen as being unfit for consumption by those pursuing a spiritual life. Orthodox Brahmans, Buddhists, Hindu widows and Jains were, and still are, prohibited from eating onions, either at any time or during certain religious festivals.

The English herbalist Gerard (1500s) said onions caused headaches, hurt the eyes, made men dim-sighted, and caused windiness and over-sleepiness. But Sydney Smith, the eminent preacher, writer and lecturer (1771−1845) who was renowned for his wit and commonsense, said in his *Recipe for a Salad*:

Let onion atoms lurk within the bowl
And scarce suspected animate the whole.

As recently as the late 1800s, onions were still arriving in English ports by the shipload. They came from Spain and were plaited into strings about 1 metre (3 ft) long. Hawkers carried them on long poles and sold them from house to house.

It is likely that onions were introduced to the Americas by the Spaniards. Sturtevant (Hendrik, 1919) suggests that they were probably among the garden herbs planted by Columbus at Isabella Island at the end of the 1400s. Certainly they were carried to the Americas on numerous occsasions by early travellers and grown by the early immigrants. There are several records of their cultivation in the 1600s and they were among the crops grown by the Iroquois at Newtown, New York. These crops were destroyed by General John Sullivan when he routed the Iroquois and their Loyalist supporters in 1779. By the start of the 1800s, at least six cultivars were described. Early in the 1900s, the American writer O. Henry wrote a short story about onions, or the lack of them, called *The Third Ingredient*. The main character says 'A stew without an onion is worse'n a matinée without candy'.

Onions landed in Australia with the first fleet. Sir Joseph Banks in his 'List of Seeds for New South Wales' records 26 bushells of Best Onion Seed, 36 bushells of Fine Onion Seed, 28 bushells of Onion Seed and 20 bushells of Onion Sorts on board the various supply ships of the first fleet—all costing a grand sum of £29. Because of the very specific climatic requirements of onions it is likely that most of these seeds and sets failed.

In 1886 a Royal Commission on Vegetable Produce was held in Victoria, Australia. In the Proceedings, a witness from California said 'We can teach you nothing about the growth of onions . . . certainly I have seen onions in the city of Melbourne that I have never seen anything to compare with anywhere else!'

Onions are now used in many different ways all over the world. Open any comprehensive cookery book and more than half the savoury recipes will include onions. In Brazil they are treated as a spice, in Honduras they are more of a herb, while Chileans use the juice as a tonic. The bulbs and stems are used in the Philippines to season foods, and in parts of Africa onions are applied as a repellent and toxin against insects, as well as being eaten.

Botanical Description

These onions are perennials which are usually grown as annuals. An onion plant is, essentially, a leaf with a root which, exposed to the correct day length and temperature, will form a bulb.

In general, onion root systems extend to about 45 cm (1½ ft) in depth and 30 cm (1 ft) across. This gives them one of the most limited root systems

Diagrammatic cross-section of (*top*) the leaf and (*bottom*) the scape of *Allium cepa* (includes common, ever-ready, potato and tree onions, as well as shallots).

0   1   2

Single onion flower with
pedicel.

among vegetable crops. The leaves are basal in their first year and are long, shiny, deep-green and hollow. They generally have a circular cross-section, except for a slight to significant flattening, or grooving, on the upper surface.

The large single bulb may be globular, oval or torpedo-shaped and can vary in colour from brown, red and yellow to green and white. The bulb forms from the swollen leaf bases when the conditions of day length and temperature are right. The outer, inedible skin of the bulb consists simply of the oldest leaf bases which have withered and dried.

Bulbs of *A. cepa* (including onions and shallots) are always made up of concentric leaf sheaths, so that a horizontal slice taken from the bulb can be separated into a number of rings. Rakkyo (*A. chinense*) is the only other cultivated species of bulb-forming allium where this happens.

If the bulbs are not harvested in the second year, a flower stem will develop from each one up to 2 m (6½ ft) high, 3 cm (1 in) in diameter and tapering towards the apex. Usually the stem will exhibit distinct swelling at the base as the flower head develops (see pp. 103, 108).

Flowers and Seeds

Flower heads form in common onions in late spring and early summer of the second year, at the top of a tall, leafless, cylindrical, hollow stalk. The persistent spathe splits into three to reveal the densely-packed spherical umbel up to 10 cm (4 in) in diameter. Flowers open irregularly over the flower head and are star-like, with green stripes on the perianth segments (petals). Stamens are exserted. Flower heads, typically, lack the bulbils which are characteristic of some other alliums.

Onions are pollinated by a range of insects. Black angular seeds occur in small capsules and are ripe when the flower stem changes from green to brown. To collect seed, the individual flower heads should be cut as the seeds ripen and placed upside-down in a paper bag in a dry airy position. Most of the black seed falls to the bottom of the bag and the rest can be released by gently rubbing the seed heads. Separate the seed from the remains of the flower head and place it in a container which excludes light. If stored in a cool dry position, seed will last for two to three years, but in warm humid climates it should be planted the following season.

Many modern hybrids do not produce fertile seed because they are grown from F1 hybrid seed. This seed is produced by crossing two inbred varieties, one of which is male sterile.

A. cepa will cross-pollinate with some wild allium species but the resultant hybrid plant is sterile.

Cultivars, Varieties and Closely Related Species
See also Appendixes 3.3 and 4 at the back of the book.

There are hundreds of cultivated varieties of onions which vary in size, colour, pungency and flavour—they also vary in keeping quality and response to temperature and day length.

Common onion, *Allium cepa* (Cepa Group), about a month before harvest, showing the swelling bulb and still vigorous green leaf growth.

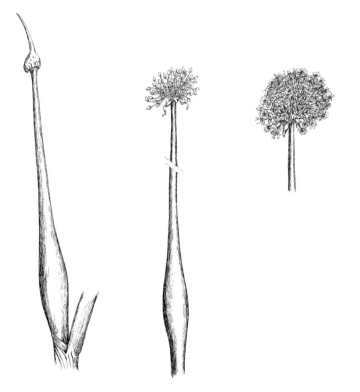

The development of the flower head and stem of common onion, *Allium cepa* (Cepa Group). Note the characteristic swelling of the lower stem.

Propagation

Choosing the Seed

Unless the cultivar chosen is one that originated in a similar climate and latitude to the one you live in, it probably won't do very well. Many cultivars are grown and available locally and, unless there is a reason to experiment with unusual or rare cultivars, it is best to stick with the local ones—this cannot be emphasised too strongly. For a general guide on which cultivars will suit particular regions, see the map on page 111, Appendix 3.3 or visit your local nursery for advice.

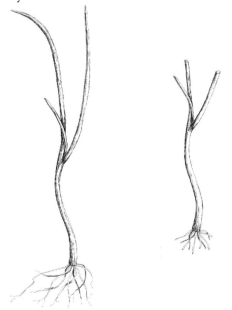

An onion seedling (*left*) untrimmed and (*right*) trimmed ready for planting.

Typical onion plants in vegetable garden.

Some of the dirt has been pulled away to reveal the bright red bulb of the 'Tango' cultivar. The white spotting on the leaves was caused by hail damage.

Red and white salad onions. They have a mild sweet flavour and are delicious in salads and sandwiches.

A bunch of onions just after harvest ready to be plaited or hung in bunches to dry.

An Explanation of Day Length and Temperature Requirements for Bulb Onions

Unlike most cultivated alliums, onions are very sensitive to the length of night darkness and are dependent upon both this and the temperature to be able to produce bulbs. Custom has decreed that day length rather than night length should be the measurement used to describe cultivars, so they are called 'long day' rather than 'short night' cultivars. For consistency this book will also refer to them in this way.

Bulb onions are divided into short day, intermediate and long day cultivars. In the British Isles, Canada, northern Europe and the northern United States, long day cultivars are predominantly used. These will initiate bulbs once there are more than 14 daylight hours. Onions grown in more tropical regions are known as short day cultivars and bulbing is initiated by 12 to 13-hour day lengths. Most onions grown in Australia are grown in the southern states where maximum day lengths are 14 to 16 hours. Long and intermediate day cultivars are best suited to these regions. The same is true of New Zealand. Short day cultivars are not actually short day plants in the botanical sense, but plants that will set bulbs under relatively shorter day conditions.

In addition to day length requirements, temperature must exceed a certain minimum before bulbing can commence. Bulbs will not form at temperatures below 15°C (59°F) but temperatures consistently higher than 30°C (86°F) will reduce bulb size. Optimum temperatures are between 20° and 25°C (68°–77°F).

Shapes of onions.
Top left: Torpedo. *Top right:* Flat globe.
Bottom left: Globe. *Bottom right:* Large Globe.

When to Plant

Bulb onions are usually grown from seed and can be planted any time from late summer through to early spring, depending on the variety being grown and the local climate. Make sure you follow closely the instructions for planting on the seed packet. Onions planted too early will go to seed and those planted too late will not form bulbs.

Sow the seed either directly into shallow trenches about 30 cm (1 ft) apart in well-prepared beds, or into seed beds or trays for later transplantation. Transplanting seedlings can cause a considerable setback, so these seeds can

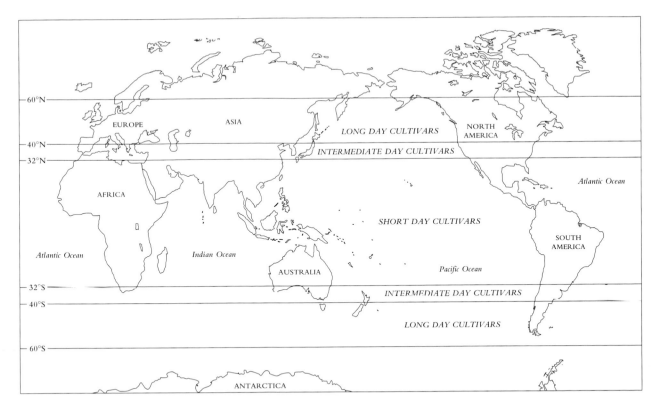

Map showing where short, intermediate and long day cultivars can be grown. Most short day cultivars can be grown in intermediate day regions and both short and intermediate day cultivars can be grown in long day regions. This map should be used only as a guide as some variation will occur with local conditions.

be sown a few weeks earlier than those sown where they are to grow. The seeds should be sown thinly and just covered with a layer of fine soil. Water carefully and keep the soil moist but not too wet. All onion seed germinates best between 15° and 25°C (59°–77°F), and will take between 7 and 10 days. Germination declines rapidly at temperatures over 27°C (81°F).

When the seedlings are large enough to handle, they can be thinned to about 5 cm (2 in) apart. Later, when they are about the size of small spring onions, remove every second plant to give a spacing of about 10 cm (4 in). The 'thinnings' can be eaten or replanted.

Seedlings

Seedlings sown into seedbeds or trays elsewhere are ready for transplanting about 12 weeks after sowing. Plant them about 10 cm (4 in) apart, in rows 30 cm (1 ft) apart. To lessen wilting it is best to trim the leaves—take about one-third off the top and the roots (see Fig. 00).

Alternatively, seedlings can be purchased. Do not plant seedlings too deeply—the bulb should not be more than 1 cm (½ in) below the surface of the soil. Choose only fresh-looking plants, as those with yellow or brown tips have been out of the ground too long. Trim these as described above.

Sets

In Europe, the British Isles and parts of the United States, where summers are often too short and too wet to allow bulbs to develop from seed, onions are often grown from sets. These are small onions that have been grown from seed in the previous year and are purchased and planted by gardeners to grow into mature onions.

Cultivation

Once you have selected suitable seed, sets or plants, you will find that bulb onions are fairly easy to grow and require little attention. They do best in rich, fine, loose soil in an open, sunny position. Good drainage is essential, as the diseases to which onions are prone thrive in wet conditions. Add well-rotted old manure to the soil before planting—and lime if the soil is acid because onions need a pH above 6.5. Heavy soil will result in smaller onions.

Different onions have slightly different nutrient requirements. For example, mild salad onions, which are not stored but usually eaten straight from the garden, benefit from some extra nitrogen to hasten growth. But too much nitrogen given to stronger, long-keeping cultivars will result in thick soft necks, and the onions will not keep well.

Onion beds should be weed-free before planting, and kept that way, as weeds will quickly swamp young plants. Top-dressings of a good all-round fertiliser and extra potash will assist growth. Fresh manure should be avoided, especially after the onions are planted, as this encourages bulb rot and can attract the onion maggot.

Onion plants with the tops bent over. This is done to encourage the plants to mature for harvest, but it also shortens the storage life of the bulbs.

During dry weather, water onions regularly. Mulching will cut down on the amount of water needed, but don't heap the mulch right up to the plant or (1) it may rot, and (2) the tops of onion bulbs will not get the sunlight they need in order to ripen. Onions are tolerant of frost but prolonged exposure to temperatures below 10°C (50°F) will make them bolt to seed in spring. The eventual size of an onion bulb depends on the size of the onion plant when the bulb begins to form—the bigger the plant the bigger the bulb will be.

Once onions are fully ripe and the green leaves begin to turn brown and fall over, stop watering. Some of the late maturing cultivars may not fall over on their own, so their leaves should be bent over late in the season. This discourages bolting and hastens bulb formation, but it may also shorten the storage life of the bulb. This is better, though, than having no bulb to store at all.

Onions should not be grown in the same position year after year. They need to be moved—preferably every year but at least every two to three years—to stop diseases and fungal spores building up in the soil.

Harvest and Storage

Onions are ready to harvest when the leaves turn yellow. This can be from early summer to early autumn, depending on the cultivar and time of planting. In a dry summer the leaves will bend and yellow on their own, but if it is wet the leaves may need to be bent over.

A typical onion flower.

Plaiting onions. This is a convenient way to dry and store onions for later use. Garlic can be plaited in the same way.

Lift the onions carefully using a fork, shake off excess dirt, and spread the bulbs out to dry in an open sunny position. If it is very hot bulbs can get sunburnt or, if the weather is unsettled, the bulbs may begin to rot. In these cases drying should be carried out under cover, such as in an airy shed or carport.

Once the leaves are brittle the onions are ready to store. Handle them carefully, as any cuts or bruises can lead to rotting. Do not store any bulbs which are damaged or showing signs of disease.

Bulbs can be hung in nets or pantyhose, placed in cardboard or wooden boxes, hung in bunches, or made into a string in the traditional way (see above). As long as the storage area is dry, cool and well-ventilated, not subject to frost, and the bulbs are inspected from time to time (to remove any that have gone soft) onions should keep for several months. Some cultivars keep longer than others. As a general rule, the stronger and more pungent onions keep longer—but the storage life of the milder onions can be increased by leaving the necks on and storing them tied in bunches. For more information on storage see Appendix 3.3 under Keeping Qualities.

Onion Sprouts

Onion sprouts grow best in a shallow tray:
(1) Soak 2 tablespoons of onion seed for 8 hours. Do not use onion seed purchased for growing bulbs as this is often treated by a fungicide. Seed can usually be obtained from health food shops.
(2) Spread the seed over a tray with tiny drainage holes.
(3) Rinse with fresh water twice a day and keep in the dark at temperatures of about 20°C (68°C).
(4) Place on a windowsill for a few hours before harvesting when about 3 cm (1 in) long.

Pickling Onions

These are small onions which differ only in that they do not develop a papery outer skin. This characteristic makes them easy to pickle. Any small onion can be pickled, but those that have to be peeled are more time consuming to prepare.

Onions intended for pickling are usually planted in late autumn or early spring. Scatter seed fairly thickly over the prepared ground or place in shallow trenches about 20 cm (8 in) apart. Cover with a fine layer of soil and water carefully. Do not thin as the crowding ensures that the bulbs remain the small size required. Pickling onions will grow in poorer drier and less fertile soil than the larger onions but they still need good drainage and full sun.

Harvest after the foliage has died back and store for short periods if necessary but the sooner they are pickled the better.

A bag of pickling onions.

Spring Onions

These onions are also called bunching onions, salad onions, green onions, scallions and even sometimes shallots, although they are more commonly called young welsh onions (*A. fistulosum*), which are misleadingly called shallots. The names salad onion, green onion and scallions are also often used for other species of onions, so it is better to call these plants, which are harvested early for their slender green and white stems, spring or bunching onions.

Spring onions are often bulb onions that are simply harvested early, like 'White Lisbon'. There are now also several hybrids with welsh onions (*A. fistulosum*) which never form proper bulbs. So some spring onions will have almost straight shanks while others have the base of the stem swollen into a small bulb.

Where the climate is mild spring onions can be sown all year round. In regions where snow and heavy frosts are a problem they can be sown under cover and transplanted in spring. Sow seeds fairly thickly into shallow trenches about 20 cm (8 in) apart. Alternatively scatter the seed randomly over a small area, about 1 m (3 ft 3 in) square, cover with soil and water carefully. As the seedlings grow, thin them to allow a reasonable space between plants.

Spring onions need much the same conditions as bulbing onions, that is full sun, fertile soil with a pH over 6.5, good drainage and no competition from weeds. They grow fast so will need extra water in dry conditions and some protection in winter in cold areas. Harvest progressively as soon as plants are large enough to use. Simply dig up those which are needed, leaving the others in the ground. In summer plants take 8 to 10 weeks to mature, in winter 12 to 14 weeks.

Pests and Diseases
See also Chapter 13.

Onions can be attacked by a number of garden pests and diseases—the most common of these are described in Chapter 13. However, if onions are grown in well-drained, healthy soil in full sun; if their position is changed every year; and if they are mixed in with other plants to create a diverse environment that will encourage predatory insects such as ladybirds, then none of the pests or diseases described should present a major problem. If the soil available is too heavy and wet so that rotting becomes a problem and an elevated bed is not possible, then choose the hardier, easier-to-grow forms, such as tree or potato onions.

The Chemistry of Onions

Mature onion bulbs contain approximately:

86% water
11% carbohydrate (including sucrose, glucose and fructose)
1.4% protein
0.2% fat
0.8% fibre
0.6% other

Bulbs also contain vitamins A and C, niacin, riboflavin and thiamine. Compared to other fresh vegetables, onions are high in food energy, rich in calcium and riboflavin, and have a reasonable protein content. Pungency of onions can vary depending not only on the cultivar, but also on where it was grown and how it was stored. So it is impossible to exactly quantify the general chemical make-up of onion bulbs.

Onions, like garlic, contain the water-soluble organic sulphur compound, **alliin**. The chemical content of alliin is identical in onions and garlic, but its structure is different. Onions contain a form of alliin which is a 'positional isomer' of the form found in garlic. Alliin in onions is also referred to as the **lacrimatory precursor (LP)**.

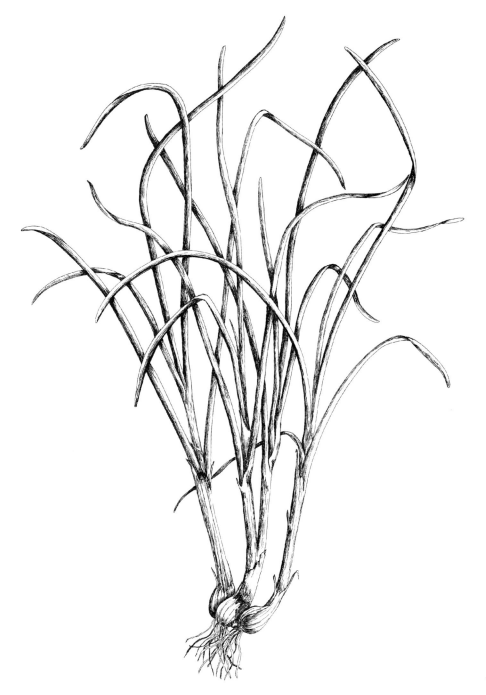

Common onion harvested as spring onions. The roots and leaves are trimmed and the whole plant used.

When the onion bulb is bruised or cut, the enzyme **alliinase**, contained within the onion, acts on the LP to produce (among other things) the **lacrimatory factor (LF)**, another complex organic sulphur compound. LF is also chemically unstable and will react with water (the moisture in the eyes) to produce, among other chemicals, sulphuric acid. It is the sulphuric acid which causes eyes to burn and sting.

Cooking eliminates much of an onion's pungency and, at the same time, some of the sulphur compounds evaporate—others convert into more complex molecules, some of which are very sweet.

Eric Block has done much of the ground-breaking research on the chemistry of onions and garlic. Greater detail is beyond the scope of this book and can be obtained from his article *The Chemistry of Garlic and Onions* (see the references at the end of the book). He confirms in this article that techniques used in the kitchen to reduce watering of eyes work because 'Chilling an onion reduces the volatility of the lacrimatory factor. Peeling an onion under running water washes the factor away; the factor is water soluble.'

Myth, Magic and Medicine in the Past

Onions have been credited with the ability to remove freckles and promote hair growth! An early recipe to prevent hair loss was to mix the juice of onions with honey and rub on the scalp night and morning. Onion juice combined with vinegar is said to remove pimples, while in the Bahamas, slices of onion are bound to the chest to relieve congestion and placed in the shoe near the heel to cure a cold. *Robinson's New Family Herbal* states that the main action of onions is as a stimulant—'promoting appetite, easing the bowels, and disposing to sleep' while 'the juice snuffed up the nostrils purges the head, and removes lethargy'.

Onions were also thought to promote sexual desire. In early Thracian society, before Thrace was annexed as part of the Roman Empire in AD 197, onions were given as wedding presents to the bride and groom to ensure fertility. Onion was a frequently mentioned erotic stimulant in an account of sexual life in Ancient Greece; and an early English writer claimed that onions 'serve for no other thing but to provoke and stirre folke to the act of carnal copulation, and to have a good appetite'!

According to Brazilian legend, onions will not grow if planted on Good Friday; and French folklore maintains that:

> When the onions grow thin skins,
> Winter cold won't freeze your shins.

Medicinal Uses

Onions have similar medicinal properties to garlic in that they are antiseptic and antibiotic—but they do not share quite the same long history of medical use.

In recent times onions have been regarded more as a vegetable or spice than a medicine, although they are considered an important part of a healthy diet. They are high in vitamin C and riboflavin as well as other vitamins, calcium and minerals. Green onion tops are an excellent source of vitamin A. Onions are often prescribed in herbal medicine and used in developing countries where other medicines are not available or affordable. They were eaten to ward off scurvy.

Regular eating is claimed to improve general health by keeping coughs, colds and other minor infections at bay. They are prescribed for bronchial complaints as an expectorant. As a home remedy, a strong, clear soup made from plenty of onions is considered useful for treating chest infections. In Trinidad, onion boiled in water is used to treat coughs, chest colds and tuberculosis.

Solutions of onion are prescribed for anaemia as a tonic, and for stomach and urinary tract infections. Raw onions can be rubbed on cracked feet, and grated onion applied externally may relieve rheumatic joints and migraine.

The juice extracted from a crushed bulb has also been used to relieve insect bites. As a quick remedy, the crushed green tops, rubbed onto a bite, will take away some of the sting and reduce itching. A book of household hints dating from 1850 recommends onions for bee stings. It says that after the bee sting has been removed, slices of raw onion applied to the bite will reduce the pain. In Yucatan, mashed bulbs are applied to scorpion and spider stings.

In Curaçao the neck of an onion stuck in the ear is believed to relieve aching and ringing in the ear. In many countries, onion juice taken after fasting is used to expel worms. A Chinese remedy for constipation says take a clean, peeled onion, stir-fry in peanut oil and eat—this should be repeated for several days.

Like garlic, onions can cause allergic contact dermatitis in some people. The likelihood of this happening increases with repeated contact.

Heartburn

The ingestion of raw onion, and to a lesser extent cooked onion, is well known to cause heartburn in some people. In tests performed in America by M. L. Allen, et al. (1990), patients known to suffer from heartburn were fed hamburgers—with and without raw onion slices. The tests showed that: 'ingestion of raw onions in subjects with [heartburn] can result in an increase in reflux episodes, oesophageal acid exposure, heartburn and belching compared with an identical meal without onions'. In contrast, the control group who did not suffer from heartburn in the first place, showed no episodes of heartburn after ingesting the hamburgers, with or without onions. It was concluded that people who already suffer from heartburn will display increased symptoms after eating onions, while those who do not suffer from heartburn can eat them with impunity.

The exact mechanism by which onions cause heartburn is not yet known, but in the *American Journal of Gastroenterology* (1992) E. Block suggested that certain thiosulphinates and disulphides contained within onions and garlic block the pathways by which acids in foods are broken down. At the same time these chemicals may relax the lower oesophagus, allowing the acid to reflux from the stomach, and they may also injure the mucus in the oesophagus which usually protects the lining from acid.

Until the mechanisms are more clearly understood it will not be possible to protect a sufferer from the symptoms of ingesting onions. Antacids sometimes help but the only real answer is not to eat the onions.

Other Uses

Dyeing

The skins and sometimes the flesh of onions are used by dyers to create different colours: yellow (in combination with an alum mordant), reddish brown (with chrome), dark-brown (with iron) and orange (with tin).
(1) Boil 100 grams (3½ oz) of dried skins for 2 hours, then strain the liquid and cool.
(2) Add wool that has been simmering for an hour in mordant solution to the dye and slowly bring to the boil.
(3) Simmer for 1 hour, remove, and rinse the wool in progressively cooler water.
(4) Hang to dry.

Pest Control

In China, the pressed juice obtained from onion leaves and stems is diluted and used as a spray against spider mites and several plant diseases. Onions have also been used to repel moths and mosquitoes in Africa. In Curaçao, onion peel and garlic are burnt to disinfect rooms following sickness. A thick border of onions can help to keep unwanted animals such as rabbits out of vegetable gardens, as they dislike the smell and taste—one of the perennial forms would be more useful for this purpose.

ONION SPRAY
Onions can be made into a useful spray against aphids and spider mites:
(1) Finely chop several onions with their skins, then add an equal amount of water.
(2) Leave to soak overnight, then strain.
(3) Dissolve 10 grams (½ oz) of an oil-based soap in 4 cups of water, slowly add this to the mixture and stir well.
(4) Strain the mixture again, this time through a fine muslin, and store in a glass bottle.
(5) Dilute at a ratio of about 5 parts water to 1 part onion mixture before use.

Stock Food

Onion wastes from fields that have been harvested can be used as a stock food. Sheep eat onions enthusiastically and will even eat bulbs that are still in the soil. However, care must be taken to prevent the onion flavour carrying over to food products. This is particularly evident in milk taken from cows which have been recently grazing in fields contaminated with wild alliums.

(2) Ever-ready Onion

Allium cepa
(Aggregatum Group)

Other Common Names

Bunching onion
Everlasting onion
False welsh onion

Derivation of Names

The common names refer to this onion's bunching habit, and the fact that it can be harvested at any time and is always ready to eat. It has also been botanically named *Allium perutile* and *Allium cepa* 'Perutile'. Perutile means very useful.

Distribution

Ever-ready onion is not known as a wild plant but it is a common garden plant in the British Isles, Europe and Australia.

History

Every-ready onion has a confused and obscure history, and it is unclear whether early references to a 'small kind of onion' (Johnson, 1633) or a 'non-flowering scallion' (Salmon's *Herbal*, 1711) are to this plant. Certainly, ever-ready onions were commonly grown in the 1800s. By the early 1900s they had largely replaced the welsh or Japanese bunching onion as a market garden plant in the British Isles, and became known as welsh onions. This is where the confusion in names began. An English plant grower and breeder, Mr Clarence Elliot, attempted to sort out the confusion in the early 1940s. He coined the name ever-ready onion for what he described as the 'perennial or old-English cottage-garden type of welsh onion'. He considered ever-ready onions to be 'the most valuable, the most easily grown and the most prolific onion in existence'.

Ever-ready and welsh onion (*A. fistulosum*) plants are alike only in the early stages of growth, and even then can be easily distinguished by looking at the leaves. Welsh onion leaves are completely rounded in cross-section, while ever-ready onions are hemispherical in cross-section. They belong to different species.

Botanical Description

Ever-ready onions grow as a very dense perennial clump. Slender, bottle-shaped bulbs produce narrow blue-green leaves, four to five to each bulb. These leaves grow to a height of about 30 cm (1 ft). A single bulb planted in early spring will produce 10 to 15 bulbs by the following autumn.

Flowers and Seeds

Flowers appear only rarely. In an experimental crop of about 30,000 clumps, less than 100 produced flowers. When flowers do appear they resemble those of the common onion except that the flower head, stalks and umbels are shorter. They rarely set seed.

Propagation

Ever-ready onions are always grown by dividing clumps, never from seed. Divide them in spring or autumn, taking groups of two to three bulbs with their green tops attached and replanting 30 cm (1 ft) apart. Firm the plants into the soil so that just the tops of the bulbs are showing. Any plants not replanted can be eaten.

Cultivation

Ever-ready onions are extremely easy to grow. They do best in full sun with a rich soil and good drainage. They will tolerate some shade and poorer soils, but under these conditions the drainage must be good or the bulbs will rot. Ever-ready onions also grow well in pots and window boxes if they are fed regularly—blood and bone, with occasional sprinklings of potash, is a good combination.

Clumps should be dug and divided every two to three years, or they become so dense that the bulbs are impossible to separate. One or two large clumps are enough to supply an average family regularly with green tops and bulbs.

Harvest and Storage

Green tops and bulbs can be harvested all year round—they are 'ever-ready' for use. To harvest the tops cut them with scissors just above the bulb. Harvest bulbs by loosening the soil around the side of the clump and pulling them from the side. If the clump is too dense and the leaves break from the bulb, then dig up the whole clump, take what is needed and replant the rest.

Medicinal Uses

No specific medicinal properties have been attributed to these onions, but being closely related to the common onion *A. cepa* (Cepa Group) they can be used in the same way.

Other Uses

Some gardeners use these like common onions as borders to vegetable and flower gardens to repel rabbits and other vermin. Ever-ready onions are particularly useful for this because they do not need to be replanted every year.

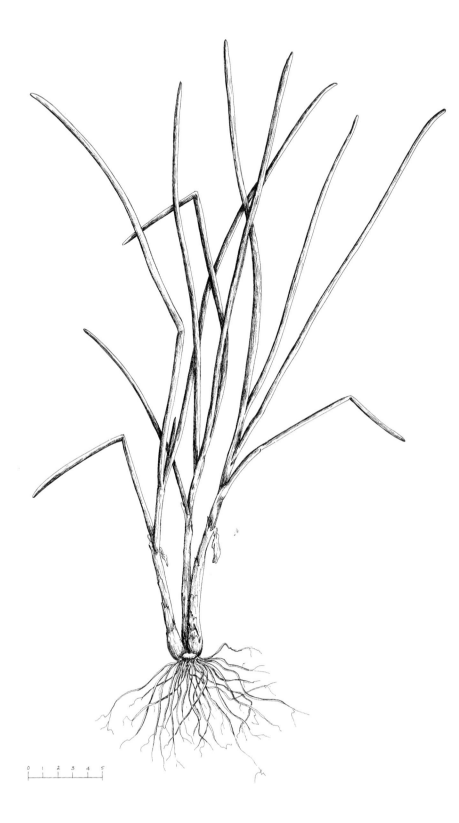

Ever-ready onion, *Allium cepa* (Aggregatum Group).

Young ever-ready onion plants grown in a pot with the dirt pulled back to show the small bulbs.

(3) Potato Onion

Other Common Names

Hill onion
Mother onion
Multiplier onion
Pregnant onion*
Underground onion

Derivation of Names

Potato onions have been called *A. cepa* var. *aggregatum*, *A. cepa* var. *solaninum* and *A. cepa* var. *multiplicans*. All these names refer to their growth habit, with *solaninum* coming from *Solanum tuberosum*, the botanical name for potatoes.

The names potato onion and underground onion came about because this onion grows further below the surface of the soil than other onions. Multiplier onion refers to the way it forms numerous lateral bulbs.

Note: Another plant known as pregnant onion, *Ornithogalum longibracteatum*, is not an onion and should never be eaten as it is poisonous.

Distribution

Potato onions are not known in the wild but were once widely grown in Australia, the British Isles, Europe and the United States. They are now fairly difficult to locate and generally only a few specialist suppliers stock them.

History

As with the ever-ready onion, the history of potato onions is obscure, because it is often not clear to which onion the early herbals and gardening books refer. The earliest clear reference to its growth and use in England is in 1796. In 1827 the Scottish botanist, George Don, described it as 'a garden form of *A. cepa*'. And in 1828, it was mentioned in an American plant catalogue as being a 'vegetable of recent introduction to this country'. By 1890, E. Watts in *Modern Practical Gardening* said that 'the underground or potato onion is so called from its habit of increasing at the bulb'. Potato onions were also popular in northern Europe and the British Isles well into the 1900s, but by 1955 were described as 'more difficult to get hold of today' in the *Complete Vegetable Gardener*.

The main advantages of the potato onion over the common onion were that they are perennial, very hardy, do not take as long to mature and are ready for use earlier in the season.

The advent of modern hybrid onions, which can be planted earlier and so harvested earlier, has meant that potato onions are no longer as useful. As a

Young potato onion plants growing in the garden. Each dense clump represents the growth from one bulb.

result of increased mechanisation, onions that can be machine-planted and harvested are more popular among growers than those like the potato onion, where nearly all the planting and harvesting has to be done by hand. In addition, potato onions can only be propagated by planting offsets, not seeds, which means that the bulbs have to be saved and replanted every year. This labour-intensiveness probably accounts for their current rarity.

In the United States, potato onions were a well-established crop in the mountainous regions of Arkansas, Kentucky, Tennessee and Virginia. They are no longer grown on a large scale but have been handed down from one generation to the next. Potato onions were certainly available in Australia early in the 1800s as they are listed in the catalogues of that period. They were commonly grown well into the 20th century.

Botanical Description

Potato onions are hardy, versatile, adaptable and perennial; they are well worth growing and preserving. They grow from underground bulbs that are usually wider than they are high. These bulbs send up hollow, blue-green leaves, which reach a height of 40 cm (1 ft 4 in). As the plant grows, the bulb produces numerous lateral bulbs which are usually enclosed within the outer thickish, brown, basal scales or skin of the original bulb—thus producing a fairly large overall bulb. Each lateral bulb will reach a diameter of up to 8–10 cm (3–4 in). In their second year, they will produce separate tops.

So, potato onions usually show an alternating growth habit. If a small bulb—about 2 cm (1 in)—is planted, it will produce one or two large bulbs, made up of several bulbs enclosed in an outer skin. If this bulb is then planted the following year, it will produce 10 to 20 small, separate bulbs.

Potato onion, *Allium cepa* (Aggregatum Group).

Flowers and Seeds

Potato onions do not usually flower. If they do, the flowers are typical of *Allium cepa*—but they are rare and usually sterile.

The Difference Between Potato Onions and Shallots

It is often difficult to distinguish between shallots and potato onions, as they are closely related and often mislabelled. The differences are subtle and mainly as follows:

Potato Onions	Shallots
Bulbs increase in size as well as multiplying	Bulbs multipy only—the individual bulbs don't grow any larger than the one originally planted
Bulbs usually multiply within an outer thin skin	Bulbs usually have marked partial or total longitudinal divisions, so that each bulb is distinct
The emerging leaves are grouped together in a sheath	Each individual leaf has its own sheath
Leaves are usually broader than those of shallots	
Bulbs tend to be wider than they are long	Bulbs are usually longer than they are wide
It is very rare to see flowers	Some will flower and produce seed (although this is unusual)

These are by no means hard-and-fast rules, and there are potato onions that don't fit one or two of the above descriptions. However, any plants that fit most of the descriptions in the left-hand column should be classified as potato onions.

White potato onion.

Brown Potato Onion. The bulbs are just beginning to swell.

Cultivars, Varieties and Closely Related Species

Potato onions are closely related to both the common onions and shallots. The main feature that distinguishes them from the common onion are the lateral bulbs. Potato onions are classified by their colour—these include red, white and yellow.

Propagation

Because potato onions rarely set fertile seed they are always grown from the individual bulbs. Each year, about one-sixth of the bulbs harvested need to be put aside for replanting. Set the bulbs in rows about 20 cm (8 in) apart each way. In very fertile soil they can be closer together, in poorer soil further apart. Each bulb should be placed so that only the dry tuft of old foliage is protruding from the soil—in very cold regions plant well below the surface.

Traditionally potato onions are planted on the shortest day, but they can be planted at any time from mid-autumn to early spring, with the optimum time being end of autumn and beginning of winter. In regions where the winter is very wet, very cold, or both, bulbs should not be planted until spring. Late planting, however, may result in lower yields.

Cultivation

Potato onions do best in the conditions that suit most of the other onions: a light, well-drained, weed-free, rich soil and a sunny position. They prefer a neutral to slightly alkaline soil and low-nitrogen fertilisers. As they grow beneath the soil, good drainage is particularly important—they should always be left slightly dry. Bulbs are hardy and resistant to pests and diseases.

In areas where the winters are very cold, 15–20 cm (6–8 in) of soil can be hilled up around the newly planted bulbs, so that the earth acts as a mulch against the winter's excesses. In very early spring, before the green tops emerge, pull the soil away. Potato onions will grow in the sub-tropics during the dry months, but tend to rot during wet and humid seasons—although they will sometimes last if grown in raised beds in an airy, sunny position.

Harvest and Storage

The bulbs take about six months to mature fully, so those planted on the shortest day are ready to harvest in mid-summer, but can be used as soon as they reach a reasonable size.

Bulbs that are to be stored must be handled carefully. Lift with a fork, shake off excess dirt and dry for several days out of direct sunlight on sheets of newspaper. Store in a dry, airy place for the bulbs to fully cure—this can take up to two months. The bulbs are then sufficiently low in moisture to withstand handling, such as packaging and transporting.

They can be stored for later use or replanting. Bulbs will not store as long as the long-keeping cultivars of common onion, but they will keep for at least six months.

Medicinal Uses

Potato onions can be used in medicine in the same way as other onions and shallots.

Allium cepa
(Aggregatum Group)

Other Common Names

Ascalonia—Spanish
Bawang merah—
    Indonesian, Malaysian
Chalota escalma—Spanish
Chung tau—Chinese
Echalote—French
French shallot
Horm lek—Thai
Khan kho—Vietnamese
Khtim kraham—
    Cambodian
Kyet-thun-ni—Burmese
Scalogna or Scalogno—
    Italian
Schalotte—German
Shalot
Sjalot—Dutch
Spanish garlic

(4) Shallots

Derivation of Names

The English name shallot comes from the French *échalotte*. This French name, most of the other common names and the botanical name often used for shallots—*Allium ascalonicum*—are derived from Askelon, a seaport city in Palestine. Shallots were thought to have originated there. However, the plant named *Allium ascalonicum* by Linnaeus is an allium found wild in

Palestine and not related to shallots, so this botanical name should never be used for them. The perennial forms of the common onion, to which the name of shallot is now applied, actually have no connection with Askelon. To add to the confusion, there are many places where the name shallot is also applied to forms of annual or spring onions—particularly the welsh onion (*A. fistulosum*). For clarity, the names shallot and eschallot should only be used to describe the perennial bulb-forming plant *A. cepa* (Aggregatum Group) Shallot.

Distribution

Shallots are no longer known as a wild plant, but are closely related to the common onion, so they would have a common ancestor. Shallots are now grown all over the world, including China, Japan and the United States. However, France is still regarded as the home of the shallot and there are more cultivars grown there than in any other country.

Shallots can be grown in any sunny, well-drained corner of the garden. Here they are growing in front of a hops vine.

History

The confusion surrounding the botanical and common names of shallots means that its history is also unclear. In the 4th century BC, the Greek philosopher Theophrastus described a plant he called 'Askalonium krommon', and in the 1st century AD the Roman scholar and author, Pliny the Elder, wrote about 'Cepa Ascalonia', which was excellent for sauces and, he said, came originally from Ascalon in Judaea (now Askelon in Palestine). Many later writers used his description as a basis for their claims concerning the origin of this plant. It was not until 1885 that the Swiss botanist, Alphonse de Candolle, suggested that shallots were actually a form of *A. cepa*—this has subsequently proved to be correct. It is not known whether the shallot of today is derived from the plant described by Pliny.

By the 1500s, the cultivation of shallots was widespread throughout Europe, but the English herbalist John Gerard does not mention them in his

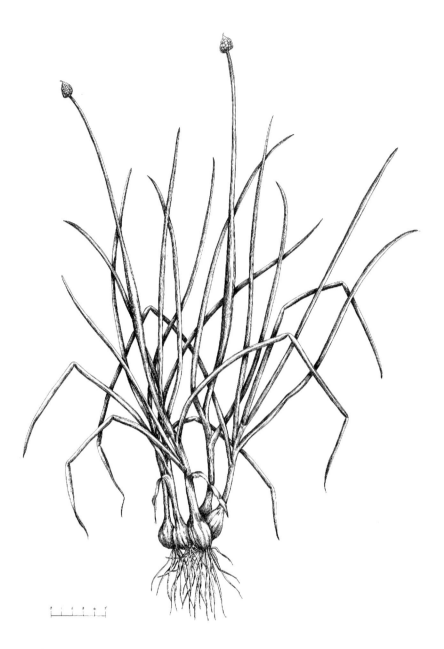

Shallots, *Allium cepa*
(Aggregatum Group).
Young plants with the bulbs
just starting to swell.

Herbal (1597). However, in the *Complete Gardening Practictioner* (1664), S. Blake mentions 'Shalot or Spanish Garlick'; and in *Husbandry* (1707), Mortimer states that 'Eschalots are now from France become an English plant'.

Shallots were taken to North America by the French and English. They were listed in garden catalogues early in the 1800s and have been grown as a commercial and garden crop ever since.

In October 1786 Sir Joseph Banks listed the fruit trees bound for Australia with the first fleet. Contained in this list were many useful plants, including 'Shalott, 2'. Shallots have been grown in Australian gardens ever since and are currently experiencing a resurgence in popularity.

Botanical Description

Shallots are perennials although they are usually grown as annuals. They grow from a bulb which can vary in colour from red to brown, yellow, grey—and even white—depending on the cultivar. The shape can also vary from long and tapering to plump and rounded.

Grey-green tubular leaves grow from each bulb to a height of about 40 cm (1 ft 3 in). These leaves are narrower than those of both common and welsh onions. During the four to five month growing season, each shallot produces many growing points within the planted bulb, and these develop into daughter bulbs which split away from each other into clusters. Each cluster consists of 2 to 20 bulbs (generally about 10), which are lightly attached at the base. Shallot cultivars with smaller bulbs seem to produce lots of small daughter bulbs in a season, while those with larger bulbs produce less but they are bigger—if compared by weight the production is much the same.

In autumn the leaves wither, turn brown and drop off. If left in the ground the bulb will remain dormant until it reshoots in late autumn, winter or early spring. In the second summer some shallots will produce stems and flowers.

Shallots are very similar to potato onions—for a detailed list of the differences see page 128.

Shallot flower head.

Immature shallot bulbs harvested after two months. Grown from one shallot bulb planted in early spring.

Flowers and Seeds

Shallots are not usually left in the ground until they flower, and many cultivars will not flower even if they are left. If they do flower, the typical white onion flowers, which densely pack the flower head, are usually sterile.

Cultivars, Varieties and Closely Related Species

See Appendixes 3.4 and 4 at the back of the book.

Propagation

From Bulbs

Shallots are usually grown from individual bulbs. Within a cultivar, it is generally found that the larger the bulb, the more new bulbs it will produce, but there is also an increased risk that it will bolt to seed. Select healthy, average-sized bulbs and plant them so that the top one-third is above the surface of the soil. Once the bulbs begin to grow the roots will sometimes push the bulbs out of the soil and they will need to be carefully firmed back in. Birds can sometimes cause problems by scratching or pulling the new bulbs out of the soil. Simply replant and cover temporarily with chicken wire or criss-crossed strands of cotton. Once the bulbs are well rooted the covering can be removed.

If the bulbs are being grown for their green tops and long white stems, then they should be planted much deeper—the tops of the bulbs need to be at least 8 cm (3 in) below the surface.

Traditionally shallots, like potato onions, are planted on the shortest day and harvested on the longest. Optimum planting time for bulbs is late winter or early spring, but they can be planted any time from autumn to spring. In very cold wet regions, shallots should only be planted in spring and may be started inside on shallow trays and transplanted later. Some cultivars will sprout in autumn, so should be planted then—although they may not survive wet, cold winters.

Bulbs grown in a bed should be spaced 12 cm (4½ in) apart, in rows 30–40 cm (1 ft–1 ft 4 in) apart depending on the fertility of the soil.

From Seed

Sow the seed in early or mid-spring directly into the soil where the plants are to grow. In sub-tropical regions it can be sown in late summer and grown through winter. If seeds are spaced 2–3 cm (1 in) apart in rows about 5 cm (2 in) apart then each seedling will result in one shallot. If the spacing is increased then clumps of bulbs are more likely to form.

Cultivation

Shallots, like other onions, prefer a sunny open position and fertile well-drained soil which is not acid (pH should be over 6.5). They do best if the soil has a high potash content and do not like too much nitrogen. If you add any animal manures they must be well rotted, as fresh manures will cause the bulbs to go soft and rot. Side dressings of fertiliser every two months will produce fatter bulbs—in Brittany shallots are fertilised with kelp. Although shallots will tolerate some frost, they will freeze and deteriorate in very cold conditions.

In the early stages of growth weeding is essential—this can be helped by mulching the soil after five or six shoots have grown. The mulch should be fairly dry, not too heavy and kept away from the bulbs or rot will set in. To encourage the bulbs to fill out and harden, gradually pull the soil away from them so that they end up sitting above the ground.

When grown from bulbs, plants will take about 20 weeks to reach maturity. New bulbs are only reliably formed at temperatures over 20°C

Shallot flowers. These shallots are being grown in an attempt to collect seed.

(68°F) and larger bulbs are produced at longer day lengths. Although shallots are not as day-length sensitive as bulb onions, they will not produce bulbs in the tropics. Spring plantings need to be made early to allow as much vegetative growth as possible before bulbs begin to form. Once the leaves begin to die back, the bulbs are ready to harvest.

When the green tops and immature bulbs are to be harvested for use in salads, shallots take less time to grow. They can be blanched by banking soil to a depth of about 5 cm (2 in) against both sides about five weeks before harvest. Repeat about three weeks later.

Harvest and Storage

Shallots grown for their mature bulbs can be harvested as soon as they are big enough to use, but must be lifted once the leaves start to die back. If they are left in the ground they will begin to grow again and the bulbs will be depleted.

Once the leaves have withered, lift the bulbs carefully with a fork and dry on the soil surface or on a screen. If there is no chance of rain, then leave them outside in an open airy position—otherwise, inside in an airy position for up to two weeks. Handle shallots carefully at all times and don't separate the side bulbs until after drying, because any bruising or injury will encourage rot. Gently brush the dry bulbs free of dirt and store on trays, in shallow cardboard boxes, hung in bags or (if harvested while the leaves are still pliable) plaited and hung in a cool, dry, airy place. Some bulbs will keep for up to a year and a few for as long as two. About one-seventh of the crop needs to be kept for replanting.

Shallots that are to be harvested green are pulled by hand when they are ½ cm (¼ in) in diameter—this is generally two to four months after planting. Peel off the outer skin and trim the roots.

Small amounts of the green tops can be picked at any time—as long as too much is not taken from the one plant and the central shoot is not cut.

Green shallot plant harvested young and used as a spring onion.

Mature red shallot bulbs.

Medicinal Uses

Shallots are low in acid, so can be useful in providing flavour and interest to dishes for people on low-acid diets, and may be better tolerated by people who suffer heartburn and are unable to eat onions. In Nepal, the bulb is rubbed on the skin to relieve itching or the pain of a burn.

Other Uses

Shallots can be used as a border or edging for the vegetable garden to protect other plants from rabbits and marauding insects.

Shallots about one month before harvest. *Yarra Glen Shallots, Yarra Glen, Victoria.*

Golden shallots with the bulbs beginning to swell.

Red shallots, about one month before harvest.

**Allium cepa
(Proliferum Group)**

(5) Tree Onion

Other Common Names

Egyptian onion
Egyptian tree onion
Top onion
Top-set onion
Walking onion

Derivation of Names

Botanical names which have been used in the past are *Allium cepa* var. *proliferum* and *Allium cepa* var. *viviparum*. *Proliferum* means prolific in Latin, and *viviparum* comes from *viviparous*, the botanical meaning of which is 'producing seeds which germinate on the plant'.

Most of the common names given to this onion refer to its unusual growth habit, where bulbils—instead of flowers—are produced in the flower heads. Bulbils sprout while still in the flower head, so that the plant looks like a tree. The weight causes the stem to bend to the ground, where the bulbs take root and grow and the cycle is repeated—thus they 'walk' over the garden. It is not clear why this plant is called Egyptian onion as it is not likely that it originated in Egypt.

Distribution

The tree onion probably originated in western Asia and spread to Europe and the British Isles, apparently during the Crusades (1095–late 1200s). Today it is mainly a plant of the home garden so it is difficult to accurately assess its distribution. It grows easily, is hardy and prolific and is likely to be found in most countries.

History

Like so many of the onion family, the history of the tree onion is confusing. The *Treasury of Botany* (1866) states that the bulb-bearing tree onion was introduced from Canada in 1820 and was considered to be a viviparous variety of the common onion. However, there are earlier references to tree onions in the British Isles and Europe and the theory that they were brought back from western Asia during the Crusades seems more likely to be correct.

In the 1500s, the Elizabethans grew tree onions in their flower gardens and delighted in their oddity. But by the 1700s they had moved back to the vegetable garden. In the 1870s the top bulbs were sold at Covent Garden for pickling, and in 1880 the 'tree onion or Egyptian onion' was mentioned in *The Encyclopaedia Britannica*.

Tree onions were taken to Australia, New Zealand and the United States by the early immigrants and by the late 1800s there were several cultivars available. They were even grown commercially but, as with the potato onion, the introduction of mechanical harvesters meant that tree onions lost their popularity as they were too difficult to harvest mechanically and cure in large quantities. They are now fairly difficult to obtain.

A patch of tree onions with the typically twisted flowering stems beginning to produce bulbils in late spring.

Botanical Description

Tree onions are a self-propagating biennial plant. They have the typical hollow onion leaves, which grow from a rounded brown bulb—this splits and forms several new bulbs. A stiff flower stalk grows from each bulb to a height of about 60 cm (2 ft). In the flower head numerous small bulbils grow, as well as the occasional flower. These reach a diameter of about 1 cm (½ in). The bulbils are initially greenish-brown, but turn to light-brown and grow more small leaves. These small leaves usually don't produce bulbils, but sometimes they will and a third tier will develop. The weight of the top-set eventually causes the stem to bend to the ground, where the bulbils take root and new plants grow. Tree onions, if well grown, make an excellent substitute for common onions and they do not have to be replanted every year.

Flowers and Seeds

Often only bulbils form in the flower head; if flowers do occur they are the typical white onion flowers and they never set seed.

Cultivars, Varieties and Closely Related Species

A. canadense is a North American species with forms which have bulbs in the flower head and this plant has been confused with *A. cepa* tree onions in some literature. For more information see Chapter 11.

Two types of tree onion are currently available. One forms a larger, more rounded bulb and grows taller but is otherwise the same as the other type; both are sold simply as tree onion, top onion or Egyptian onion. There is also

Tree onion bulbils forming. Some bulbils are already growing green shoots.

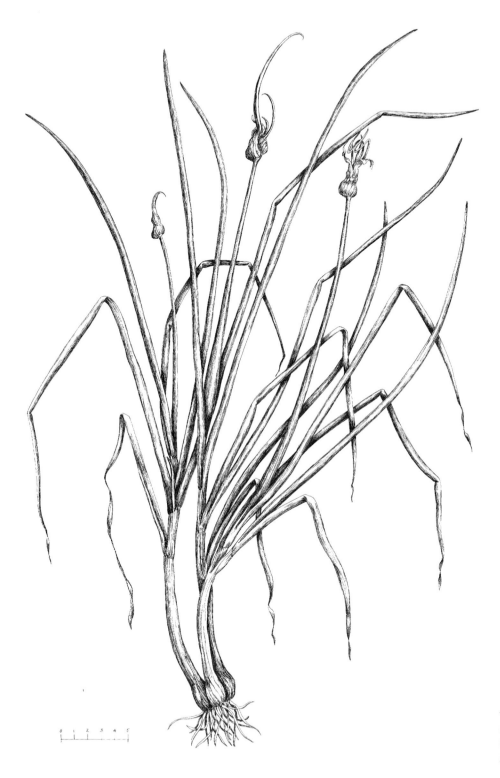

Tree onion, *Allium cepa* (Proliferum Group), with the bulbils in the flower head just starting to develop.

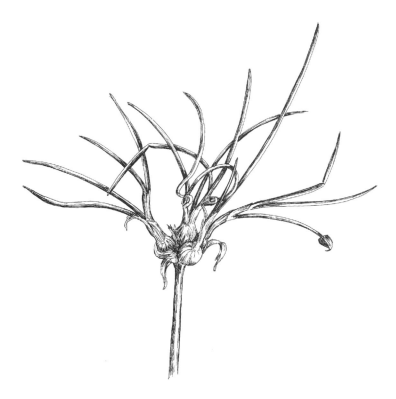

A typical tree onion flower head, showing the bulbils and daughter shoots.

a tree onion derived from the welsh onion usually called *Allium fistulosum* var. *viviparum*. This can be distinguished from the *A. cepa* tree onion by looking at the leaves, which are circular in cross section. Those of the *A. cepa* tree onion are semi-circular with a flattened side.

Propagation

Tree onions can be grown either from the bulbils that form in the flower head or by dividing the bulbs formed in the soil and replanting. Plants seem to grow more quickly and vigorously when grown from the bulbils. If they are small, the whole clump should be planted; if large, separate the bulbils and plant just below the soil surface about 25 cm (10 in) apart each way. Bulbils and bulbs can be planted in spring or autumn, or in winter in mild climates. Plants grown from bulbils will take about a year to produce bulbils of their own.

Cultivation

Tree onions are probably the hardiest onions and the easiest to grow. They will survive in soil that is completely frozen and will tolerate very dry conditions. Even if the parent plant dies, the bulbils will start growing when it rains. However, like all onions they will not tolerate bad drainage and constantly wet soil.

Tree onions do best in a light fertile soil in a sunny position. They are heavy feeders so give them lots of well-rotted manure and compost with additional potash. The more fertile the soil, the more succulent the leaves and the bigger the bulbs. Once established, tree onions need little attention other than weeding. Add mulch to lessen the need for water, but make sure it's a light mulch that does not cover the actual bulbs or they may rot. Tree onions grow well in the sub-tropics during the dry season, but they tend to rot in the wet season.

Every three years or so, thin out the clumps drastically, or dig them up completely and replant. They are most conveniently planted in a single row—anything else can become very congested because of the plant's random self-rooting habit.

Harvest and Storage

The bulbs, leaves and bulbils of tree onions can all be eaten. As they are hardy, and grow all year round in mild climates, you can pick them as needed and don't need to store them. In fact, harvesting keeps the multiplying clumps of new shoots under control. However, if you do harvest them and leave them for a few days in a dry airy position, tree onion bulbs will keep for long periods. Bulbils still attached to their flower stalks and hung upside down under the same conditions will last up to two years.

Medicinal Uses

Tree onions are closely related to common onions and can be used medicinally in the same way.

Culinary Uses of Onions

Onion Flavours

Onions provide one of our most common vegetable flavourings and are the most widely grown of all the cultivated alliums. However, they are used more because of their distinctive smell and flavour than for their nutritive value.

The alliaceous or onion odour, and in part the flavour, come from complex organic sulphur compounds that are formed only after an onion is cut or bruised. Cutting or bruising releases the enzyme alliinase, this acts on a sulphur containing amino acid which produces several more sulphur containing compounds. These compounds are unstable and can be further altered by heat. For more information on the chemistry of onion bulbs see page 116. Garlic also produces organic sulphur compounds when cut or bruised which, though they are similar to those produced in onions, differ sufficiently for the odours and flavours of the two plants to be quite distinct.

Cooking onions alters or suppresses chemical changes. It will also alter or reduce the formation of odours and flavours. The flavour also alters depending on the *way* onions are cooked, and on whether they are cooked whole, sliced or chopped into small pieces. So, raw onions taste quite different from cooked ones, boiled onions taste different from fried onions and whole onions taste different from finely sliced ones. It is important to prepare and cook onions in the way specified in a recipe or the flavour of the dish will differ from that intended.

Which Onion to Use

Flavour also varies enormously between cultivars. The milder spring and short-keeping salad onions should be used in salads or dishes such as stir-fries, which do not involve much cooking. Some of these onions are so sweet

Tree onion bulbils. These can be eaten as they are, pickled or used for replanting.

that they are eaten fresh, like apples. The more pungent, longer-keeping onions are best used in soups, stews and sauces.

Common, ever-ready, potato, tree onions and shallots can be used interchangeably in many recipes. Ever-ready onions are used in the same way as spring onions—either raw in salads where their flavour is sweet but strong, or the whole plant can be lightly boiled and served cold as a hors d'oeuvre. The flavour of potato onions is mild and sweet, while that of tree onions is stronger and more pungent. Tree onion bulbils can be pickled or added whole to stews. The leaves of all onions and shallots can be used as a garnish for soups and stews, or added to stir-fries and salads.

The flavour of shallots is generally mild, sweet and subtle although this will vary considerably with the variety, and the soil and climate in which it is grown. Shallots soften more readily than onions, which makes them particularly good for sauces. In France some dishes call for specific shallots. Shallots must never be browned as this makes them bitter. They are often pickled and their delicate flavour makes them suitable to be used fresh or pickled in salads and shallot butter, or cooked in soups and sauces such as French Beurre Blanc Sauce and Sauce Bernaise.

Onion seed is sometimes used as a spice although the seed of love-in-a-mist (*Nigella sativa*) is also called wild onion, so it may be this seed which is intended for use in some recipes. Onion seed can also be grown as sprouts (see p. 114) and these add a delicous tang to salads and sandwiches.

Preparation

Onions should not be cut well before use, as lengthy exposure to the air creates a stale flavour. If onions need to be prepared in advance, cook them gently in butter or oil, cool them, and keep refrigerated until needed. Alternatively, onions can be minced, blanched for 2 minutes, cooled and then frozen in small portions. They can then be added to sauces, soups and stews as needed.

To Prevent Tears

The chemical that causes tears when cutting onions is not the same as the one that causes the odour and flavour, although it is also enzymatically produced (see p. 116). Cold will render this chemical less volatile and water will wash it away. So, if onions are chilled first, or cut under water, then tears are not such a problem.

To Remove Onion Odours

Rubbing hands with celery leaves, chervil leaves, chopped parsley, or lemon segments, followed by washing with soap and cold water, will also remove onion odours from the skin.

A recipe from last century 'to remove onion and fish odours from the hands'
Combine ¼ teaspoon of dried mustard powder with 1 tablespoon of moistened salt. Rub this mixture into the hands and wash off with soapy water.

Onions

Recipes

*Appetisers and
Light Meals*

3 spring onions
3 cups self-raising flour
salt
4 tablespoons butter
½ cup strongly flavoured
   cheese, grated
1 cup milk

Onion and Cheese Scones

Trim and finely chop the onions, including some of the green tops.
Sift the flour and a little salt into a bowl and rub in the butter
until the mixture resembles coarse breadcrumbs. Add the spring
onions and cheese. Pour in most of the milk and mix quickly with
a knife. Add the remaining milk only if the mixture is too dry.

Turn the mixture onto a floured board and pat into a round
about 2 cm (1 in) thick. Cut out the scones with a scone cutter.
Place the scones close together on a lightly greased baking tray,
brush the tops with a little milk and bake in a pre-heated very hot
oven until they are well risen and golden in colour—about 10
minutes.

Eat hot, liberally buttered, or cool on a wire rack.

Sweet Onion with Lemon Thyme

2 tablespoons mild olive oil
1 tablespoon butter
2 teaspoons fresh lemon
   thyme, chopped
salt and freshly ground
   black pepper
500 grams (1 lb 1½ oz)
   sweet salad onions

Serve as an appetiser, a light lunch or with fish or chicken.

Combine the olive oil, butter, lemon thyme, salt and pepper in a
bowl. Peel the onions and cut into 1-cm-thick (½-in) horizontal
slices. Brush the mixture on one side of the onion slices and lay
them on the grill buttered-side down. Brush the mixture on the
tops and cook under the grill until they are just tender—this takes
about 20 minutes. Brush the tops with more of the mixture every
5 minutes or so, but do not attempt to turn or the slices will fall
apart.

Crispy Onion Rings

These onions can be served as an appetiser or to accompany a main dish.

Cut the onions into thin slices and soak in the milk for 2 hours. Mix the flour with salt and pepper and dredge the onion rings in the seasoned flour. Put enough oil in a heavy-based frying pan or saucepan to give a good depth and heat. Drop in the floured onion rings a few at a time. Fry until crisp and golden. Drain carefully and serve hot.

1 or more very large strongly flavoured onions
milk
flour
salt and freshly ground black pepper
cooking oil

Glazed Onions

Soak the onions in cold water for a few minutes. Peel and trim the ends and put them in the frying pan with the melted butter. Stir over a medium heat for about 10 minutes and add the sugar, salt and pepper. Continue cooking and stirring gently without a lid. Add the port or sherry and water and continue cooking until the onions are tender and the liquid syrupy.

750 grams (1 lb 10 oz) small onions
4 tablespoons butter
2 tablespoons sugar
salt and freshly ground black pepper
½ cup port or sherry
1 cup water

Stuffed Roast Onions

This recipe is typical rural fare—particularly good for cold winter's days. In England last century, parsley was used to remove the smell of onions from the breath and often when onions were a major part of the meal, a bowl of finely chopped parsley would be passed around afterwards.

Peel the onions, remove the roots and tops and partially boil, about 15 minutes. Drain well. Scoop out the centre of the onions with a pointed knife. Finely chop some of the centre of the onions and mix with the minced meat. Fill the cavities of the onions with the mixture and arrange in a baking tray. Sprinkle with flour, salt to taste and chopped herbs. Place butter on top of each onion and bake in a moderate oven for 40 to 45 minutes. Serve the onions with tomato sauce or a brown gravy, with boiled rice and a green vegetable.

1 large onion per person
30–60 grams (1–2 oz) of minced chicken, beef or lamb per onion
flour
salt
2 tablespoons mixed sage, parsley and thyme, chopped
1 tablespoon butter per onion

Braised Onions

500 grams (1 lb 1½ oz)
   onions
2 cloves garlic
2 tablespoons olive oil
1 tablespoon white wine
½ teaspoon ground
   cardamon
½ teaspoon ground red
   pepper
salt
1 tablespoon fresh parsley,
   chopped
¾ cup sour cream

Peel and slice the onions very finely. Peel and crush the garlic cloves. Combine the onions, garlic, oil, wine, cardamon, red pepper and salt in a large casserole dish. Mix thoroughly, cover and cook in a pre-heated moderate oven for about 1¾ hours. Transfer to a serving dish, sprinkle with parsley and serve with sour cream.

A bunch of young salad onions.

Soups

Onion soup is a common dish in many countries and there are as many versions as there are countries. The following five recipes give an idea of the range of possibilites.

French Onion Soup

250 grams (9 oz) onions
6 tablespoons butter
1 level tablespoon flour
4 cups water
salt and freshly ground
   black pepper
3 tablespoons parmesan
   cheese
croutons

Although this soup is called French Onion Soup, its equivalent can be found in several European countries.

Peel the onions and chop very finely. Melt the butter in a heavy frypan and add the onions. Fry slowly until the onions are tender and slightly golden—they must not be brown. Add the flour and stir well for 1–2 minutes. Add the water a little at a time until a thick paste is formed. Transfer the mixture to a saucepan and add the remaining water. Bring to the boil—stirring to prevent lumps from forming—and simmer for half an hour, season with salt and pepper. Strain, sprinkle liberally with parmesan cheese and serve with croutons.

Simple Creamed Onion Soup

Cut the onions into eight vertical slices and put them in a saucepan with the cloves. Add the stock and bring slowly to the boil—simmer for 1 hour. Pour the stock and onions into a bowl. Melt half the butter in the saucepan, carefully stir in the flour and slowly add the milk. Bring to the boil. Strain out the onions and cloves and add the stock to the milk. Bring to the boil again. Add the other half of the butter and serve very hot with croutons and grated cheese.

500 grams (1 lb 1½ oz) onions
4 cloves
3 cups chicken or vegetable stock
4 tablespoons butter
3 tablespoons flour
1 cup milk
croutons
tasty cheese, grated

Traditional Polish Onion Soup

This soup is traditionally served with pancakes cut into squares.

Dice the bread and make croutons by placing the pieces in a baking tin, sprinkling them with half the butter and drying in a warm oven—turning from time to time until golden brown. Sweat the onions in a saucepan with the remaining butter until they are transparent. Add the croutons to the onions and pour the water over them. Simmer for 40 minutes and strain. Push the onions and croutons through a sieve and return to the pan. Reheat the mixture. Blend the cream with the egg yolks and use this mixture to thicken the soup. Season with salt. Do not boil hard.

90 grams (3 oz) bread, preferably rye
4 tablespoons butter
250 grams (9 oz) of onions, peeled and sliced
4 cups water
½ cup cream
4 egg yolks
salt

Mrs Thorpe's English Onion Soup

This recipe dates from 1815.

Soak the peas overnight. The next day drain them and simmer in the water with the salt until tender. Put through a liquidiser with the liquid. Lightly brown the sliced onions and then the small onions in half the butter. Add the onions to the liquidised peas. Simmer until the onions are quite tender (30–40 minutes). Season with salt and pepper to taste. Fry the slices of bread in butter until crisp and float one in each bowl when serving.

120 grams (4 oz) split peas
4 cups water
1 teaspoon salt
3 large onions, peeled and thinly sliced
8 tiny onions, peeled but left whole
8 tablespoons butter
salt and freshly ground black pepper
a slice of bread for each person

Iranian Onion Soup

4 onions, finely sliced
½ cup good vegetable oil
2 tablespoons flour
2 tablespoons dried
**   fenugreek leaves (or dill**
**   if these are hard to find)**
1 teaspoon tumeric
6 cups water
3 potatoes, peeled and
**   quartered**
salt and freshly ground
**   black pepper**
3 eggs

Brown the onions in the oil in a large saucepan—this should take about 15 minutes. Add the flour, fenugreek and tumeric. Stir with a wooden spoon for a minute. Add the water, potatoes, salt and pepper to taste. Cook over a medium heat for about 30 minutes. Check the seasoning and add more if necessary. Ensure that the potatoes are cooked and, 5 minutes before serving, break the eggs into the soup. Stir constantly with a wooden spoon. Pour the soup into a tureen and serve with yoghurt and bread.

Salads

English Salad Dressing

1 shallot, finely chopped
1 dessertspoon parsley,
**   finely chopped**
1 dessertspoon chives,
**   finely chopped**
1 mixed dessertspoon
**   tarragon, thyme and**
**   chervil, finely chopped**
salt and freshly ground
**   black pepper**
3 tablespoons wine or cider
**   vinegar**
4 tablespoons olive oil

This is a versatile salad dressing which dates from the 19th century. It is particularly good with leafy salads.

Put the shallot and all the other herbs with the salt and pepper into a bowl. Pour on the vinegar and mix well. Gradually stir in the oil and beat very well. Leave to stand for a few hours before using.

Green and Blue Creamy Potato Salad

Mix all the ingredients together and place in the refrigerator for several hours or overnight.

750 grams (1 lb 10 oz) new
  potatoes (preferably
  small red ones), cooked
1 cup sour cream
½ cup plain yoghurt
½ cup spring onions, finely
  chopped—use the green
  stalks, as well as the
  white part
120 grams (4 oz) blue
  cheese, crumbled
salt and freshly ground
  black pepper

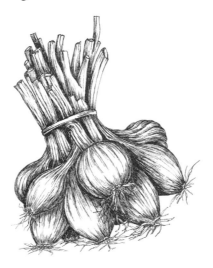

Shallot Butter

Place the shallots with a little cold water in a small saucepan and bring to the boil. Remove them and plunge them into cold water. Drain and crush into a pulp in a bowl or mortar. Add the butter and mix thoroughly. Serve with steak or fish, or simply spread on toast or biscuits as a snack.

Sauces and Relishes

100 grams (3½ oz) shallots,
  peeled
6 tablespoons butter

Bedfordshire Onion Butter

Melt the butter, add the onion juice, mix well together and serve very hot with meat. The easiest way to extract the juice from the onion is to cut the onion in half and squeeze out the juice using a lemon squeezer. Alternatively the juice can be obtained by scraping the cut surface with the back of a knife.

8 tablespoons butter
juice of a medium-sized
  onion

Russian Egg and Shallot Sauce

Serve hot or cold with poultry or fish.

Peel, trim and coarsely chop the shallots. Fry gently in the butter until the shallots are transparent—do not brown. Chop the hard-boiled eggs and mix with the shallots, add salt and pepper to taste.

500 grams (1 lb 1½ oz)
  shallots
8 tablespoons butter
4 hard-boiled eggs
salt and freshly ground
  black pepper

French Ravigote Butter

1 shallot, finely chopped
3 mixed tablespoons chives,
    chervil, parsley and
    tarragon, finely chopped
10 tablespoons unsalted
    butter
1 tablespoon lemon juice
salt and freshly ground
    black pepper

Serve with chicken, fish or potatoes.

Blanch the shallot by covering with boiling water, leave to stand for a couple of minutes, then drain and cover with cold water. Drain again and add, with the herbs, to the butter. Mash with a fork, slowly adding lemon juice. Season with salt and pepper. Chill.

Ravigote Sauce

3 tablespoons wine vinegar
salt
3 teaspoons french mustard
²/₃ cup virgin olive oil
1 tablespoon capers
1 shallot, finely chopped
2 tablespoons tarragon,
    parsley, chives and
    chervil, combined and
    finely chopped
black pepper, freshly
    ground

Serve with cold meat.

Place the vinegar into a bowl and whisk in a little salt until it is dissolved. Add the french mustard and whisk, then slowly add the oil, whisking all the time. Stir in the remaining ingredients and pour into a jug. Leave to stand for about 1 hour.

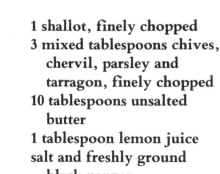

Onion, Shallot and Garlic Sauce

1 tablespoon onion, finely
    chopped
1 tablespoon shallot, finely
    chopped
1 clove garlic, finely
    chopped
2 tablespoons butter
1 tablespoon plain flour
1½ cups milk

Serve with strong flavoured fish, corned beef or add to tinned salmon or prawns for a snack. Alternatively, add grated tasty cheese and serve with vegetables such as cauliflower and zucchini (courgette).

Place the onion, shallot, garlic and butter into a saucepan. Slowly melt the butter and gently cook the vegetables until they are transparent but not brown. Remove the pan from the heat and stir in the plain flour until it is well blended. Return to the heat and add the milk, stirring constantly. Continue to stir until the sauce thickens and cook gently for several minutes.

Persian Shallots with Yoghurt

This is served as a side dish with a main meal or sometimes as an appetiser.

Peel and chop the shallots and soak in cold water overnight. Drain shallots and combine with the yoghurt, salt and pepper to taste. Chill for several hours before serving.

4 shallots
2 cups yoghurt
salt and freshly ground
   black pepper

Spanish Tomato and Onion Sauce

Serve with hot grilled meat and fish.

Peel and dice the onions and chop the tomatoes. Heat the olive oil in a heavy frying pan until it is very hot. Add the onions and tomatoes, salt and pepper. Simmer until the onions are well cooked. Rub the mixture through a sieve to remove the skins and seeds. Add the parsley. This sauce will keep for several days in the refrigerator and is best heated before use.

500 grams (1 lb 1½ oz)
   strong onion (not mild
   salad onion)
500 grams (1 lb 1½ oz) ripe
   tomatoes
½ cup olive oil
salt and freshly ground
   black pepper
1 tablespoon plain-leaf
   parsley, chopped

Sweet Onion Pickle

Serve with grilled beef or fish.

Heat the oil and cook the onions for about 10 minutes until they are soft but not brown. Add the sugar, salt and vinegar and cook the onions until they turn a deep golden brown. Serve them hot or warm.

3 tablespoons mild olive oil
500 grams (1 lb 1½ oz)
   young sweet onions,
   sliced
2 tablespoons brown sugar
salt
2 tablespoons balsamic
   vinegar

Fresh Onion Relish

This relish will keep in the refrigerator for about 3 days and is delicious served with poultry, eggs or fish.

Slice the onion into very thin rings. Place in a bowl and add the lemon juice, paprika and salt and pepper. Mix thoroughly and cover tightly. Leave to stand for at least 1 hour before serving.

1 medium onion
juice of one lemon
½ teaspoon paprika
salt and freshly ground
   black pepper

Traditional Onion Sauce

3 medium onions
1½ cups milk
6 tablespoons butter
3 tablespoons plain flour
salt and freshly ground
  black pepper

This sauce is usually served with mutton or lamb.

Peel the onions and cut downwards into quarters. Pour the milk into a saucepan and add the onions. Stew them over a low heat for 20 minutes. Pour the milk and the onions into a bowl, and in the saucepan they were in, melt the butter over a low heat—do not brown. Stir in the flour, being careful not to colour it, and stir until completely smooth. Slowly add the milk with the onions to the butter and flour, stirring well. Season and simmer for 2–3 minutes. If too thick add a little extra milk. Serve hot.

Soubise

8 medium onions
8 tablespoons butter
2 tablespoons flour
1 cup hot water
salt and freshly ground
  black pepper

This is the simplest form of this French onion sauce; variations can be achieved by substituting stock for the water, and adding an egg—beaten with 2 tablespoons of cream—to the boiling sauce just before serving. This sauce is usually served with boiled meats and poached fish.

Peel and finely slice the onions. Gently fry in the butter until the onions are transparent. Sift the flour onto the onion and butter mixture and stir until there are no lumps. Slowly add the hot water and stir until smooth. Add salt and pepper and simmer gently for about 15 minutes. If a smooth sauce is required pass it through a sieve before serving. If the sauce is too thick add more water. If too thin add more flour.

Bread Sauce

2 medium onions
16 cloves
2 cups milk
1 cup breadcrumbs
2 tablespoons thick cream
salt and freshly ground
  black pepper

This simple sauce is served with boiled meat, fish and chicken. It may have originated in Britain, but versions are also seen in early European cookbooks.

Peel the onions, cut in half and stick the cloves in them. Pour the milk into a saucepan and add the onions and cloves. Bring slowly to the boil. Add the breadcrumbs and simmer for half an hour. Remove the onions and add the cream and salt and pepper to taste. Stir vigorously and serve immediately.

Onion Bread Stuffing

This stuffing is traditionally used with poultry.

Peel and slice the onions. Fry them gently with the garlic in the butter until soft but not brown. Rub the bread into crumbs and add it to the onions with the parsley, thyme, salt and pepper. Continue to heat gently and stir this mixture until it is evenly mixed. Cool.

3 onions
1 clove garlic, crushed
1 tablespoon butter
1 loaf stale white bread,
  crusts removed
1 teaspoon parsley, chopped
½ teaspoon lemon thyme,
  chopped
salt and freshly ground
  black pepper

Caramelised Onions and Eggs

This is a Turkish dish which was traditionally eaten by the Ottoman Sultans on the fifteenth day of Ramadan. The cook's reputation and life-expectancy often depended on preparing it correctly!

Cut the onions into quarters and then into wafer-thin slices. In a heavy-based frying pan, heat the butter and add the onions. Sprinkle with salt and cook over a very low heat, stirring occasionally, for at least 40 minutes—until the onions turn a reddish-brown colour and just begin to crisp. It is crucial that the onions are not burnt during this time. As the onions cook and dry out, sprinkle with a little water.

When the onions are caramelised, remove from the heat and add the vinegar, allspice, cinnamon, pepper and sugar and mix thoroughly. Return to the heat and make 4 depressions in the onions. Break an egg into each and season with a little salt and pepper to taste. Cover and cook on the same low heat until the eggs are covered with a thin transparent film. Serve immediately.

Serves two.

Main Courses

2 large red onions
4 tablespoons unsalted
  butter
salt
water
½ teaspoon balsamic
  vinegar
⅛ teaspoon ground allspice
¼ teaspoon ground
  cinnamon
freshly ground black
  pepper
½ teaspoon of sugar
4 eggs
extra salt and freshly
  ground black pepper

Lemon Chicken with Onions

1 large chicken, cut into
　pieces and the skin
　removed
4 large onions, thinly sliced
6 limes or lemons
1 teaspoon freshly ground
　black pepper
1 teaspoon cayenne pepper
1 tablespoon vinegar
⅓ cup groundnut (peanut)
　oil
salt

This is a traditional recipe from Senegal which combines the pungency of strong onions with the tartness of lemon or limes.

Put the chicken pieces into a large bowl. Add the sliced onions, juice of six lemons or limes, black and cayenne pepper and vinegar. Mix all these ingredients together, ensuring that the marinade coats all the pieces of chicken. Leave to stand for 30 minutes.

Remove the chicken and grill, turning several times, for 15 minutes.

Heat the oil in a saucepan and fry the chicken on a low heat for a few minutes. Add the onion and fry with the chicken until it is soft. Add the rest of the marinade and a cup of water. Simmer for 20 minutes until the liquid is reduced. Season with a little salt. Serve with fluffy white rice and a salad.

Serves four.

Spicy Indian Chick Peas

2 cups chick peas
3 cloves garlic, peeled and
　crushed
2 cups of onions, chopped
2 fresh green chillis, seeded
　and chopped
⅓ cup vegetable oil
1 tablespoon coriander
　seed, ground
1 tablespoon cumin seed,
　ground
1 teaspoon garam masala
1 teaspoon tumeric
3 medium tomatoes,
　chopped
salt and freshly ground
　black pepper
1 tablespoon lemon juice
1 tablespoon fresh
　coriander leaves,
　chopped

Wash and drain the chick peas then soak in cold water overnight. Drain. Fill a pan with salted water, add half the garlic and all the chick peas. Cook until tender. Drain. Fry the remaining garlic, onions and chilli in the oil until the onions soften. Add the spices, tomatoes and salt and pepper to taste. Cook for a few minutes then add the chick peas and cook for a further 5 minutes. Just before serving add the lemon juice and garnish with coriander leaves.

Onions and Braised Beef

This is a rich, sweet dish where the meat is flavoured by onions and garlic, with small pickling onions being a major ingredient.

Remove any excess fat and cut the beef into 4-cm-thick (1½-in) cubes. Pour the oil into a frying pan, add the beef and brown on all sides—cook one layer of beef at a time. Transfer the meat to a casserole dish.

Put the sliced onion and crushed garlic into the frying pan and cook gently until the onion is soft. Add the tomato paste, red wine and wine vinegar and stir for a minute. Pour over the meat in the casserole dish and add the bay leaf, herbs, cinnamon, cloves and sugar. Season with salt and pepper. Cover and cook in a low oven for an hour.

While the beef is cooking, top-and-tail the small onions, and cut a cross in the root end. This allows the flavour to penetrate and stops the centre from popping out. Pour boiling water over the onions and leave to sit for a few minutes, then drain. The skins can now be removed easily. Add the small onions and sultanas to the casserole, re-cover and continue to cook for another 1–1½ hours. Meat and onions should be tender and the sauce thickened. Serve with salad and crusty bread.

Serves six.

1 kilogram (2 lb 3 oz) stewing beef
¼ cup olive oil
1 medium onion, finely sliced
2 garlic cloves, crushed
¾ cup tomato paste
½ cup red wine
2 tablespoons wine vinegar
1 bay leaf
1 sprig thyme, rosemary and parsley
8-cm (3-in) cinnamon stick
4 whole cloves
1 tablespoon sugar
salt and freshly ground black pepper
750 grams (1 lb 10 oz) small onions
2 tablespoons sultanas

Armenian Meatballs

Fry the onions, parsley and 3 tablespoons of the meat in the butter until the onions are cooked. Mix the rest of the meat with the cracked wheat and divide the mixture into egg-sized balls. Flatten a ball on the hand and make a hollow in the centre. Into the hollow place a flat tablespoon of the onion mixture. Fold the meat ball over the mixture and press the edges together so that the onion mixture is enclosed in the centre of the ball. Repeat this process until all the mixture is used up.

Place the hot water in a large saucepan and add the tomatoes. Bring to the boil and then gently lower the meatballs into the liquid. Season with salt and pepper and simmer, uncovered, for about 30 minutes. The liquid should be cooked down until there is just enough for a sauce. Serve hot.

Serves four to six.

6 onions, finely chopped
6 parsley stalks, chopped
1 kilogram (2 lb 3 oz) ground beef or lamb
2 tablespoons butter
½ cup cracked wheat (burghul)
4 cups hot water
2 large ripe tomatoes, peeled and chopped, or 1 tin of tomatoes, chopped
salt and freshly ground black pepper

Chicken with White Wine and Shallots

1½ kilograms (3½ lb) of chicken pieces
200 grams (7 oz) butter
5 shallots, peeled and chopped
⅓ cup white wine
⅓ cup wine vinegar
salt and freshly ground black pepper

This is a simple, quick recipe which makes the most of the subtle, more delicate flavour of shallots.

Heat half the butter in a pan and gently cook the chicken pieces until just beginning to brown. Cover and place in a pre-heated hot oven for about 20 minutes until cooked. Remove the chicken pieces and keep them warm. Add the rest of the butter to the pan and fry the shallots until they are soft—do not allow them to brown.

Add the wine and vinegar and stir. Simmer gently to reduce the liquid by about ⅓, season with salt and pepper. Just before serving, pour the sauce over the chicken.

Serves four.

Basic Onion Flan

Pastry:
250 grams (9 oz) flour
salt
120 grams (4 oz) butter
1 egg yolk
a little water

Filling:
1 kilogram (2 lb 3 oz) onions
1 tablespoon butter
2 eggs, beaten
½ cup cream
1 tablespoon sharp cheese, grated

Sift the flour with a little salt into a bowl. Rub the butter into the flour until it has the consistency of breadcrumbs. Beat the egg yolk with a little water and add to the mixture. Knead thoroughly and put in the refrigerator until required.

Peel and slice the onions very finely and fry slowly in butter until soft. Do not brown. Remove the pan from the flame and allow to cool slightly. Add the 2 beaten eggs, cream and grated cheese. Line a pie tin with the pastry, fill with the onion mixture and bake in a moderate oven until the egg mixture is set and golden on top.

Other ingredients can be added to this tart to add flavour and colour, for example ham, bacon, olives, mushrooms and assorted fresh herbs.

Serves four to six.

Imitation Worcestershire Sauce

Roughly chop the shallots and garlic, add them to the vinegar and boil for 20 minutes. Add all the other ingredients, cover and boil for a further 20 minutes. Transfer to a wide-mouthed bottle, seal and store in a cool dark place for 1 month. Occasionally shake the bottle. After a month, strain and rebottle. The sauce is now ready to use.

100 grams (3½ oz) shallots
4 cloves garlic
2 cups vinegar
2 teaspoons horseradish, freshly grated
4 small pieces fresh ginger
6 cloves
6 whole cardamon seeds
10 black peppercorns
2 teaspoons cayenne pepper
2 tablespoons soy sauce

Pickled Shallots

Pickled shallots are best served with plain foods and combine very well with chunks of tasty cheese and wholemeal bread—the traditional 'Ploughman's Lunch'.

Gently top-and-tail the shallots and carefully peel—any bruising or cut will result in a dark blemish. Make a brine from the water and salt and pour over the shallots. Leave to soak overnight, drain and rinse carefully—if not properly rinsed the pickle will be very salty.

Meanwhile add the peppercorns, ginger, chillies, coriander and bay leaves to the vinegar. Bring to the boil and simmer for 20 minutes. Leave to cool, then strain.

Pack the shallots into sterile jars, cover completely with the spiced vinegar and seal. These shallots will keep in a cool dark place for up to 6 months, but are at their best in 2 to 3 months. Store for at least 6 weeks before using.

1 kilogram (2 lb 3 oz) shallots
4 cups water
4 heaped tablespoons salt
4 cups malt vinegar
10 peppercorns
small piece chopped root ginger
4 small dried chillies
10 coriander seeds
3 bay leaves

Spiced Vinegar with Shallots

16 cups white wine vinegar
1 whole nutmeg
3-cm-piece (1-in) fresh
   ginger, peeled
2 tablespoons yellow
   mustard seed
8 whole cloves
1 tablespoon grated orange
   peel
1 heaped tablespoon salt
6 shallots cut in half

This vinegar can be used to pickle a range of vegetables. It also makes an interesting addition to salad dressings or can be drizzled over grilled steak just before serving.

Combine all the ingredients in a large glass or pottery bowl with a close-fitting lid. Stir well and cover tightly. Store in a warm place for about a month. Strain the liquid through a sieve, squeezing the remains to extract as much of the flavour as possible. Pour into clean, sterile bottles, label and seal. The vinegar is now ready for use.

Pickled Onions

500 grams (1 lb 1½ oz) salt
20 cups water
2 kilograms (4 lb 6 oz)
   pickling onions
6 cups vinegar
2 tablespoons mace blades
1 tablespoon whole allspice
1 tablespoon whole cloves
2 whole cinnamon sticks
10 peppercorns
5 dried red chillies
1 bay leaf

Dissolve half the salt in half the water. Place the unskinned onions in a large bowl and cover with the water. Leave overnight. Drain the onions and remove the skins. Dissolve the remaining salt in the remaining water and pour over the the onions—leave for 2 days.

On the second day prepare the spiced vinegar by putting the vinegar, all the spices and the bay leaf into a large saucepan. Bring to the boil and pour into a bowl. Cover and leave to marinate for 2 hours. Strain the vinegar through muslin.

Drain and carefully rinse the onions. Pack them into warm, sterile jars and cover with the spiced vinegar. Cover and seal the jars and store for 3 months before use.

7. Onion Weed

Allium triquetrum

Other Common Names

Angle onion
Three-cornered garlic
Three-cornered leek
Triquetrous garlic
Wild garlic

Derivation of Names

THIS PLANT DERIVES ITS NAMES FROM THE ONION-GARLIC SMELL OF ITS LEAVES, ITS invasive habit and the triangular shape of its flower stems.

Distribution

Onion weed is a native of the Mediterranean region and parts of Europe near the Atlantic (to an altitude of 1000 metres/0.6 miles). It is now naturalised in damp shady places and woods in Australia, the British Isles, other parts of Europe, New Zealand and the United States.

History

Onion weed, although edible, has little recorded use, being regarded as a wildflower rather than a vegetable or herb.

Botanical Description

Onion weed grows from white ovoid bulbs with keeled, rather fleshy bright-green leaves growing to a height of about 50 cm (1½ ft). It looks very like the snowflake (*Leucojum aestivum*), but can easily be distinguished by the strong onion smell which emanates when it is crushed or broken. The flower stem, which grows from the centre of the bulb, is obviously three-sided or triquetrous. The plant increases vegetatively by producing new bulbs as well as growing from seed.

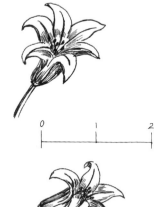

Onion weed flowers with pedicels.

161

Onion weed naturalised on the foreshore. Although it looks attractive it can be a considerable problem in temperate regions.

Flowers and Seeds

Flowers occur in one-sided umbels at the tops of the rather flaccid three-sided flower stems. There are 3 to 15 long-stemmed bell-shaped flowers in each flower head. The flowers are white with a green stripe on each perianth segment (petal). When the seed is fertilised and begins to mature, the flower stem wilts and bends over until the flower head touches the ground. Seed dispersal is carried out by ants who are attracted by the aril (a special covering of certain seeds), which is impregnated with an aromatic oil. The seeds are carried long distances and germinate easily.

Propagation and Cultivation

Onion weed grows easily in damp, shaded places, although in colder climates it does better in drier, well-drained positions. British authors have described

Onion weed, *Allium
triquetrum*, drawn in spring
with the buds and flowers.

Diagrammatic cross-section of (*top*) the leaf and (*bottom*) the scape.

onion weed as a useful, attractive garden plant. It is considered a problem weed, however, in the warm, temperate regions of Australia, New Zealand and the United States, particularly in highly cultivated areas, on roadsides and in waste places. In these regions cultivation should not be attempted.

Harvest and Storage

When onion weed is needed it should be collected from the wild. Take care to ensure that its spread is not encouraged. If it is in flower, seed may be present, so be sure not to collect any flowers that will not be used. Leaves and bulbs should be harvested and used fresh. They do not keep well and the leaves cannot be dried.

Medicinal Uses

Onion weed has not been used medicinally, but as it shares some of the chemical characteristics of other alliums, it may also share some of the medicinal uses.

Culinary Uses

Onion weed can be used in much the same way as chives, although the flavour is not as sweet.

Onion weed flowers.

Recipes

Leafy Salad

Use equal amounts of as many of the leafy herbs as are available. Sorrel and onion weed should be limited to about 6 leaves each, as they have a fairly strong flavour. Carefully wash all the leaves, drain and pat them dry. Either leave them whole or tear them roughly and combine in a large bowl.

In a small bowl beat the oil, vinegar, mustard, salt and black pepper together. Pour over the leaves and garnish with a handful of nasturtium and onion weed flowers. Serve immediately.

corn salad, young dandelion, small lettuce, mizuna, plain-leaf parsley, rocket and sorrel
young onion weed leaves, chopped
4 tablespoons virgin olive oil
2 tablespoons balsamic vinegar
½ teaspoon mustard
salt and freshly ground black pepper
nasturtium flowers
onion weed flowers

Onion Weed and Potato Soup

Place the onion weed bulbs in a saucepan and fry in the butter for a few minutes. Add the potatoes and stock. Season with salt and pepper. Cover and simmer until the potatoes are soft—about 20 minutes.

Purée the mixture. Return it to the saucepan and add the cucumbers. Bring back to the boil and add the milk and cream which have been scalded in a separate saucepan. Stir, add the caraway seeds, stir again and simmer for about 5 minutes. Garnish with a sprig of caraway leaves and serve hot with crusty bread.

about 15 bulbs of onion weed, topped, tailed, washed and chopped
4 tablespoons butter
3 large potatoes, peeled and diced
2 cups chicken or vegetable stock
salt and freshly ground black pepper
2 medium cucumbers, peeled, seeded and sliced
1 cup milk
½ cup cream
1 teaspoon caraway seeds, roughly crushed
caraway leaves to garnish (use parsley if caraway is not available)

8. Rakkyo

Other Common Names

Baker's garlic
Ch'iao t'ou—Mandarin
Chinese scallions
Garden shallot
Hiai or Hsieh—Mandarin
Japanese scallions
K'iu t'au—Cantonese
Namemira—early
  Japanese
Pickled scallions
Rak kioo
Rakkiyo

Derivation of Names

AT ONE STAGE RAKKYO WAS ASSUMED TO BE A CULTIVAR OF THE SHALLOT, *A. CEPA* (Aggregatum Group). Other botanical names which have been used for rakkyo are *Allium bakeri* and *Allium exsertum*.

The Chinese names *ch'iao t'ou* and *k'iu t'au* are the modern or household names used for this plant, while *hiai* (old Mandarin) and *hsieh* (standard Mandarin) are the names given to this plant in classic Chinese literature. All are Anglicised spellings of the way Chinese characters are pronounced. The plants are also called scallions and shallots because the bulbs are like small shallot bulbs and are used in similar ways.

Distribution

Rakkyo is still found growing wild in the mountainous regions of the eastern Chinese provinces Zhenjiang and Jiangxi, and less commonly in northern parts of the Indo-Chinese peninsula and northern India. It is widely cultivated in Japan and in central and southern parts of China, and to a lesser extent on some Pacific Islands.

History

Rakkyo is indigenous to central-eastern China and was probably first cultivated there. One of the earliest written references to this plant was in the Han dynasty (206 BC—AD 220), when several cooking methods are recorded in a book of manners from that era, but it has been used medicinally for much longer. It is also mentioned in one of the first Chinese dictionaries.

Pickled rakkyo. The bulbs in the bowl on the left have been pickled in a mixture containing soy sauce. The bulbs in the bowl on the right are hana-rakkyo, the smallest, finest rakkyo which can take up to four years to produce.

A document known as the *Yo-Yang Tsa-Tsu* (about AD 800), which discusses plants as indicators of the presence of metals, says, 'Whenever there is hiai one will find gold beneath'. At about this time rakkyo was introduced to Japan and it is listed in a 9th-century Chinese-Japanese dictionary under the name of *namemira*. Its medicinal uses are mentioned in a book of the Heian Court (794–1185).

Diagrammatic cross-section of (*left*) the leaf and (*right*) the scape of rakkyo.

Rakkyo is a widely used vegetable crop in China and Japan. Both countries also export hundreds of tonnes of the pickled bulbs. Seventy per cent of the rakkyo grown in Japan comes from the area surrounding the town of Mikuni, north-west of Tokyo. Production of rakkyo in Japan is diminishing each year as a result of the intensive nature of its cultivation and more is being imported from China.

Rakkyo is grown as a home garden plant by Japanese and Chinese immigrants to Western countries but it is not grown commercially in these countries—except for the United States, where some small areas are cropped around California.

Botanical Description

Rakkyo grows as a dense clump of narrow, tubular, thin-walled leaves, which closely resemble chives (*A. schoenoprasum*), except that rakkyo leaves are not as erect, they are bright green instead of blue-green, and in cross-section they are 3-5 angled instead of circular (see p. 167). The bulbs are narrow, ovoid in shape and usually asymmetrical. In cross-section they are made up of concentric rings like common onion bulbs (*A. cepa*). They form a dense clump which is held together by a common stem at the base and there are about three leaves to each bulb. The size and number of new bulbs formed each season varies enormously between cultivars.

In early to mid-summer the leaves die back completely, and in late summer or autumn solid flower stalks emerge from the centre of the old leaves. New leaves appear at the same time or soon after, but these grow from the new lateral bulbs and do not sheathe the flower stem. This arrangement of leaves and flower stems does not occur in other cultivated alliums, and rakkyo is the only cultivated allium to have hollow leaves and a solid scape. The plant continues to grow right through winter.

Rakkyo flowers.
Photograph by Yoshitaka Kamikura.

Flowers and Seeds

The solid stalk that appears in autumn is topped by the flower head, which is covered by a spathe. The spathe splits in two and remains attached, revealing the flattened umbel of 15 to 20 nodding rose-pink to lavender-coloured flowers. Each flower has a long stem or pedicel and the styles and stamens

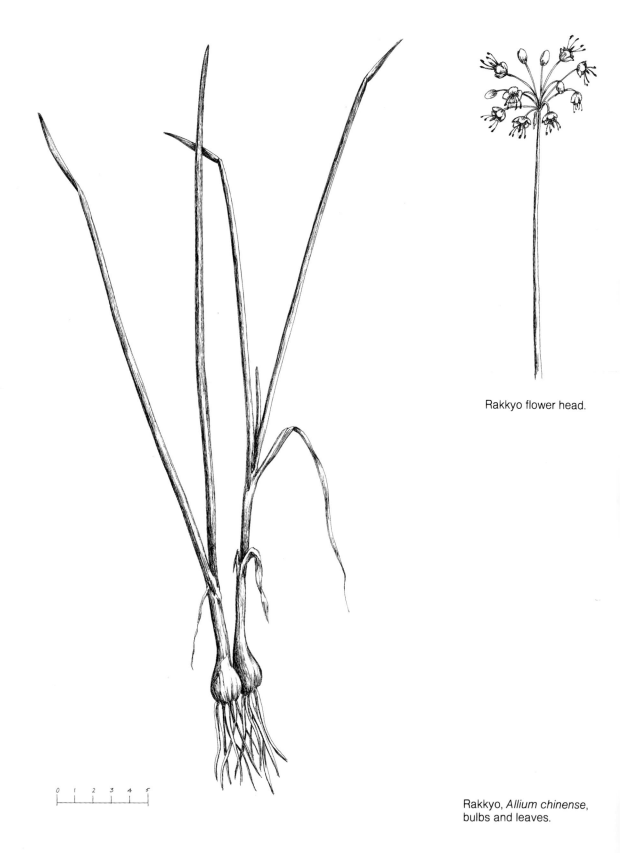

Rakkyo flower head.

Rakkyo, *Allium chinense*, bulbs and leaves.

are long and exserted. The flowers open irregularly over the surface of the umbel. Flowers either do not set seed or the seed is sterile. Plants will often grow for several years without flowering, especially if water is scarce in summer.

Cultivars, Varieties and Closely Related Species

Rakkyo is not readily available in Western countries, although the pickled bulbs, labelled as scallions, are often sold in Asian groceries. The plants are grown in home gardens by people of Japanese and Chinese descent and bulbs are sometimes listed by the seed savers' networks. The main cultivars grown in Japan are listed below:

'Kuzuryu' (new cultivar)
High yield.

'Rakuda'
High yield.
Forms a few large, lateral bulbs, often blanched and eaten raw.

'Tama-rakkyo'
Tama means ball and refers to the shape of the pure white bulbs.
Introduced to Japan from Taiwan.
High yield.
Forms many small bulbs of good texture.
This is the main cultivar used for pickling.

'Yatsubusa' (old cultivar)
Low yield, inferior quality.
Produces many small offsets with narrow necks and has largely been replaced by 'Tama-rakkyo'.

Note: Hana-rakkyo is not a cultivar but a name given to processed bulbs. They are so named because of the way the rakkyo bulbs are cut at both ends. Both 'Kuzuryu' and 'Tama-rakkyo' are used to make hana-rakkyo.

Propagation

Rakkyo is always propagated by planting bulbs because it never sets fertile seed. Bulbs are usually planted in late summer or autumn just below the surface of the soil, about 10 cm (4 in) apart, in rows about 60 cm (2 ft) apart.

If they are grown commercially to be blanched for the fresh market, they are planted 20 cm (8 in) apart in beds made up of double rows 30 cm (1 ft) apart. These beds are separated by an irrigation furrow and are about 1 metre (3 ft 3 in) apart.

Cultivation

Commercial growers of rakkyo plant it in light sandy soils in full sun. The sandy soil needs to be heavily fertilised, but it is preferred because it encourages the formation of numerous small bulbs which are the best for pickling. In Japan, the soil is fertilised when the crop is planted in autumn, and then again in winter as the bulbs develop.

The small fine bulbs required for hana-rakkyo can take up to four years to produce. The first three years are spent cultivating bulbs that are as large as possible, then in the final year each clump of large bulbs is dug up and the individual bulbs replanted at the spacing indicated above. Each bulb will divide into about 20 small bulbs.

In the home garden, rakkyo will grow in any reasonably light, well-drained soil in full sun. Dig in some compost and well-rotted manure a few weeks before planting and add some good general fertiliser when the bulbs are planted. Rakkyo also grows well interplanted with other crops.

The 'Rakuda' cultivar can be blanched by piling soil at the base of the stem as the plants grow so that the bulb and stem are tender and white.

Harvest and Storage

Generally, rakkyo is harvested after the leaves have died back in the late summer of the first year, because any bulbs left in the ground will reduce in size as they multiply the following season. However, hana-rakkyo attracts higher prices for smaller bulbs so they are sometimes harvested after two years' growth, and often as many as four.

If you are growing plants for the fresh bulbs and white stems, harvest them one or two months earlier in early summer—before they die back. These are usually marketed as shallots in Japan. Keep enough bulbs to replant for the following year's harvest. Replant them just as they begin to shoot.

Medicinal Uses

The dried rakkyo bulb is used in Chinese medicine specifically to treat problems of the lungs, stomach and large intestine. It is considered pungent, bitter and warming.

Culinary Uses

The part of rakkyo used for food is the long egg-shaped bulb. More than 80 per cent of the rakkyo grown commercially is pickled—mostly in vinegar. Some are pickled in salt, soy sauce and sugar or in sugar alone. A small number of bulbs are used as relish in curry dishes. The rest are eaten fresh. The taste is difficult to describe but its main characteristics are the crisp

Rakkyo plants with the rakkyo crop behind, near Mikuni in Japan. *Photograph by Yoshitaka Kamikura.*

texture of both fresh and pickled bulbs and the strong distinctive, but basically onion-like, odour. The strong taste and odour make fresh rakkyo an acquired taste.

Chinese and Japanese cooks also use common onions (*A. cepa*) but will not accept them as a substitute for rakkyo. The smell of rakkyo is reduced by pickling in vinegar, which is why so much of the crop is treated in this way.

In China, rakkyo is eaten both fresh and fried, pickled in vinegar with or without sugar or honey, and pickled in brine. In Taiwan, rakkyo is always boiled before being used, while further south, bulbs pickled in brine are reprocessed with vinegar and eaten in curries.

In Japan, most rakkyo is pickled and called rakkyo-zuke. There are many variations in the pickling process, but the bulbs are usually first steeped for several days in brine and then transferred to a vinegar and sugar, or vinegar and salt pickle. A few small red peppers are often added. The commercial product will be heat sterilised, but home pickling recipes usually do not involve heat.

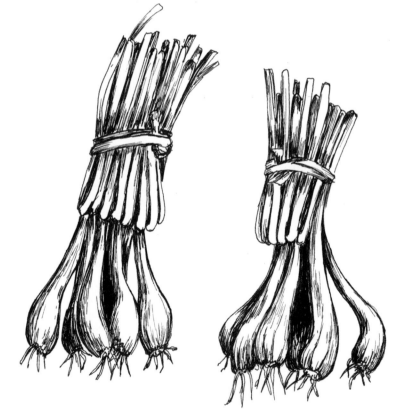

Fresh rakkyo bulbs and stems prepared for sale. Usually sold as 'shallots'.

Recipes

Rakkyo-zuke (Basic salted scallions)

Other pickling recipes begin with this basic one.

Clean the rakkyo bulbs and place in a clean dry wide-mouthed glass or glazed pottery jar—do not cut the ends of the bulbs at this stage. Combine water, vinegar and salt and mix well. Pour over the rakkyo bulbs making sure they are well covered. Place a saucer or lid which is smaller than the mouth of the jar on top and weight it down. Leave for 10 days. If any scum appears, scrape it from the surface.

   Before serving, cut off the stem and roots.

500 grams (1 lb 1½ oz) raw rakkyo bulbs with roots and short stalks
2 cups water
2 cups rice vinegar
2 tablespoons salt

Rakkyo with Honey

Peel off the outer skin of the pickled rakkyo bulbs and scrub gently. Remove roots and stalks. Rinse several times. Combine the vinegar, sugar, honey, peppers and lemon and mix well. Place the rakkyo bulbs in a large sterile jar and pour the vinegar and honey mixture over the top. Cover and shake gently every second day for about 2 weeks. The bulbs are now ready to eat. Refrigerate once opened.

500 grams (1 lb 1½ oz) rakkyo-zuke
1 cup rice vinegar
½ cup sugar
¾ cup honey
1 red chilli pepper, seeds removed, or ½ tablespoon of chilli paste
half a lemon, thinly sliced

Pickled rakkyo.

Allium ursinum

9. Ramsons

Other Common Names

Bärenlauch—German
Bear's garlic
Broad-leaved garlic
Buckrams
Cheremsha—Russian
Daslook—Dutch
Gipsy onion
Hog's garlic
Ramps
Rams
Ramsay
Wild chive
Wild garlic
Wood garlic

Derivation of Names

THE SPECIES NAME, *URSINUM*, COMES FROM THE LATIN *URSUS* MEANING BEAR AND IS probably derived from the fact that bears fed on this plant in the wild. The common names *bärenlauch* (bear's leek) and bear's garlic have the same origin, while hog's garlic suggests that hogs also grazed on it or dug up the bulb. Ramsons, ramps, rams, ramsay and buckrams all come from the Old English word *hramsa* which means wild garlic.

Distribution

Ramsons are indigenous to most parts of the British Isles and Europe from Finland in the north to Greece in the south. They extend as far east as the Caucasus and northern Asia. They grow naturally and in great abundance in damp woods and along stream banks up to an altitude of 1600 metres (1 mile).

History

Ramsons have been used as a food plant since at least the 1st century AD. In botanical literature they are mentioned as edible plants in the 700s and more regularly after the 1400s. The bulbs were boiled and the leaves used in salads in England, while the leaves were eaten in Holland, as reported in Gerard's *The Herbal or General History of Plants* (1597). In Russia the bulbs were gathered and stored as a winter stand-by.

Alice M. Coats in her *Flowers and their Histories* quotes an earlier authority: 'the leaves may very well be eaten in April and Maie with butter, of such as are of a strong constitution, and labouring men'. However, an English book

Ramsons, *Allium ursinum.*

on health in 1547 listed ramsons along with other onion plants as not to be eaten, and Tomlinson in *Renou's Dispensary* described it as a 'poysonous medicament'. Ramsons have gradually fallen into disrepute in Britain — so much so that some herb books describe their flavour as rank — and although they still grow prolifically in some areas they are seldom used.

Ramsons do not grow wild in Australia, New Zealand and the United States, but it is possible to obtain the seed. Because of their prolific growth in their countries of origin, anyone growing them should not allow them to set seed, as they may escape into the wild and add to the weed problem.

Botanical Description

Ramsons are perennial plants which grow to a height of about 40 cm (1 ft 3 in) when in flower. From each narrow, white, bottle-shaped bulb, two to three leaves grow on long, white, basal stalks. The bulbs divide during the growing season to produce dense clumps. Leaves are bright-green, broadly elliptical, taper to a point and have parallel veins. In the ground they are similar to lily-of-the-valley (*Convallaria majalis*), but confusion is impossible once the leaves are crushed because of the powerful garlic smell. The leaves die back in winter and re-shoot again in spring.

Flowers and Seeds

The flowers, which occur in late spring and early summer, grow on two to three angled stems. The spathe splits into two, revealing loose umbels of glistening white star-like flowers. The flower heads can be quite large — up to 6 cm (2½ in) across — with up to 25 flowers. Small, black seeds are contained in a three-chambered capsule and are impregnated with an aromatic oil. As the seed matures, the stem flops over onto the ground and (as in the case of onion weed, *A. triquetrum*) the oil attracts ants to the seed. They carry the seed away, dropping some in the process, and this seed grows into new plants.

Propagation

Ramsons can be grown from seed or by dividing clumps. Unless the seed is very fresh it is difficult to get it to germinate. Soak it overnight on damp cotton wool and then nick the hard seed case with a sharp blade. The optimum temperature for germination is 6°C (43°F). Plant the seed 1 cm (½ in) deep in humus-rich, moist, well-drained soil. It should begin to shoot in two weeks. Planting of seed and division of bulbs is best done in late winter and early spring.

Cultivation

Ramsons grow best in shady damp places, but they do not like to be water-logged. They need a humus-rich soil and will grow well in pots. They are frost-tolerant and, given the right conditions, they do not need any attention, except to be divided and replanted from time to time.

Harvest and Storage

Harvest the leaves by cutting them just above the ground—they are at their best in spring. Dig the bulbs in autumn and wash before use. Both the bulbs and leaves should be used as soon as possible after harvest but they will keep for up to a week in the refrigerator. The flavour of the leaves almost disappears when they are dried. In some regions the bulbs are salted for winter use.

Medicinal Uses

The bulbs and leaves of ramsons have been used medicinally instead of garlic. Their main action seems to be on the intestinal and respiratory systems. In the form of a syrup or a decoction, this plant has been used for coughs, colds, sore throats and bronchitis. Several early slimming diets involved the use of the freshly pressed juice of wood garlic (ramsons). Steinmetz's *Materia Medica Vegetabilis* lists ramsons as being used against asthma and arteriosclerosis, to reduce blood pressure and to aid digestion.

Culinary Uses

Both the leaves and bulbs can be used in any dish that would benefit from the garlic-like flavour of ramsons. The leaves can be used as a garnish and bulbs and leaves can be chopped and added to omelettes, casseroles and sauces. A traditional use was to combine the leaves with a white sauce and serve with fish. Young leaves can also be added to salads.

Ramsons

Recipes

Ramsons Butter

8 ramsons leaves with stalks
4 tablespoons butter
black pepper, freshly ground

Carefully wash and dry the leaves and chop very finely. Cream the butter, add pepper to taste and stir in the finely chopped leaves. Place in a small butter dish in a refrigerator until firm. Serve with grilled or roast meat and strong flavoured fish.

Mayonnaise and Ramsons

2 heaped tablespoons ramsons leaves, finely chopped
1 heaped tablespoon parsley, finely chopped
1 cup mayonnaise

Wash and dry the ramsons and parsley. Chop the herbs separately and then add them both to the mayonnaise, stirring until evenly mixed. Serve with cold fish, cold chicken or hard-boiled eggs.

10. Welsh Onion

Allium fistulosum

Other Common Names

Atasuki—Japanese
Bawang daun—
    Indonesian, Malaysian
Bunching onion
Chang fa—Chinese
Chibol
Chinese small onion
Ciboule
Cong—Chinese
Evergreen bunching onion
Green onions
Japanese bunching onion
Japanese leek
Negi—Japanese
Onion-leek
Rock onion
Scallion—American
Self-perpetuating onion
Shallot
Spanish onion
Spring onion
Stone leek
Sybow—Scottish
Two-bladed onion
Welsch zwiebel or Winter
    zwiebel—German

Derivation of Names

FISTULOSUM MEANS TUBE-LIKE AND REFERS TO THE LARGE, HOLLOW LEAVES AND flower stem. The common name, welsh onion, has nothing to do with Wales except that both words have the same origin, coming originally from the Anglo-Saxon *welise* and the old German *welsche*—both meaning foreign. When welsh onions were introduced to Germany in the Middle Ages— probably carried across Russia from Asia, they were seen as foreign onions or *welsch zwiebel*. As they moved into other European countries and the British Isles, the name welsh continued to be used. The other common names refer to this plant's growth habit, bunching and evergreen, and its re-semblance to other onions: leeks, shallots and spring onions.

Distribution

Welsh onions probably originated in eastern Asia but are no longer found as a wild plant. They are now grown around the world, both as a commercial crop in countries such as Australia, the British Isles, China, Japan and the United States and in home gardens. They also thrive in a variety of climates, being grown from the cold regions of Siberia to the tropical parts of Asia.

History

This onion has been cultivated since prehistoric times and was the main garden onion of China and Japan. It is mentioned in Chinese literature as early as 100 BC and in Japan by AD 918. Over the centuries many variants have been selected and grown and their uses have been wide ranging. The array of welsh onion cultivars in Asia is probably as diverse as that of the

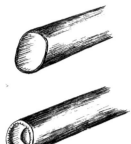

Diagramatic cross-section of (*top*) the leaf and (*bottom*) the scape of welsh onion.

0   1   2

Single welsh onion flower with pedicel.

bulb onion in Europe and America. In China and Japan, where they are mostly grown for their long white stems, welsh onions are still the most important onion crop.

Welsh onions probably reached Europe in the 1400s and Britain and Ireland in the late 1600s. They were widely grown in both places until the beginning of this century. Then, they stopped being grown as a market garden plant in Britain and the name welsh onion was often used for the ever-ready onion instead. Welsh onions have been grown in the United States, New Zealand and Australia since colonisation, originally by Chinese immigrants but now much more widely.

Today in Western countries welsh onions are grown in home gardens and as a commercial crop. They are used as a green bunching or spring onion. There are many cultivars, some of which are the result of cross breeding with *A. cepa*, and several of these are grown as commercial crops to produce larger bunching or spring onions.

Botanical Description

Welsh onions grow in large, robust, perennial clumps from a short rhizome with tapering roots. They have no obvious bulb but, like the leek, are grown for their thickened stems, which are made up of elongated leaf bases. In some cultivars the stems can reach 50 cm (1½ ft) and are often blanched. Each plant produces a hollow stem with two to six hollow cylindrical leaves, which sheathe the stem for up to one-third of its length. The flower stem reaches a height of 15–80 cm (½–2½ ft) and the leaves are usually slightly shorter. This onion often multiplies at the base, producing numerous side-shoots, and usually remains green all winter, although some cultivars will yellow or die back.

Flowers and Seeds

The short spathe has no long tip and remains attached to the base of the flower head. It splits to reveal the spherical flower head which is up to 5 cm (2 in) in diameter and densely packed with pale yellow bell-shaped flowers. Flowers open in a regular progress from the top of the umbel to the base. The only other cultivated onion that shows this characteristic is chives (*A. schoenoprasum*). In the individual flowers the stamens protrude well past the perianth segments (petals) which remain more of less erect instead of opening out like those of *A. cepa*.

Welsh onions have been known to cross-pollinate with common onions, so if seed is to be collected they must be grown apart. Seed is best used within two years of harvest.

Cultivars, Varieties and Closely Related Species
See also Appendixes 3.5 and 4 at the back of the book.

There are many cultivars of welsh onion, some of which are hybrids with common onions and shallots. These hybrids are usually sterile. There is also

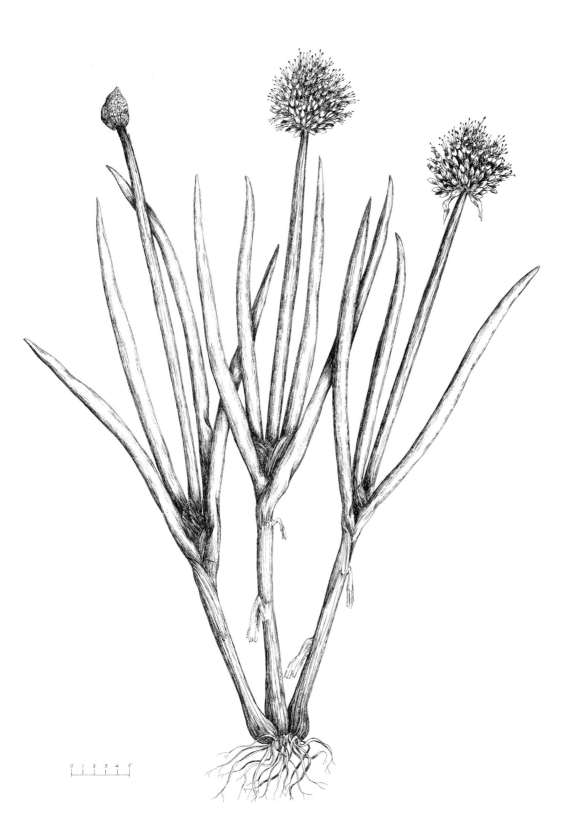

Welsh onions, *Allium fistulosum*, with long slender stems and
narrow bulbs. Flowers start to appear in early spring.

considerable variation in growth habit between the different varieties, cultivars and hybrids. Forms with tender leaves are grown for their edible tops. Those with long, thick stems like leeks are grown for their blanched leaf bases. Some cultivars lose their leaves in winter, so do best in cold regions. Others are harvested at the seedling stage when only 10 cm (4 in) high and are sold in bunches. There are even varieties which produce top-sets or bulbils, like tree onions, instead of flowers in the flower head. These cultivars are usually smaller and are grown for their green leaves. Other forms are erect and some are floppy and sprawling. Others produce many new side-shoots, some only a few. Most cultivars are grown as annuals, although some are perennials and can be cultivated from side-shoots.

Propagation

Welsh onions are grown from seed which can be sown for most of the year in mild climates, but they are best sown in spring or summer where winters are severe. Simply plant the seed about ½ cm (¼ in) deep in good, friable soil. Plants should be thinned in stages to 20 cm (8 in) apart.

New plants can also be propagated by dividing clumps and replanting the younger plants in groups of two or three. This division is most successful in late winter or early spring. If the leaves are large, then cut them back before replanting.

Cultivation

Welsh onions grow well in a fertile, well-drained soil in full sun. They do not like a soil which is too acid and do best with a soil pH between 5.5 and 7.0. In very acid infertile soils, add dolomite and well-rotted animal manure about six weeks before planting.

Welsh onions are very hardy and some cultivars will survive cold winters—especially if thickly mulched. Others may be damaged by frost, but will reshoot. However, once the plants have reached a certain stage, low temperatures may cause them to bolt to seed in spring. If the winters are very severe, treat welsh onions as annuals and resow in spring, or dig them up and plant them in a greenhouse or cold frame until the worst of the winter is over.

They do best in temperate regions and, if they are to remain tender, need plenty of water during hot, dry weather. Some cultivars grow continually by producing side-shoots throughout most of the warm season. Short, bunching types, grown for their stems and tops, are mainly a summer crop and can be interplanted with other vegetables or used as an edging.

Blanching the Stems   Welsh onions grown for their white stems can take much longer to grow and also produce fewer side-shoots than those grown for their green tops. In Japan, great care is taken to produce long white stems, and the plants may stay in the ground for up to a year.

Welsh onion flowers are attractive to bees and many other useful insects. They occur in spring and last right through summer.

The upright leaves of welsh onions look dramatic with the nasturtiums surrounded by a box hedge.

Welsh onions with the developing flower buds.

A clump of welsh onions in early spring before the flowers begin to appear.

To grow welsh onions with long blanched stems, start the plants in a seedbed. When they are about 12 cm (3 in) high, transplant into furrows just deeper than the height of the plants, and space them about 5 cm (2 in) apart. As the stem grows, push the dirt into the furrow to just below the point where the leaves divide from the stem. This will eventually result in large mounds, with deep furrows in between which allow for irrigation and good drainage. Some modern cultivars are self-blanching.

Harvest and Storage

The green tops can be harvested at any time—simply cut what is needed. New growth is the most tender so the best leaves are picked in spring and summer.

Stems from perennial clumps can usually be harvested by pulling the growth at the edge of the clump out sideways. In heavy soil this may be difficult, so it is best to dig up the whole clump, use what is needed and replant the rest. Cultivars which are grown for spring onions, are ready to harvest from 8 to 10 weeks after planting in summer, and 12 to 14 weeks in winter.

Short, bunching types which don't survive the winter are usually ready to harvest in autumn—about four months after planting. Those grown for their very long, white stems are often grown through the winter and harvested the following spring, spending up to a year in the ground. The whole plant has to be dug very carefully so that the tender stem is not damaged.

In China some cultivars have the soil pulled back from the clump and the stalks cut about 2 cm (1 in) above the bulb. The tops are then left to regrow. Usually, though, the whole plant is harvested.

Pests and Diseases
See also Chapter 13.

Very few insects attack welsh onions. Onion thrips and onion maggot are the most likely, although thrip is less of a problem with welsh onions than other cultivated allium species. They are also resistant to diseases such as pink root, smudge and smut—all of which cause problems with bulb onions. Diseases such as downy mildew and Alternaria leaf spot can cause problems with welsh onions.

Medicinal Uses

Welsh onions have a long history of use in Chinese medicine. The whole plant can be used and contains volatile oils, vitamins C, B1, B2 and a little vitamin A. These onions are regarded as being antiseptic and having an affinity with the lungs and stomach. They are used internally to treat colds,

Young welsh onion plants. Harvested at this stage they are sold as spring onions.

chills and stomach aches. Crushed, fried and made into a poultice they are applied warm to boils and to relieve the swollen and painful breasts of new mothers. A paste made from the fresh stem pounded with honey is applied to abcesses and weeping infections.

Welsh onions do not have a history of medicinal use in Western countries, but they share most of the attributes of common onions and can be used in many of the same ways.

Other Uses

In China the diluted pressed juice from the whole plant is used as a spray against aphids.

Culinary Uses

Welsh onions have a mild sweet onion flavour. The stem contains some vitamin C and small amounts of carotene, potassium and dietary fibre. In China and Japan, the white and green stems are commonly used in stir-fries because they cook quickly. Overcooking can make them bitter. The leaves are used as a garnish.

Elsewhere, they are mainly used like spring onions to supply young growth for salads, stews and soups. They are particularly good in potato soup in winter when other onions are harder to get, or combined with cheese and bacon in omelettes and quiches.

Welsh onions can be used as a substitute for spring onions in any of the recipes at the end of Chapter 6 and spring onion stems can be used instead of welsh onions.

Recipes

Oriental Green Onion Pastries

Serve as a snack or with stir-fried vegetables.

Sieve the flower, sugar and salt into a bowl. Add the oil and enough water to make a smooth dough. Knead gently and divide into 6 pieces. Roll out until ½ cm (¼ in) thick, spread sesame oil, welsh onions and salt evenly over the top of each pastry and roll each into a tight roll. Stretch each roll until it is about 3 times the original length and then shape into a coil. Sprinkle lightly with flour and roll each coil to a 1 cm (½ in) thickness. Brush more sesame oil onto the base of a wide flat pan and place the pastries into the pan. Brush the top of each with cold water and sprinkle thickly with sesame seeds. Cook over a medium heat until the bottom is golden, then turn and cook the other side. Remove when golden and crisp. Serve hot or cold.

Welsh Onion Stems in Dill Sauce

Put the welsh onions into a saucepan and pour the stock over the top. Season with salt and pepper and bring to the boil. Simmer for about 10 minutes, partially covered, until the onions are cooked but still firm. Drain the onions and place them in a warm serving dish. Reserve the stock.

Rinse the saucepan and use it to melt the butter over a low heat. Stir in the flour to make a smooth paste and cook gently for a minute. Add a cup of the reserved stock, stirring carefully. Return to the heat and bring to the boil. Simmer, stirring all the time for a few minutes. Add the cream and continue to heat but do not allow to boil, then add the chopped dill. Stir and pour over the onion stems. Garnish with whole chive flowers and eat as an entree or serve with other vegetables with chicken or fish.

Appetisers and Light Meals

2 cups plain flour
½ teaspoon sugar
½ teaspoon salt
2 tablespoons vegetable oil
sesame oil
1 cup chopped welsh onions, white and green
1 teaspoon salt
cold water
2 tablespoons white sesame seeds

300 grams (10½ oz) welsh onion stems, cut into 4-cm (2-in) lengths
1½ cups chicken or vegetable stock
salt and freshly ground black pepper
2 tablespoons butter
1 tablespoon plain flour
¼ cup cream
2 tablespoons dill, finely chopped
chive flowers to garnish

Onion Bread

2 breadsticks
10 tablespoons butter
½ cup young welsh onion
leaves, finely chopped

Cut the bread sticks in half lengthways and butter the tops and bottoms. Sprinkle the chopped leaves onto the bottom of the bread, cover with the top and tightly wrap each breadstick in foil. Place in a moderate-to-hot oven and cook for about 15 minutes until the bread is crisp and the butter melted. Remove from the oven, unwrap and cut the bread into slices. Serve as an appetiser or to accompany a main course.

Salads

4 cups bamboo shoots,
cooked
¼ cup coconut milk
3 tablespoons lime juice
1 tablespoon fresh red
chilli, minced
2 cloves of garlic, crushed
1 cup welsh onion stems
and leaves, finely
chopped
1 tablespoon basil leaves,
roughly chopped
1 tablespoon coriander
leaves, roughly chopped
3 small shallots, peeled and
thinly sliced

Bamboo Shoots and Welsh Onion Salad

Carefully drain the bamboo shoots. Mix the coconut milk and lime juice with the sugar, chilli, garlic and welsh onion. Pour this mixture over the bamboo shoots, mix and leave to stand for about 1 hour. Sprinkle the basil, coriander and shallots over the top just before serving.

150 grams (5 oz) crushed
wheat (burghul)
6 welsh onion stems,
chopped
250 grams (9 oz) tomatoes,
skinned and chopped
6 tablespoons parsley,
finely chopped
4 tablespoons mint, finely
chopped
4 tablespoons olive oil
juice of 1 lemon
salt and freshly ground
black pepper

Burghul Salad

Pour the wheat into a fairly large bowl and cover with fresh cold water. Leave to soak for 45 minutes, drain well and squeeze out any excess moisture. Transfer the wheat to a salad bowl and add the onions, tomatoes, parsley and mint. Mix well. Add the oil, lemon juice, salt and pepper to taste. Mix thoroughly again. Leave to stand for a couple of hours, so that the flavours are thoroughly absorbed by the wheat and serve with cold or barbecued meat.

Chinese Ginger and Welsh Onion Sauce

This sauce is usually served with poached or steamed chicken.

Warm the oil in a small pan on low to medium heat. Add ginger, welsh onions and salt and cook for 1–2 minutes. Cool briefly and serve in small side dishes.

Korean Barbecue Sauce

This sauce needs to be prepared several hours before it is to be used and is delicious with all barbecued meats.

Mix all the ingredients together, seal in a jar and leave to stand for at least 4 hours.

Steamed Schnapper with Onion and Chilli Sauce

With a sharp knife make several slits on either side of the fish. Rub the sugar over the fish, inside and out, and put it onto a plate that will fit inside a steamer or wok. Place the whole cloves of garlic inside the fish and sprinkle the ginger over the top. Place the plate inside the steamer or wok, sitting on a trivet, and pour in boiling water to just below the plate. Cover the steamer or wok with a tight-fitting lid and cook the fish on a low heat for about 15 minutes, until cooked.

While the fish is cooking, lightly toast the sesame seeds in a small dry frying pan. Remove the seeds and pour the olive oil into the pan. Heat the oil and add the welsh onions and chillies and cook for a few minutes. Remove from the heat and allow to cool a little. Remove the fish from the steamer or wok, pour off any juice that has accumulated on the plate and clean. Add the soy sauce and sesame oil to the onion mixture, whisk together and pour over the fish. Garnish with the toasted sesame seeds and serve with steamed white rice.

Serves two.

Sauces and Relishes

⅓ cup good vegetable oil
2 tablespoons ginger, peeled and minced
4 tablespoons welsh onions, finely chopped
1 teaspoon salt

2 tablespoons soy sauce
1 tablespoon rice vinegar
2 tablespoons welsh onions, minced
1 clove garlic, crushed
1 teaspoon sweet chilli sauce
1 tablespoon white sesame seeds, toasted

Main Courses

1 whole schnapper, cleaned and gutted
1 teaspoon sugar
2 cloves garlic, peeled
small piece ginger, peeled and finely chopped
1 tablespoon sesame seeds
1 tablespoon olive oil
2 welsh onion stems, sliced into short lengths
2 fresh red chillies, finely sliced or 1 teaspoon of chilli paste
2 tablespoons soy sauce
1 tablespoon sesame oil

11. Other Edible Alliums

ALL ALLIUMS ARE EDIBLE BUT WHETHER THEY ARE ALL WORTH EATING IS ANOTHER question altogether. The following alliums are either available from ornamental bulb suppliers or common in their country of origin. All are recorded as having been eaten on a regular basis at some stage in history.

Allium akaka

Valik
Wolag

Wolag is a low growing plant with wide, glaucous leaves and solid short flower stalks to 30 cm (1 ft). Flower heads are spherical with many soft mauve-pink to whitish flowers. It is native to parts of temperate Asia (Iran, Turkey and the Caucasus) and grows in rocky, dry places up to 3000 metres (almost 2 miles). In Iran, bulbs are eaten in much the same way as the common onion. The whole young plant is also used and treated as a delicacy. Until fairly recently plants could be seen for sale in the markets of Teheran.

Allium ampeloprasum

Wild leek
Levant garlic

Wild leek is a plant from which several cultivated food alliums are derived. These include elephant garlic, leeks and kurrat.

The species name *ampeloprasum* is derived from two Greek words, *ampelos* meaning vine and *prason* meaning a leek, signifying that this leek-like plant grew among grapevines. They may have self-sown there, or perhaps they were an early attempt at companion planting—allium species have been used for centuries to protect more tender plants from hungry insects.

Wild leek is an extremely variable plant. It reaches 45–180 cm (1½–6 ft) in height and has flat, keeled leaves with rough margins. The bulbs are ovoid and a number of bulblets grow among the foliage leaf bases. These bulblets are outside and completely separate from the larger bulbs. Flower heads are large and globular and consist of numerous pink or dark-red cup-shaped flowers. Bulbils are not usually present. The solid scape is somtimes over 1 metre (3 ft 3 in) tall and is never coiled or curved in the early stages.

In the wild, wild leek ranges from southern Europe and northern Africa eastwards through Turkey, Iran and the Caucasus. It grows in rough, untended places, near cliffs and sandy shores, and on cultivated land. It has been eaten both raw and cooked in most of the countries where it can be found growing wild.

Kurrat closely resembles leeks, will cross-fertilise with leeks and is often confused with them. Kurrat plants are small with virtually no bulbs. The leaves are smaller and narrower than those of leeks and the leaf base is shorter. Kurrat is believed by some to be the leek of ancient Egypt, the plant which has been found in tombs of this time. It is the young leaves of Kurrat which are usually eaten. They make an appetising vegetable on their own, or with other dishes. Uncooked they are used in salads.

Kurrat is occasionally seen in Western gardens. In Egypt, where it is grown as a commercial crop, the first leaves are cut and harvested about four months after sowing. Successive cuttings are made every three to six weeks for the next year and a half. After this the crop is resown.

Allium ampeloprasum (Kurrat Group)

Kurrat
Kurrat-nabati
Salad leek

Allium giganteum, showing the very tall growth habit and spectacular flower heads.

Allium giganteum flower head.

Allium angulosum

Mischei-tschesnok
Mouse Garlic

Mouse garlic reaches a height of 20–50 cm (8 in–1½ ft). Slender elongated bulbs are clustered on a rhizome. Basal, linear, rich-green leaves are up to ½ cm (¼ in) wide, have a blunt tip and a sharp keel on the underside. Numerous cup-shaped, white to rose-purple flowers grow in hemispherical umbels in summer.

This allium is indigenous to all the countries from northern Europe to Siberia. It grows naturally in damp grasslands, is very hardy and will grow easily from seeds or by dividing bulbs. In Siberia the bulbs are eaten fresh and salted for later use.

Allium canadense

Bulb-bearing onion
Canada garlic
Egyptian onion
Meadow garlic
Meadow leek
North American garlic
Rose garlic
Rose leek
Tree onion
Wild garlic
Wild onion

Canada garlic grows to about 30 cm (1 ft), with three or more leaves to each bulb and bell-shaped pink or white flowers. It is extremely variable—some varieties have only bulbils in the flower head, others a mixture of bulbils and flowers. This onion is indigenous to the north-east of North America and was eaten by the Iroquois, Menominee and Meskwaki Indians as well as the early explorers and settlers. The strongly flavoured bulbs were eaten boiled and pickled, while the stalks were eaten fresh. The white bulbs are at their best before the flowers appear.

In 1876, the eminent botanist, Baron Ferdinand von Mueller, published a long list of *Select Plants Readily Eligible for Industrial Culture or Naturalisation in Victoria (Australia)* in which he said that 'North American garlic could be cultivated or naturalised on moist meadows for the sake of its top bulbs, which are much sought for pickles of superior flavour'.

Allium cernuum

Lady's leek
Nodding onion
Wild onion

The botanical name, *cernuum*, comes from Latin and means drooping or nodding, a reference to the growth habit of the flowers. Nodding onion grows from long slender bulbs which are grouped on a short rhizome. Flattened leaves, up to six per bulb, grow to about 40 cm (1 ft 4 in). Flowering stems are slightly longer and carry a drooping umbel of 20 to 30 pale-pink to dark-rose cup-shaped flowers. When the seed forms, the flower heads suddenly straighten, forming numerous distinctive angles. If they are growing in the garden, flowers should be removed at this time to prevent self-sowing.

Nodding onion is easy to cultivate. In its natural habitat it does best in cool, mountain regions. It is indigenous to Canada, northern Mexico and North America and was widely used by native Americans. One group of north-western native Americans harvested the bulbs and ate them fresh, either raw or cooked; or they plaited them together and dried them for winter use. Sometimes the whole plant was rubbed over the body as an insect repellent. Early explorers and settlers also ate the strongly flavoured bulbs raw, in soups or pickled.

Allium geyeri

Geyer's onion
Omoir

This onion is named after Carl Andreas Geyer (1809–1853), an Austrian botanist who travelled in America in 1843 and collected this plant. It grows from an ovoid bulb, with delicate flattened leaves, to a height of 15–50 cm (½–1½ ft). White to pink bell-shaped flowers occur in umbels, with up to 25 per umbel. Some varieties also have bulbils in the umbel.

Geyer's onion is native to the western United States where it grows along streams and in moist meadows. The Nez Percé called it *omoir*, and they and several other indigenous peoples including the Apache ate the bulb, usually dried and later cooked, steamed in pits.

Allium giganteum

This allium is similar to elephant garlic, *A. ampeloprasum* (Ampeloprasum Group), except that the leaves are broader, it grows taller and the flowers are bright-purple rather than rose-pink.

A. giganteum grows from large ovoid bulbs which can reach 8 cm (3 in) in diameter. The tall ribbed flower stems can be as high as 2 metres (6½ ft), with the leaves sheathing them to one-third of their length. Leaves are linear, large and floppy, and 5–10 cm (2–4 in) wide. Flower heads are enclosed by a single spathe, which splits to reveal the densely-packed, spherical umbel. The flowers are star-like and purple, occasionally white. Once the flowers appear the leaves have mostly died back. The bulbs do not have much flavour and the flowers do not dry well, but they create a very impressive display in the garden.

A. giganteum is a native of central Asia and needs a warm corner to thrive.

Allium ledebourianum

Asatsuki
Siu yuk

A. ledebourianum has small bulbs which cluster on a rhizome. Semi-cylindrical hollow leaves sheathe the scape to about half its height, which is about 60 cm (2 ft). Numerous rose-violet flowers occur in umbels. This allium is found from Russia through China to Japan. It is cultivated in Japan. The leaves and bulbs are eaten fresh and boiled, and the bulbs are often pickled. They taste like mild onions with a little garlic.

Nodding onion (*Allium cernuum*) flowers in summer showing the typical nodding head.

Allium macleanii

Bulbs of *A. macleanii* have papery coats, and the leaves are green, basal and up to 8 cm (3 in) across. Flower stems grow to 1 metre (3 ft 3 in) high with distinct ribbing while the flowers are star-shaped and purple with exserted stamens. This allium is native to Afghanistan and central and south-west Asia and grows in stony mountainous regions. The bulbs are eaten in parts of central Asia.

Allium neopolitanum

Daffodil garlic
Flowering onion
Naples garlic
Naples onion

Naples onion grows to a height of 10–40 cm (4 in–1 ft 4 in) from a small round bulb with two to three flat, keeled leaves. Flower stems are slightly triangled and can grow up to 60 cm (2 ft). Glistening white cup-shaped flowers occur in slightly nodding umbels and are sweetly scented. It will grow well in a pot. Naples onion is native to the Mediterranean region—from Portugal to Israel—where it flowers in spring.

Naples onion is regarded as either an ornamental or a weed, depending on where it grows. It is one of the most readily available decorative alliums and is often grown for cut flowers. It can also be eaten cooked as a vegetable, and is used in this way in the Mediterranean region.

Allium obliquum

Twisted-leaf garlic

The botanical name of this allium comes from the Latin, *obliquus*, meaning lopsided or oblique. Plants grow from a single thickened oblong bulb with a long flower stem up to 1 metre (3 ft 3 in), half of which is sheathed by a series of leaves. These leaves are linear and v-shaped in cross section. Flowers, which grow in densely-packed spherical umbels at the top of the stalk, are bright yellow-green and cup-shaped, with exserted stamens.

A. obliquum is a native of temperate Europe and Asia where it grows in meadows and woods. In Siberia it was cultivated and used as a substitute for garlic.

Allium oleraceum

Field garlic

The botanical name, *oleraceum*, comes from the Latin *oleraceus* and means of the vegetable garden, where it may be either a crop or weed. Field garlic grows from a small egg-shaped or rounded bulb, 20–100 cm (8 in–3 ft 3 in) in height. Narrow, linear leaves sheathe the lower half of the flower stem. The flowers occur in rather messy spherical umbels. They are cup-shaped and white in colour, tinged with green, pink or brown. Flowers are often replaced either partially or completely by bulbils. Seed is rarely produced.

Field garlic is native to most of Europe (including parts of Russia) where it grows in waste and scrub land, roadsides and rocky places. It is naturalised in some parts of America and Australia, but is an occasional weed in others. Because of the bulbils, field garlic is almost impossible to control in the garden and should never be deliberately planted. It was eaten in Sweden, where the leaves were added to soups and stews, and the bulbs are also added to soups in other parts of Europe. It is very similar to two other species—*A. scorodoprasum* and *A. vineale*, but in *A. oleraceum* the spathe splits in two, while in the others it splits down one side only and stays in one piece.

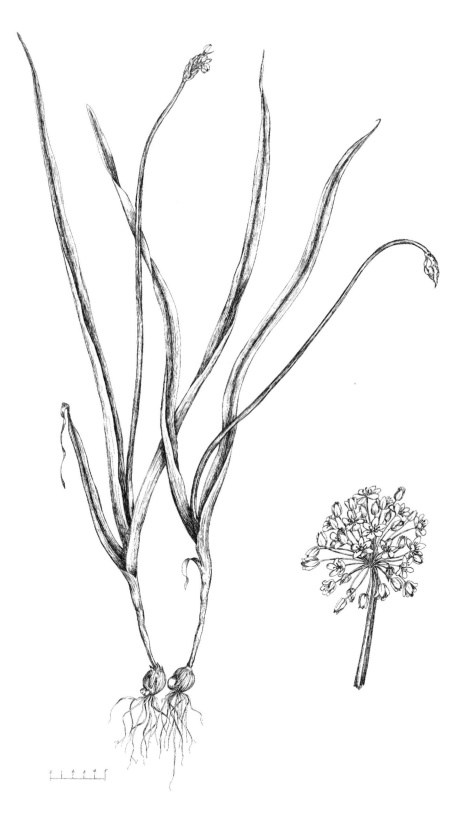

Naples garlic, *Allium neopolitanum.*

Allium ramosum

Chinese chives
Chinese leeks
**Fragrant Chinese
chives**
Fragrant flowered
garlic

The botanical name, *ramosum*, comes from the Latin *ramosus*, meaning branched, and probably refers to the rhizome. *A. ramosum* is very similar to *A. tuberosum* (garlic chives) and at one time both plants were classified under the name of *A. odorum*.

A. ramosum grows from cylindrical bulbs clustered on short rhizomes. The leaves are long and tubular, semi-circular, hollow in cross-section, and sheathe the stem for about one-third of its length. The flowers, which occur in funnel-shaped umbels, are bell-like and white with a dark-red mid-rib. This allium blooms in early summer, is native to central Asia and is easily grown. It can be used in the same way as garlic chives (*A. tuberosum*).

Sometimes plants sold as Chinese leeks are in fact *A. ramosum*, but mostly they are *A. tuberosum* (garlic chives). For a list of the differences between *A. tuberosum* and *A. ramosum* see page 65.

Allium roseum

Rose garlic
Rosy flowered garlic

The botanical name and the common names describe the rose-coloured flowers. Rose garlic grows from egg-shaped bulbs, which are usually surrounded by numerous bulblets. Linear leaves sheathe the lower part of the solid stem, which can grow to a height of 70 cm (2½ ft). Broad, cup-shaped flowers occur in large, hemispherical umbels and are pink or white. Flower heads may also contain bulbils and, if cultivated in the garden, non-bulbiferous forms should be used so that they are not invasive. Select forms with good flowers and few or no bulbils.

Rose garlic is native to Europe and northern Africa where it grows easily in well-drained, stony, warm places up to an altitude of 700 metres (almost ½ mile). It is naturalised in some waste places elsewhere. Bulbs are eaten in the Mediterranean region.

Allium rubellum

Himalayan onion
Pharna

The botanical name, *rubellum*, means reddish-coloured and refers to the flowers. Himalayan onion grows from small bulbs with hollow thread-like leaves. Numerous pink bell-shaped flowers occur in hemispherical umbels. It is native to temperate Europe and Asia where it grows in dry semi-desert regions. In northern India and the Himalayas it is also called *pharna*. Here, leaves are harvested and dried, and used as a condiment. Bulbs are also eaten, both raw and cooked.

Allium scorodoprasum

Sand leek

The botanical name, *Allium scorodoprasum*, has often been mistakenly used to describe a form of garlic with a coiled scape (see pp. 1, 6). From 1700, *A. scorodoprasum* has been given the common names rocambole and serpent's garlic, as well as sand leek. Only sand leek is correct and rocambole and serpent's garlic should only be used for forms of *A. sativum*. *Scorodoprasum* comes from the Greek *skorodon*, meaning garlic, and *prason*, meaning the leek.

Sand leeks grow from egg-shaped bulbs which can be dark-violet in colour and surrounded by reddish-black bulblets. Linear leaves sheathe the lower part of the stem, which can grow to a height of 80 cm (2 ft 8 in). The umbel is densely packed with purplish bulbils and some purple-red flowers. *A. scorodoprasum* is a native of Europe (including parts of Russia) and parts of Asia. *A. scorodoprasum* has not been cultivated.

The vibrant white flowers of *Allium neopolitanum*.

Allium angulosum coming into flower.

Round-headed garlic (*Allium sphaerocephalon*) combines beautifully with English lavender. *Photograph by Dave Pomare.*

This plant grows naturally in waste places, and plants which produce bulbils should never be planted in the garden. Dr Dilys Davies in her book *Alliums: The Ornamental Onions* describes *A. scorodoprasum* as a 'self-perpetuating garden thug'. There are some sub-species that do not produce bulbils—these will not spread through the garden. Bulbs have been used for flavouring in many countries.

Allium senescens

German garlic
Mountain garlic

Mountain garlic grows in tufted clumps from bottle-shaped bulbs which are clustered together on a rhizome. Basal, linear leaves are rounded on the underside with no strong keel. Flowers occur in hemispherical to spherical umbels on stalks up to 40 cm (1 ft 4 in) long. They are densely-packed, lilac-purple and cup-shaped. This allium is native to Europe and central Asia where it grows in mountain pastures and damp, rocky places. The bulbs are eaten as a vegetable and the leaves used as a flavouring.

Allium sphaerocephalum

Ballhead onion
Round-headed garlic
Round-headed leek

Sphaerocephalum is from Greek and means round head, referring to the shape of the flower head. Round-headed garlic grows from egg-shaped bulbs with additional yellow bulblets. It can reach a height of up to 90 cm (3 ft) when in flower, but is a very variable plant and may only grow to 5 cm (2 in). The semi-cylindrical leaves sheathe the lower part of the flower stem, which is topped by a small spherical umbel, packed with reddish-purple tubular flowers and occasional bulbils. This is an easy plant to grow in a sunny border and is ideal for planting in clusters interspersed with other perennials.

Round-headed garlic is native to sandy and rocky places in Europe, north Africa and south-west Asia where both the leaves and bulbs are used as food. It is known as a garden escape in many countries.

Allium stellatum

Prairie onion

Stellatum comes from the Latin *stellatus*, meaning starry or star-like, and refers to the shape of the flowers. *A. stellatum* grows from an ovoid bulb to a height of up to 70 cm (2 ft 4 in). Basal leaves are linear and keeled and the pink, star-shaped flowers grow in a hemispherical umbel. This allium is a native to rocky hilly parts of North America and edible bulbs were consumed by both the indigenous peoples and the early colonists.

Allium textile (syn. *A. reticulatum*)

Prairie onion

The bulbs of this prairie onion grow in clusters with each bulb producing two leaves which grow to about 30 cm (1 ft). Bell-shaped pink or white flowers grow in umbels on the top of flower stems, which reach the same height as the leaves. *A. textile* is a native of western North America, where it can be seen forming thick carpets on the dry plains and hills. The bulbs were eaten raw and cooked by indigenous North Americans in the north-west.

Allium tricoccum

Native garlic
Ramps
Wild leek

The specific name, *tricoccum*, comes from the deeply three-lobed fruit—*tri* meaning three. Slender ovoid bulbs are grouped on a short rhizome and from each bulb two or three broad, stalked, shiny bright-green leaves grow. When flowers appear the leaves die back. Flower stems grow up to 40 cm (1 ft 4 in) and are topped by a hemispherical umbel of white star-shaped flowers.

Ramps is a native of North America where it grows in dampish woodlands and hillsides. It is this plant which gave Chicago its name. In the mid-1600s the indigenous people who farmed this region called it *chicagou*, which means skunk. Apparently, it was called this because when the big broad leaves were trodden on, they spurted their pungent perfume in a manner similar to skunks.

The bulbs were eaten raw or dried for later use, often with fish, by the Iroquois and other North Americans. In Virginia, ramps-eating festivals were held when the bulbs were at their best—this was just as the leaves began to grow. In 1939, the *Baltimore Sun* described them as 'tasting like the food of the gods and smelling a dozen times worse than Limburger cheese and burning rubber'!

Allium neopolitanum.

Allium victorialis

Alpine leek
Long-root onion
Victory root

Victory root grows from narrow bottle-shaped bulbs which form dense clumps to a height of 30–60 cm (1–2 ft). The leaves are lance-shaped, leathery and sheathe the lower part of the stem. Two or three leaves grow from each bulb. White star-like flowers grow in mostly spherical umbels. The whole plant has a pungent garlic smell.

Victory root is found in the cooler regions of Europe and Asia, where it grows on stony mountain slopes. The bulbs were worn by German miners to protect them from the evil spirits that lived underground, and in Russia it was believed to protect the eater from scurvy. Fresh and pickled bulbs have been eaten in many countries. In Japan it was used by the Ainu (aboriginal people who once dominated the northern part of Japan) in incantations to prevent infections and diseases. In northern India and the Himalayas the brittle stems and bulbs are eaten raw and cooked.

Allium vineale

Crow garlic
False garlic
Field garlic
Stag's garlic
Wild garlic

The botanical name, *vineale*, means belonging to vines, and suggests that this plant was a weed of vineyards. Crow garlic grows from an egg-shaped bulb with cylindrical leaves which sheathe the lower part of the stem. Flower stems can reach a height of 1 metre (3 ft 3 in) but they are usually shorter than this. The hemispherical umbel is densely packed with bulbils and a few to many pink to red, bell-shaped flowers.

In the past the leaves and bulbs have been used for flavouring, but today crow garlic is regarded as a noxious weed of cultivated land. It is a problem weed throughout much of Europe, to which it is endemic, and Asia, Australia, New Zealand and the United States, where it is naturalised. It will taint the milk of dairy cattle who feed on it and produce 'off' flavours in beef and poultry. The bulbils can also contaminate wheat fields, finding their way into the harvest and spoiling flour. Bears will dig up the bulbs and wild grazing animals, such as deer and elk, eat the green tops.

Allium sphaerocephalum.

12. Other Onion or Garlic Flavoured Plants

THERE ARE MANY PLANTS THAT HAVE THE WORD ONION IN THEIR NAMES, BUT THESE are so called because they have bulbs that resemble onions, not because they have an onion flavour. Examples of these are onion grass or onion couch (*Avena elatior*), dog's onion (*Ornithogalum umbellatum*) and pregnant onion (*Ornithogalum longibracteatum*). The following are brief descriptions of three other plants which have been grown and used for their onion-garlic flavour. This use is reflected in their common and botanical names.

Garlic mustard is a perennial which grows from a tap-root with erect stems 30–100 cm (1 ft–3 ft 3 in) high. The leaves grow in rosettes and are heart-shaped with long stalks and wavy margins. White flowers occur in flat-topped clusters. The whole plant smells of garlic and both the roots and the leaves have been used to impart garlic flavour to sauces and stews. They have also been used medicinally—internally to produce a sweat and externally to relieve itching from stings and bites.

Sage-leafed germander has square stems with opposite, greyish-green pebbled leaves, similar to sage except that the tips are rounded and the leaves more green. It grows to about 50 cm (1½ ft) high, and has small greenish-yellow flowers in spike-like clusters. The whole plant has a faint smell of garlic. It has been used as a substitute for hops in beer making and medicinally to help with rheumatism, fevers and colds.

Alliaria petiolata

Alliaria
Donkey's foot
Garlic mustard
Jack-by-the-hedge
Onion nettle
Sauce-alone

Teucrium scorodonia

Ambroise
Garlic sage
Hind heal
Large-leafed germander
Sage-leafed germander
Wood sage

Tulbaghia violacea

Society garlic

Society garlic is named after Rijk Tulbagh (1699–1771) who was a Dutch governor of the Cape of Good Hope.

This plant is a perennial which grows from thick white tuberous roots. The strap-like grey-green leaves grow from a basal sheath and form dense clumps. When not in flower it looks fairly similar to garlic chives (*A. tuberosum*) and has a similar smell. The leaves stay green all year and there is also a variegated variety. Round stems grow up to about 30 cm (1 ft) and are topped by clusters of narrow tubular lilac-mauve flowers in spring and summer.

The leaves can be used in the same way as chives and garlic chives, chopped into salads or as a garnish for soups and stews. The flowers steeped in vinegar give it a mild garlic flavour and they too can be used as a garnish. Society garlic makes an attractive border or edging plant and cut flowers last well in water.

Society garlic, *Tulbaghia violacia.*

The mauve of the society garlic flowers contrasts well with the large dark green comfrey leaves.

The delicate mauve flowers are not only beautiful and long lasting in the garden but they can also be eaten.

13. Pests and Diseases

AT FIRST GLANCE IT MAY SEEM THAT A FORMIDABLE LIST OF PROBLEMS CAN BESET edible alliums. But don't worry, because many of these only attack commercial crops where intensive monocultures are practised. They are included here though because they do occasionally crop up in the home garden and from the descriptions you should be able to work out what's wrong. As a general rule, diseased plants should be dug up and burnt to stop the pest or disease from spreading.

Pests

Cutworms

Brown in colour, up to 3.5 cm (1½ in) long, cutworms are nocturnal and feed on the leaves of plants. They can destroy small seedlings but only if present in large numbers.

Lucerne Flea

The lucerne flea is a yellow-green wingless insect about 3 mm (⅛ in) long. In areas where gardens are surrounded by pasture, lucerne flea can appear from late autumn to spring—usually after rain. They attack young onion seedlings and heavy infestations can kill seedlings overnight.

Malathion and maldison are used to control the flea on commercial crops, but in the garden pyrethrum is effective.

Mite (*Aceria tulipae*)

This mite, also known as the wheat curl mite, is so tiny it cannot be seen with the naked eye. The first signs of its presence may be that the shoots emerging from affected cloves are twisted and streaked with yellow. The injury to the leaves occurs during storage and once the young garlic plants have overcome the initial setback, they seem to grow quite normally. In storage, bulbs that are badly infected by the mites will shrink and wrinkle.

You can control the spread of infections to other bulbs by dusting with sulphur, but this will not kill the mites inside the cloves. It is a good idea to destroy any diseased or less-than-perfect bulbs before planting.

Of the thousands of nematodes, there is one that is attracted to garlic, onions and other alliums. It is usually called the stem-and-bulb eelworm or nematode. The nematodes burrow into the bulbs and stems, which swell and go soft and spongy. Leaves are sometimes malformed and twisted.

Remove and burn all the infected plants and avoid planting in affected soils for at least five years where the soils are heavy and two years where soils are light. Nematodes can be introduced on seed and bulbs, so ensure that any you buy are disease-free. Lucerne and some other pasture species can act as hosts of these nematodes.

Nematodes (Ditylenchus dipsaci)

The onion fly is small—about ½ cm (¼ in) long—with transparent wings. It lays eggs into cracks in the soil or on the neck of a young plant. A small white grub up to 1 cm (½ in) long emerges from the egg. It burrows into the root and stem of young onion seedlings and newly sown garlic cloves and kills them. Onion maggots are encouraged by fresh animal manure and large quantities of unrotted organic matter in the soil close to planting. It attacks most bulb onions and welsh onions, while shallots and leeks are less susceptible.

To lessen the chances of maggot attack, prepare the bed well before use and do not add fresh organic matter, blood and bone or green manure crops after planting. Handle the onion plants as little as possible, as the smell of onions seems to attract the onion fly. Parsley grown with onions will help to keep the onion fly away and, if onions are planted after other crops from the *Apiaceae*, such as celery, the chance of attack by onion maggot is greatly lessened. If plants are attacked they should be removed immediately and burnt.

Onion Fly and Maggot (Hylemya antiqua)

Thrips are yellow in the nymph stage and grey-black when mature. They can be carried long distances by prevailing winds and are at their worst from late spring to late summer. They can do considerable damage to all edible alliums and seriously reduce the resultant crop. The leaves will show silvery streaks or spots as the thrip sucks the moisture from the plant. Severe attacks can result in shrivelling of the plant. During the day they hide right down in the heart of the plant and can be difficult to see.

You can control small infestations by squashing the thrip or by spraying with soapy water. For larger infestations, you may need several applications of pyrethrum.

Welsh onions are more resistant to these pests than most of the other cultivated alliums.

Thrip (Thrips tabaci)

The wireworm can be up to 3 cm (1 in) long with a white or brown body and brown head. It mainly attacks commercial crops when onions are planted following cereal or pea crops. To prevent this, the soil is usually treated with an insecticide before planting.

Wireworms (Limonius genus)

Diseases

Alternaria Leaf Spot (*Alternaria porri*)	This disease usually occurs in summer. The first signs are dark-brown or black spots with yellow edges on the leaves. The whole spot can be up to 3 cm (1 in) in diameter. Warm weather encourages the disease and spores are spread by wind and water. To control the disease, destroy the affected plants and spray with fungicides. Easier still, grow resistant cultivars.

Black Mould (*Aspergillus niger*)

Black mould develops on onion, shallot and garlic bulbs which have not been properly dried or have been stored in damp sheds. Prevention is the only cure. Dry the bulbs properly before storing, do not store damaged bulbs, and ensure that the storage space is well-ventilated and dry.

Downy Mildew (*Peronospora destructor*)

This is the disease most likely to cause problems with onions. It is less likely to occur if the onions are grown in an open, sunny spot. Downy mildew usually attacks in spring, summer or autumn, especially if there are long periods of humid weather.

Symptoms are a grey mould that develops into purple patches on the leaves, which later turn yellow. The entire leaf may die if not treated. A black, secondary fungus may develop on the dead leaf. Downy mildew usually develops from previously infected crop residues.

At the first sign of mildew, destroy the affected plants, preferably by burning. Affected leaves should never be used in mulch or composted for later use on onions. Alternatively, spray with copper oxychloride plus a wetting agent. A fine spray sticks better to the waxy surface of the onion leaves.

There are some species and culivars which are more resistant than others. For example welsh onions are known to be less affected. This disease can affect all alliums and, if it becomes a problem, the best way of dealing with it is not to re-use affected soil and to choose a sunny, open, windy spot for planting so that leaves do not remain wet after dew or rain.

Fusarium Root Rot (*Fusarium oxysporum*)

This root rot is carried in the soil and attacks during moist warm spells. It rots the bulb at its base, but the first obvious symptom is a yellowing of the leaves, followed by a reddish discolouration at the base of the plant. It mainly attacks damaged bulbs and is at its most prolific around 30°C (86°F).

Bulbs affected by fusarium root rot late in the season may be mistakenly put into storage, but the rot will spread. As soon as you detect it, destroy the affected bulbs. This particular fusarium is specific to allium species, so onions, leeks, chives, garlic and shallots can all be affected. It can be controlled by long rotations between crops. Also, avoid very fertile soils and store only undamaged bulbs in an airy shed at cool temperatures—4°C (39°F) is ideal.

This disease usually occurs during storage to onions which have been topped too close to the bulb. The bulbs start to look shrunken and soggy. Later a grey mould develops. Once this happens, affected bulbs should be discarded. You can avoid neck rot by ensuring that bulbs to be stored are properly dried and that the leaves are not cut too close to the bulb. All bulb-forming plants in *A. cepa* are susceptible to this disease, but chives (*A. schoenoprasum*) are immune.

Neck Rot (*Botrytis allii*)

Penicillium may attack garlic bulbs in the field or in storage. Many bulb onions are also affected. The thick fleshy part of the clove will soften, shrivel and eventually show patches of dust-like blue-green spores. This disease is carried by the bulbs, not in the soil. Even seemingly healthy bulbs may carry the spores.

Any bulbs showing signs of infection when split apart to plant should be discarded. High soil moisture-levels at the time of planting seem to inhibit the growth of the penicillium, so irrigate the soil when you plant the bulbs.

Penicillium Decay (*Penicillium corymbiferum*)

Pink root affects only the roots, which turn pink, shrivel and die. As new roots grow they also die if affected. The diminished food supply caused by the lack of roots results in undersized bulbs. This disease attacks chives, garlic, leeks, onions and shallots, as well as other alliums—but welsh onions seem to be resistant to it. It also attacks other crops such as maize and sorghum.

Pink root is still mainly a disease of commercial crops but, as it can be spread on seedlings and bulbs, it is possible that it will occur in the home garden. It can survive in soil for up to 10 years, becoming more severe with successive crops.

In the home garden it is best to abandon the growth of susceptible species in affected areas, until there is no longer any chance of the disease being active.

Pink Root (*Pyrenochaeta terrestris*)

The first sign of a rust attack is seen as patches of orange spores on leaf surfaces. It is difficult to control. Leeks and, to a lesser extent, garlic seem to be the worst affected.

Plants that show patches of orange spores should be dug up and destroyed. Rust seems to be encouraged by high nitrogen-levels in the soil. It is very variable from year to year so that some years it will be a problem, but other years it will be unnoticeable. Even so, once detected it is better not to plant leeks or garlic in that bed for several years. Bordeaux mixture, sprayed at the first sign of rust, may help to stop rust spreading to other plants.

Rust (*Puccinia porri*)

This is a disease of white onions and garlic. It takes the form of black spots on the bulb scales. It will build up in the soil if successive crops are grown in the same area, and extra moisture in the soil before harvesting aggravates the problem.

Smudge (*Colletotrichum circinans*)

To prevent the occurrence of smudge ensure bulbs are properly dried before storing, store in an airy position, do not water just before harvest, and do not regrow onions in affected soil for several years.

Smut (*Urocystis cepulae*)

Onion smut is first seen as black streaks of mould just below the surface of the first leaves that emerge. The leaves bend and twist and appear bumpy. If the leaves are broken open, masses of black spores are seen. Any affected plants should be destroyed.

Soot (*Embellisia allii*)

Soot grows on the outer scales of garlic bulbs, so that the whole bulb has a black sooty covering. Often there is no sign of the attack until the bulbs are harvested, although those badly affected may be stunted and the leaves show tinges of purple and orange. Preventive measures are careful culling of any affected cloves before planting, reducing or ceasing watering just before harvesting, and ensuring good drainage at all times.

White Rot (*Sclerotium cepivorum*)

White rot attacks onions through the roots. The first signs are stunted plants, with the older leaves turning yellow and dying back at the base. At later stages a white fungal growth may be seen around the base of the plant. White rot has been known to remain viable in the soil for up to 20 years, even if onions are not grown in the soil. It is triggered into new growth by secretions from onion roots. Optimum conditions are temperatures between 10° and 20°C (50°–68°F) and high air moisture-content. Conversely, higher soil temperatures and low moisture-levels will retard the spread of the disease.

Although there is no measure offering total control, onion oil has proved effective in some areas of commercial cropping. If an area in your garden is affected, destroy the diseased material and don't use this area for onions again.

White rot affects chives, garlic, leeks, onions and shallots—but garlic chives (*A. tuberosum*) are immune.

Viruses

Garlic Virus

This virus affects both bulb growth and crop yields. The first signs are yellow streaking on the leaves. Unfortunately garlic virus is nearly endemic in some areas. Crops can still be grown but yields are reduced.

If it is not already present in your area, take care to purchase only virus-free cloves for planting. If plants do become affected, remove and destroy them immediately. Take steps to control aphids and thrip, which will spread the viruses.

Shallot virus

This virus shows first as yellow streaks on the leaves and then plants are dwarfed. Onions are occasionally affected. There is no cure, so affected plants should be removed and burnt. The virus is spread by aphids so these need to be controlled.

Glossary

Acid (of soils) Peaty and sandy soils are generally acid in character. Acid soils have a pH reading below 7. Lessen acidity by adding lime.

Alkaline (of soils) Chalk, lime and clay soils are generally alkaline in character—they have a pH reading higher than 7. Lessen alkalinity by adding organic matter such as compost and manure.

Annual A plant that completes its life cycle within one year.

Bactericidal Capable of killing bacteria.

Basal At or forming at the base.

Biennial A plant that requires two years to complete its life cycle and produces flowers and seeds in its second year.

Blanching To make white or prevent from becoming green by excluding light. With alliums this is usually achieved by hilling soil around the stem of the plant or by completely covering the whole plant with a pot or similar container.

Bolt To flower and set seed prematurely.

Bract Small or modified leaf.

Bulb A storage organ, made up of a short underground stem surrounded by swollen leaf bases usually with a dry outer protective skin also consisting of leaf bases.

Bulbils Small bulbs usually formed in the flower head.

Bulblets Small bulbs produced beside the parent bulb.

Capsule A dry fruit derived from at least two united carpels which break open when mature.

Carpel The central female organ of a flower made up of the ovary, style and stigma.

Cellulose A carbohydrate which is the main constituent of cell walls in plants.

Corm Swollen solid fleshy stem base.

Cultivar A cultivated variety.

Decoction An extract obtained by boiling plant material in water for a certain length of time.

Diaphoretic Producing perspiration.

Dicotyledon A member of the Dicotyledonae which is the larger of the two classes of Angiosperms (flowering plants). The main characteristic is the presence of two seed leaves in the embryo.

Diuretic Increasing the volume of urine.

Elliptic In the shape of an ellipse.

Endemic A native of one country or specific area.

Entire leaf One with a continuous margin, not indented.

Enzyme A protein which is capable of acting as a catalyst to a chemical reaction.

Exserted Projecting beyond the surrounding organs. Often used to describe stamens which project beyond the length of the perianth segments.

F1 hybrid F1 hybids are based on an inbred male sterile line (female) which is pollinated by a selected male line. The resultant hybrid seed shows a high level of genetic uniformity. The plant grown from this seed does not produce fertile seed.

Flower head A cluster of flowers arising from a primary branch.

Fungicidal Capable of killing fungi.

Genus The major division of a family usually made up of more than one species all basically similar to one another and genetically close. The first part of the botanical name gives the genus, e.g. *Allium* in *Allium cepa*.

Hybrid The result of a cross between two species or varieties, may be natural or artificial.

Inflorescence A flower head or group of flowers with a common stalk borne at the end of a stem.

Infusion An extract obtained from plant material by steeping it in water.

Intermediate day cultivar (onions) Bulbing occurs when the day lengths are between 13 and about 14 hours.

Keel A longditudinal ridge, usually on the underside of a leaf.

Linear leaf Narrow leaf with near-parallel sides.

Locule One of the cavities or chambers in an ovary.

Long day cultivars (onions) Bulbing occurs when day lengths are between about 14 and 16 hours.

Monocotyledon A member of the Monocotyledonae which is the smaller of the two classes of Angiosperms (flowering plants). The main characteristic is the presence of one seed leaf in the embryo. Includes grasses, palms, tulips and alliums.

Mucilage Gelatinous substances or gummy secretions found in plants.

Naturalised A plant which has been introduced into an area and flourished as if it were an indigenous plant.

Oblate Flattened at the poles, wider than it is high.

Open pollinated (seed) Random natural pollination.

Ovoid Egg-shaped, in three dimensions.

Pectin A substance which occurs in ripe fruits, soluble in water, forming a jelly after evaporation.

Pedicel Stalk of an individual flower within a flower head.

Peptide Compound formed by two or more amino acids.

Perennial Living for more than two years.

Perianth The outer part of a flower which encloses stamens and carpels, usually made up of two whorls. In dicotyledons the perianth is usually made up of an outer green calyx (a whorl of sepals) and an inner corolla (a whorl of petals). In monocotyledons, including alliums, there is usually no differentiation between the calyx and corolla (or petals and sepals).

Perianth segment   The sepals and petals combined and then divided into segments, also called tepals. There are six perianth segments in each allium flower.

Petals   Generally the white or coloured part of the flower. In the *Alliaceae* they are combined with the sepals and more correctly called tepals or perianth segments.

Rhizome   A horizontal, underground stem bearing roots, scales and nodes.

Scape   A leafless flower stalk, originates from the ground or from basal leaves.

Sepals   Outer perianth segments, in the *Alliaceae* they are combined with the petals and called tepals or perianth segments.

Short day cultivar (onion)   Cultivars where bulbing occurs when day lengths are between 12 and 13 hours.

Softneck (garlic)   Cultivars of garlic which do not produce a scape or flower head.

Spathe   The bract which encloses the flower head of some monocotyledons.

Species   A group of plants which is closely related and will freely cross with each other. The second part of the botanical name gives the species, e.g. *cepa* in *Allium cepa*. Species which are closely related are grouped together in a genus.

Tepals   The floral leaves of a monocotyledon, also called perianth segments. The same as sepals and petals in a dicotyledon.

Tillers   Side-shoots arising from the root or around the base of the original stalk.

Top-setting (garlic)   Cultivars of garlic which produce scapes and flower heads.

Tuber   Swollen underground organ of solid tissue. Contains stored food and is an organ of vegetative reproduction.

Umbel   An indeterminate flat-topped umbrella-shaped inflorescence, in which the flower stalks arise from a common point.

Variety   A distinct form of a species which is found in the wild as a true breeding entity.

References Consulted and Further Reading

The following is a list of the major references consulted and, in particular, those that may be of interest to anyone who wants to know more about a certain topic. It would not be sensible to include every reference consulted. Those books or articles which are unlikely to be available to the general reader have not, with a few exceptions, been included.

Books

Alger, C., *The Chase Organics Manual of Fruit and Vegetable Cultivation*. Ian Alland Ltd, Surrey, England, 1989.

Baumann, H., *The Greek Plant World in Myth, Art and Legend*. Translated and augmented by W. T. Stearn and E. R. Stearn. Timber Press, Portland, Oregon, 1993.

Bricknell, C. D. (Ed.), *International Code of Nomenclature for Cultivated Plants*. Bohn, Scheltema and Holkema, The Hague, 1980.

Brouk, B., *Plants Consumed by Man*. Academic Press, London, 1975.

Chang, C., Q. Cao and B. Li, *Vegetables as Medicine*. The Rams Skull Press, Kuranda, Australia, 1989.

Coats, A. M., *Flowers and their Histories*. A. & C. Black, 1968.

Crawford, S., *A Garlic Testament*. Harper Collins, New York, USA, 1992.

Culpeper, N., *Culpeper's Complete Herbal and English Physician*. J. Gleave and Son, Deansgate, UK, 1826.

Davies, D., *Alliums: The Ornamental Onions*. Timber Press, Portland, Oregon, USA, 1993.

Engeland, R. L., *Growing Great Garlic: The Definitive Guide for Organic Gardeners and Small Farmers*. Filaree Productions, Okanogan, WA, USA, 1991.

Fanton, M. and J., *The Seed Savers Handbook*, The Seed Savers Network, Byron Bay, Australia, 1993.

Frost, A., *'Sir Joseph Banks' And the transfer of plants to and from the South Pacific 1786–1798*. The Colony Press, Victoria, Australia. 1993.

George, A. S., *Flora of Australia, Hydatellaceae to Liliaceae*. Australian Government Publishing Service, Canberra, Australia, 1987.

Greg-Wilson, C. and Mathew, B., *Bulbs: The Bulbous Plants of Europe and their Allies*. Collins, London, 1981.

Griffiths, M. (Ed.), *Index of Garden Plants: The New Royal Horticultural Society Dictionary*. MacMillan, London, 1994.

Grigson, J., *Jane Grigson's Vegetable Book*. Penguin, London, 1980.

Halpin, A. M. (Ed.), *Unusual Vegetables*. Rodale Press, Emmaus, Pennsylvania, USA, 1978.

Hendrik, U. P. (Ed.), *Sturtevant's Notes on Edible Plants*. J. B. Lyn and Co., New York, 1919.

Herklots, G. A. C., *Vegetables in South East Asia*. Allen and Unwin, London, 1972.

Hsu, Hang-Yen. *Oriental Materia Medica—A Concise Guide*. USA, 1986.

Hyams, E., *Plants in the Service of Man*. J. M. Dent and Sons, London, 1971.

Johnson, A. T. and Smith, H. A., *Plant Names Simplified*. Landsmans Bookshop Ltd, Herefordshire, UK, 1986.

Jones, H. A. and Mann, L. K., *Onions and their Allies: Botany, Cultivation and Utilization*. Leonard Hill, London, 1963.

Kunkel, G., *Plants for Human Consumption: An Annotated Checklist of the Edible Phanerogams and Ferns*. Koeltz Scientific Books, Koenigstein, West Germany, 1984.

Lamp, C. and Collet, F., *A Field Guide to Weeds in Australia*. Inkata Press, 1984.

Larkcom, J., *The Salad Garden*. Doubleday, Sydney, Australia, 1984.

Lazarides, M. and Hince, B. (Eds), *CSIRO Handbook of Economic Plants of Australia*. CSIRO, East Melbourne, Australia, 1993.

Mendelsohn, O. A., *A Salute to Onions: Some Reflections on Cookery … and Cooking*. Sydney, Rigby, 1965.

Michael, P., *A Country Harvest*. Peerage Books, London, 1986.

Montagné, P., *New Larousse Gastronomique: The World's Greatest Cookery Reference Book*. Hamlyn, London, 1977.

Morton, J. F., *Atlas of Medicinal Plants of Middle America, Bahamas to Yucatan*. Charles C. Thomas, Illinois, USA.

Mueller, Baron F. Von, *Select Plants Readily Eligible for Industrial Culture or Naturalisation in Victoria*. McCarron, Bird & Co., Melbourne. 1876.

Painter, G. and Power, E., *A Garden of Old-fashioned and Unusual Herbs*. Hodder & Stoughton, London, 1982.

Painter, G. and Power, E., *The Herb Garden Displayed*. Hodder & Stoughton, London, 1978.

Pearson, C., Cunningham, G. and King, D., *A Plain English Guide to Agricultural Plants*. Longman Cheshire, Melbourne, Australia, 1993.

Perry, L. M. (Compiled by), *Medicinal Plants of East and Southeast Asia*. MIT Press, London, 1980.

Phillips, R. and Foy, N., *Herbs*. Pan Macmillan, London, 1990.

Phillips, R. and Rix, M., *Vegetables*. Pan Macmillan, London, 1993.

Plowden, C. Chicheley, *A Manual of Plant Names*. Allen and Unwin, London, 1968.

Proceedings from the Royal Commission on Vegetable Production. Victoria, 1886.

Purseglove, J. W., *Tropical Crops: Monocotyledons*. Longman, London, 1979.

Robinson, M., *Robinson's New Family Herbal and Botanic Physician*. William Nicholson and Sons, London, 1890.

Romer, E., *The Tuscan Year*. Weidenfeld & Nicholson, London, 1984.

Shimizu, K., *Tsukemono, Japanese Pickled Vegetables*. Shufunotomo Co. Ltd, Tokyo, 1993

Simmonds, N. W. (Ed.), *Evolution of Crop Plants*. Longman, London and New York, 1976.

Smith, I. L. L., Revised and enlarged by Stern, W. T., *A Gardeners Dictionary of Plant Names*. Cassell, London, 1972.

Steinmetz, E. F., *Materia Medica Vegetabilis*. Steinmetz, Amsterdam, Holland, 1954.

Stobart, T., *Herbs, Spices and Flavourings*. Penguin, New York, 1977.

Stuart, D. C., *The Kitchen Garden*. Robert Hale, London, 1984.

Uphof, J. C. T., *Dictionary of Economic Plants*. Stechert-Hafner, New York, 1968.

Vilmoran-Andrieux, C., *Les Plantes Potagères*. Marchand Grainiers, Paris, 1904.

Visser, M., *Much Depends On Dinner*. Penguin, London, 1989.

Yanovsky, E., *Food Plants of the North American Indians*. The Redwood City Seed Co., Redwood City, California, USA, 1993.

Journals, Magazines and Agricultural Notes

Allen, M. L., et al. 'The Effect of Raw Onions on Acid Reflux and Reflux Symptoms', *The American Journal of Gastroenterology*, 85, 4, pp. 377–80, 1990.

Apitz-Castro, R., et al. 'Ajoene, The Anti-platelet Principle of Garlic', *Thrombosis Research*, 42, pp. 303–311, 1986.

Ave, R. D., 'Garlic Preparations and Processing', *Cardiology in Practice*, 10, pp. 7–8, 1989.

Block, E., 'The Chemistry of Garlic and Onions', *Scientific American*, 252, pp. 114–19, 1985.

Block, E. and Purcell, P. F., 'Letters to the Editor: Onions and Heartburn', *The American Journal of Gastroenterology*, 87, 5, pp. 697–8, 1992.

Bordia, A., et al. 'Protective Effect of Garlic Oil on the Changes Produced by Three Weeks of Fatty Diet', *The Indian Heart Journal*, 34, pp. 86–8, 1982.

Dausch, J. G. and Nixon, D. W., 'Garlic: A Review of its Relationship to Malignant Disease', *Preventive Medicine*, 19, pp. 346–61, 1990.

Farbman, K. S., et al., 'Antibacterial Activity of Garlic and Onions: A Historical Perspective', *The Pediatric Infectious Disease Journal*, Vol. 12, 7, pp. 613–14, 1993.

Fogarty, M., 'Garlic's Potential Role in Reducing Heart Disease', *British Journal of Clinical Practice*, 47 (2), pp. 64–5, 1993.

'Healthy Eating', *World Cancer Research Fund Newsletter*, June, 1990.

Lembo, G., et al. 'Allergic Contact Dermatitis Due to Garlic (*Allium sativum*)' *Contact Dermatitis*, 25, pp. 330–1, 1991.

Lomman, G., 'Onions and Allied Crops in South Australia' *Market Development Paper No. 13*, Department of Agriculture, South Australia, 1990.

Mansell, P. and Reckless, J. P. D., 'Garlic: Effects on Serum Lipids, Blood Pressure, Coagulation, Platelet Aggregation, and Vasodilation', *British Medical Journal*, 303, pp. 379–80, 1991.

McElnay, J. C. and Li Wan, A., 'Dietary Supplements: (8) Garlic.' *The Pharmaceutical Journal*, March, pp. 324–6, 1991.

Pitman, D. and Burt, J., 'Growing Garlic', West Australian Department of Agriculture, Agdex 256, 20, 1994.

Appendix 1

A Botanical Explanation

Description and Classification

There may be as many as 1000 species of allium. The exact number is not clear. This confusion arises because many alliums have been collected from politically or geographically inaccessible places such as Iran, Siberia and Afghanistan. This has made it difficult to check and compare species. So it is quite possible that plants have been given different specific names when they are actually the same species, or a variety of the same species. Also, new species are still being discovered and named in some of these countries.

Plants with bulbs usually come from regions where the climatic extremes necessitate periods of time spent below the ground—either hot dry summers or cold freezing winters. These plants die back and rely on their underground storage vessels or bulbs to survive. Usually, the larger the bulb the more climatic extremes the plant is capable of surviving. Those alliums with small or almost non-existent bulbs generally come from regions with more moderate climates.

All alliums are perennial or biennial. They can range in height from 10 cm (4 in) to 2 metres (6½ ft). Most produce the characteristic smell of onions when broken or crushed and this is caused by organic sulphur compounds contained within the plant's cells. Some plants which are *not* alliums have similar odours—see Chapter 12 for some examples.

The botanical family to which the alliums belong is still a matter of contention. For many years they were placed in the *Liliaceae*. In the late 1960s the botanist Cronquist proposed that, along with many other genera in the *Liliaceae*, they should be placed in the *Amaryllidaceae*. This is the system followed by some institutions. However, others have elected to follow parts of a later reclassification suggested by the Danish botanist Rolf Dahlgren in 1985. This divides the *Liliaceae* into about 20 smaller family units, with Alliums placed in the family *Alliaceae*, along with *Agapanthus*, *Nothoscordum*, *Tulbaghia* and 28 other genera. All these plants have flowers which are borne in umbels, with the fruiting stages consisting of dry capsules.

Many of the *Alliaceae* also have a similar basic chemistry. A brief botanical description of the genus follows:

All alliums have either bulbs, rhizomes or storage roots (never corms).
The **bulbs** are either solitary or clustered, covered with papery or fibrous tunics, and are occasionally grouped on a short rhizome.
The **scapes**, which carry the flower heads, are solid or hollow and unbranched.
Leaves are basal or sheathe the flower stem; they are flat, grooved or cylindrical, linear to elliptic, solid or hollow.
The number of **flowers** varies enormously, but they all occur in umbels supported by a scape. In some species the flowers are either partially or completely replaced by bulbils.
Flower heads are initially sheathed by a spathe, which splits into one or more bracts as the flower head develops.
Petals and **sepals** are similar, and joined together to form a **perianth**. The perianth is split into six free **segments**, which are often called **tepals** or **perianth** segments. These perianth segments closely resemble petals.
Each flower has six **stamens**, the filaments of which are sometimes toothed and can be united at the base or free. The structure of the stamens is important in distinguishing one species of allium from another.
The **ovaries** have three locules, and when fertilised they develop into capsules which contain the seeds. These are numerous, black and angled, round or flat.

Nomenclature

Although most alliums have botanical names which are accurate and clearly convey the identity of the plant being discussed, there are two species, *Allium cepa* and *Allium ampeloprasum* which include a diverse range of plants where confusion can easily arise. For this reason a slightly different botanical nomenclature is used for these two groups. This is described and explained below.

The botanical name *Allium cepa* includes the common onion, ever-ready onions, potato onions, shallots, spring onions and tree onions. In the past these plants have been labelled as varieties (wild forms) or cultivars (cultivated forms) of the common onion. For example *Allium cepa* 'Ailsa Craig', a widely-grown long-lasting form of yellow-skinned onion, is a cultivar. *Allium cepa* var. *viviparum* is a name used for the tree onion, supposedly a wild variety of onion. The tree onions we see today do not, however, represent wild forms or populations presently in existence. They are probably the result of cultivation, so it is technically inappropriate for them to be classed as a variety. This is just one of several examples where confusion or inaccuracy exists in the naming of plants belonging to *A. cepa*.

The same confusion exists among those plants belonging to *A. ampeloprasum* (leeks, elephant garlic and kurrat). The *International Code of Nomenclature for Cultivated Plants* (Bricknell, 1980) in article 26 states:

> When a species, interspecific hybrid or intergeneric hybrid includes many cultivars (or varieties), an assemblage of similar cultivars (or varieties) may be designated as a group. This category is intermediate between species and cultivar. It is not an essential part of the cultivar name. If used between the specific name or collective name and the cultivar name, the name of the group is placed within parentheses.

Using this system, the correct way to write the name for golden shallots is *Allium cepa* (Aggregatum Group) 'Golden Shallots'.

A. cepa and *A. ampeloprasum* can be divided in the following way.

Allium cepa

Cepa Group	Aggregatum Group	Proliferum Group
Common onion	Ever-ready onion Potato onion Shallots	Tree onion

Allium ampeloprasum

Porrum Group	Ampeloprasum Group	Kurrat Group
Leeks	Elephant garlic Pearlzwiebel	Kurrat

These classifications are clearer and more accurate than the numerous alternative botanical names that exist. They also indicate the closer relationship which exists between plants such as shallots and potato onions—both of which are in the Aggregatum Group.

The group names imply no more than that certain morphological similarities exist between plants within these groups. They actually have no official standing as part of the scientific name, but they are inserted where their descriptive value is important.

Group names for these plants have been adopted by most botanical authorities in Australia and overseas, and they are gaining in acceptance.

Botanical varietal names can still be used by those who wish to, as they convey some information and they form an important part of the historical literature.

In several chapters, previous or alternative botanical names are mentioned. For example *A. chinense* has also been called *A. bakeri* and *A. exsertum*. Both these names were given to rakkyo after it was called *A. chinense*. The rules of botanical nomenclature say that the first botanical name given to a plant is the one that stands.

Appendix 2 Easy Identification Chart

Name	Botanical Name	Bulb	Leaf	Flower Head	Flower Stalk	Height	Edible Part	Comments
Garlic	*Allium sativum* softneck	Bulbs vary in size from 2–6 cm. Clove numbers vary from 6 to 20. Colours vary red, purple, cream and white.	Flat, linear, grey-green, folded longitudinally.	Does not produce flowers.	None.	To about 60 cm (2 ft).	Dried bulbs, young leaves, stems and immature green bulbs.	
Garlic	*Allium sativum* top-setting	Bulbs often smaller than softneck cultivars, usually fewer cloves, flavour not as strong.	Flat, linear, grey-green, folded longitudinally. Usually more slender than softneck cultivars.	Flower heads usually packed with mauve bulbils, occasionally a few flowers of white, purple or pink. Much smaller than elephant garlic. Early summer.	Solid, cylindrical. In some cultivars, a peculiar loop in the stem which straightens as the spathe splits.	To about 1.2 m (4 ft) when in flower.	Dried bulbs, young leaves, stems and immature green bulbs.	Usually matures slightly later than softneck garlics.
Chives	*Allium schoenoprasum*	Bottle-shaped, clustered.	Slender, hollow, cylindrical, blue-green.	Spherical, flowers pink/purple in spring and summer. Open progressively from the top of the umbel to the base.	Hollow, cylindrical.	30–60 cm (1–2 ft) depending on the cultivar.	Leaves, flowerbuds and flowers.	Will self-sow.
Garlic Chives	*Allium tuberosum*	Conical bulbs on short, branched rhizomes.	Solid, flat, bright green leaves with a keeled undersurface.	White, scented, star-like in hemispherical umbels. Summer and autumn.	Solid, angular, erect.	60 cm (2 ft) when in flower.	Leaves, young flower stems with bud, flowers.	
Elephant Garlic	*Allium ampeloprasum* (Ampeloprasum Group)	Very large, 4–6 cloves. Also rounds and bulblets. Bulbs solid, not made up of concentric rings.	Large, blue-green, linear, central dividing rib.	Large, to 10 cm (4 in), spherical, densely packed. Purple, pink and red flowers. Usually sets seed which is sometimes sterile.	Solid, cylindrical.	Up to 2 m (6½ ft) in flower.	Cloves and rounds. Leaves when young.	Very hardy, can become a pest in the garden.

Appendix 2 Easy Identification Chart continued

Name	Botanical Name	Bulb	Leaf	Flower Head	Flower Stalk	Height	Edible Part	Comments
Pearlzwiebel	*Allium ampeloprasum* (Ampeloprasum Group)	Rounded bulbs from ½–6 cm in diam. No cloves. Solid, not made up of concentric rings.	Large, blue-green, linear, central dividing rib. Small offsets around original plant.	Fairly large, mauve–pink. Seldom sets seed, always sterile.	Solid, cylindrical.	To about 1 m (3 ft 4 in) when in flower.	Round bulbs, young stems and leaves.	Very easy to grow.
Leeks	*Allium ampeloprasum* (Porrum Group)	Flat, elongated bulb formed from the foliage leaf bases which encircle each other. Bulb usually called stem or stalk.	Flat, broad linear leaves, folded longitudinally. Usually broader than elephant garlic.	Globular umbel packed with hundreds of pink to white cup-shaped flowers. Spring and summer.	Stout, solid, cylindrical.	1.5 m (5 ft) when in flower.	Blanched foliage leaf bases (stems).	
Onion, Common	*Allium cepa* (Cepa Group)	Large, single, made up of concentric leaf sheaths. Red, brown, yellow, purple and white. Globular, flattened and torpedo-shaped.	Long, shiny, deep green, cylindrical and hollow with a grooving or flattening on the upper surface.	Densely packed spherical umbel up to 10 cm (4 in). Flowers white and star-like with green stripes, no bulbils. Late spring and early summer (2nd year).	Cylindrical, hollow, swelling in lower stem.	To 2 m (6½ ft) when in flower.	Bulbs, young leaves and stems.	
Onion, Ever-ready	*Allium cepa* (Aggregatum Group)	Slender, bottle-shaped, white with a brown skin.	Narrow, hollow, cylindrical, blue-green, flat on the upper surface.	Very rare. Resembles the common onion.	Very rare, cylindrical, hollow, shorter than common onion.	Leaves to 30 cm (1 ft).	Bulbs and leaves.	
Onion, Potato	*Allium cepa* (Aggregatum Group)	Usually wider than long. Red, brown or yellow. Several bulbs often enclosed in the papery outer casing.	Hollow, cylindrical, blue-green, flattened on the upper surface, broader than shallots.	Very rare. Resembles the common onion. Almost never sets seed.	Very rare, but similar to the common onion only shorter.	Leaves to 40 cm (1 ft 4 in).	Bulbs and leaves. Strong sweet flavour.	Very similar to shallots, see p. 128

		Bulb	Leaf	Flower	Stem	Height	Used parts	Notes
Onion, Shallots	*Allium cepa* (Aggregatum Group)	Usually longer than wide. Red, golden, grey, white. Each bulb is usually enclosed in its own papery sheath.	Hollow, cylindrical, blue or grey-green, flattened on the upper surface, narrower than potato and common onions.	Most cultivars do not flower. Some do, usually in the second year with globular umbels of white star-like flowers. Often does not set seed.	Cylindrical, hollow.	Leaves to 40cm (1ft 4in), flowers to 80cm (2ft 8in).	Bulbs, leaves and whole young plants as spring onions.	
Onion, Tree	*Allium cepa* (Proliferum Group)	Round, elongated, brown, divides into several bulbs during the season.	Hollow, cylindrical, blue or grey-green, flattened on the upper surface.	Green bulbils to 1cm (½in) diam. Usually turn brown and replace the flowers. If flowers present they are white and star-like.	Cylindrical, hollow, tapers towards the top.	60cm (2ft) when in flower.	Bulbs, leaves and bulbils.	Probably the hardiest of all the onions.
Onion Weed	*Allium triquetrum*	Small, ovoid, white.	Fleshy, keeled, bright green.	Long stemmed, bell-shaped, white with a green stripe in 1-sided umbels.	Flaccid, 3-sided.	Up to 50cm (1ft 8in).	Leaves, flowers and bulbs.	An invasive weed in some places. Should never be planted.
Rakkyo	*Allium chinense*	Narrow, ovoid, usually asymmetrical, made up of concentric rings.	Narrow, tubular, bright green. 3 to 5 sided in cross-section.	Flattened umbel, 15–20 nodding pink to lavender flowers. Does not set seed.	Solid, cylindrical.	Up to 50cm (1ft 8in).	Bulbs and lower young stems.	Dies back in summer. May not flower for several years.
Ramsons	*Allium ursinum*	Narrow, white, bottle-shaped.	Bright green, broadly elliptical, tapering to top on long white stems.	Loose umbels of bright white star-like flowers, up to 25 in each.	2–3 angled, solid, bright green.	Up to 40cm (1ft 4in) in flower.	Bulbs and leaves.	Difficult to grow from seed. May not flower for several years.
Welsh onion	*Allium fistulosum*	No obvious bulb, grown for thickened stem, often multiplies at the base.	Hollow, cylindrical, blue-green, no flattening on the upper surface.	Spherical flower heads up to 5cm (2in) in diam. Flowers pale yellow, bell-shaped, open from the top of the umbel to the base.	Cylindrical, hollow, tapers toward the top.	Up to 80cm (2ft 8in) when in flower.	Young leaves, young stems.	

Appendix 3.1   Garlic Cultivars

Cultivar Name (other names in italics)	Description	When to Plant	Harvest and Storage	Comments	Suppliers (see also Appendix 4)
Brown Tempest	Top-setting. About 6 cloves per bulb. Brown with a rose-blush tint. Hot intense flavor when raw, milder when cooked.	Fall or early spring.	Mid to late summer or fall.	Form of *Allium longicuspis*, a wild garlic, the possible ancestor of cultivated garlic.	Southern Exposure.
California White *White*	Softneck. Large bulbs with 10–20 cloves. White skin.	Fall.	Mid to late summer.	Best in central and coastal regions.	Jung's, Redwood City.
Chesnok Red	Top-setting. Large bulbs. Very aromatic.	Fall.	Mid to late summer.	Comes from the Republic of Georgia. Excellent for baking.	Southern Exposure.
Chet's Italian Purple	Softneck. Large bulbs with an average of 15 cloves per bulb. Skin white with purple streaks. Mild flavor.	Fall.	Mid to late summer. Stores well.	Selected from Italian Purple. Very productive.	Southern Exposure.
Dixon Strain	Softneck. Large bulbs with purple brushed cloves.	North: Aug. to Oct. South: Nov. to Jan.	Late summer. Stores well.	Good for braiding.	Garden City.
German Extra-Hardy	Top-setting. Large bulbs. White outer skin and red skin covering the cloves. Good flavor.	North: fall. South: Nov. to Jan.	Late summer. Stores well.	Old-world variety. Very vigorous. One of the most winter-hardy cultivars.	Johnny's.
German Red *Red German*	Top-setting. Large bulbs with 8–12 cloves per bulb. Deep green leaves. Easy to peel. Large top-set bulbils. Fine hot spicy flavor.	Late Aug. to mid Oct.	Stores well.	Can be grown in mild climates but best where winters are cold.	DeGiorgi, Southern Exposure*.
Gilroy	Softneck. Large white-skinned bulbs. Large, easy-to-peel cloves. Very pungent.	Fall.	Stores very well.		Shepherd's.
Inchelium Red	Softneck. Very large bulbs with 8–22 cloves in 4–5 layers. Skin white with purple patches. Mild lingering flavor.	Fall or very early spring.	Mid to late summer. Stores well.	Originally from the Colville Indian Reservation, Inchelium, WA. Rated best of 20 in a 1990 test at Rodale kitchens. Flavor sharpens with storage.	Garden City, Gourmet Gardener*, Southern Exposure*.
Italian Late	Softneck. White bulb. Very pungent	North: Oct. South: Nov. to Jan.	Mid to late summer. Stores well.	Good for braiding.	Territorial.
Italian Purple Skin	Softneck. Thick-skinned bulbs with large cloves. Purplish stripes at the base. Good flavor, crisp texture.	Fall.	Stores very well.	Widely adapted to many climate zones.	Shepherd's.

*For specific times of availability, contact the supplier.

Appendix 3.1   Garlic Cultivars continued

Cultivar Name (other names in italics)	Description	When to Plant	Harvest and Storage	Comments	Suppliers (see also Appendix 4)
Korean Red	Top-setting. Plants grow to 41 cm (16 in) with dark green leaves. Rocambole type with typical curled flower stem and bulbils in the flower head. Bulbs have purple striped skin and 6–11 cloves. Hot taste.	North: Oct. South: Nov. to Jan.	Mid to late summer. Does not store well.	Mid-season. Very easy to peel.	Territorial.
Lorz Italian	Softneck. About 16 cloves per bulb. Spicy hot flavor.	Fall.	Mid to late summer.	Came from Italy before 1900. Hotter than most. Ideal for Italian food.	Southern Exposure.
Machashi	Softneck. Large, plump cloves usually in a single layer.	Fall.	Mid to late summer.	Comes from the Republic of Georgia. Sometimes produces bulbils low on the stem. Very large cloves.	Southern Exposure.
Mild French Silverskin	Medium bulbs with about 14 cloves in layers. Pungent flavor.	Fall.	Mid to late summer.	Very good for hot dry southern regions. Easy to clean and braid.	Southern Exposure.
Montana Roja	True gourmet flavor.	Spring, as soon as the ground can be worked.	Beginning of Sept.	Specifically tested for spring planting.	Garden City.
New York White *Polish White*	Softneck. White skin with purplish blush.	Fall.	Summer.	Good for the north and east coast. Quite winter-hardy. Good for braiding.	Johnny's.
Purple	Purple-tinted skins.	Fall.	Summer.	Good for southern regions.	Redwood City.
Red Toch	Softneck. Large bulbs streaked in pink and red.	Fall.	Late summer.	From the Republic of Georgia. One of the best to use raw.	Southern Exposure.
Romanian Red	Top-setting. Plants grow to 51 cm (20 in) with 3–5, easy-to-peel, fat cloves. White skins. Pungent lingering garlic taste.	North: Aug. to Oct. South: Nov. to Jan.	Late summer. Stores well.	Late season. In cold regions purple splashes on skin.	Southern Exposure, Territorial.
Silver Rose	Softneck. Pink to rose striped bulbs. 7–10 larger cloves surround the small central cloves. Sharp garlic flavor.	North: Oct. South: Nov. to Jan.	Late summer. Stores very well.	Very late-season. Good for braiding. Can be spring planted but does not do as well.	Territorial.
Spanish Roja *Greek garlic, Roja Spanish Red, Spanish Red*	Top-setting. Thick blue-green stalks and leaves. Rocambole type with typically curled stem. Bulbs 4–6½ cm (1½–2½ in) in diam. 6–11 cloves per bulb. Light color. 'True' garlic flavor.	North: Aug. to Oct. South: Nov. to Jan.	Mid to late summer. Medium storage.	Introduced in the 1800s. Very popular mid-season type. Best in cold regions. Cloves peel easily.	Garden City, Southern Exposure, Territorial.

Pinetree supplies an unnamed cultivar of garlic and Deep Diversity an unnamed top-setting cultivar. Filaree Farm cultivates hundreds of different forms of garlic. Many of these are available by mail order within the U.S.A. but listing them is beyond the scope of this book.

Appendix 3.2 Leek Cultivars

Cultivar Name (other names in italics)	Description	When to Plant	When to Harvest	Comments	Suppliers (see also Appendix 4)
Alaska *Winter Giant, Alaska*	Long tender white stems to 20 cm (8 in). Broad dark blue-green foliage. Sweet flavor.	Late winter inside. Spring outside. Also fall.	Fall, winter, spring. About 115 days.	Very winter hardy. Will tolerate sub-freezing temps. Disease and bolt resistant.	Gourmet Gardener, Stokes.
Arcona	Long white stems to 20 cm (8 in). Upright dark blue-green leaves. Non-bulbing.	Feb. to Mar. inside. Apr. to June outside.	100 days.	Frost and disease tolerant. Stores well.	Stokes.
Arkansas	Medium white stems to 15 cm (6 in). Semi-upright, blue-green foliage. Non-bulbing.	Feb. to Mar. inside. Apr. to June outside.	108–120 days.	Good, non-bulbing, winter hardy strain. Stores well.	Stokes.
Bulgarian Triumph *Bulgarian*	Long thick stems up to 36 cm (14 in). Light green leaves.	Early spring.	Summer to early fall.	Frost sensitive, so will not over-winter. Good for dehydration.	PSR.
Durabel	Medium, tender, white stalks to 15 cm (6 in). Non-bulbous. Dark blue-green leaves. Mild flavor, tender texture.	Feb. to Mar. for transplant or direct seed in May.	Fall, winter, early spring. About 125 days.	Bred to handle bad weather. Slow growing and very late to bolt.	PSR, Territorial.
Furor	Long thick uniform stem. Tall dark green foliage. Quite pungent flavor.	Early spring.	Fall.	Medium maturity.	Pinetree.
Giant Carentan *Carentan, Carentan Winter, De Carentan*	Short creamy white thick stems. Delicate dark blue-green leaves. Very mild flavor.	Late winter inside. Early spring outside.	Fall and winter.	Very old French cultivar. Excellent winter leek. Mulch in late fall. Can be eaten raw in salads.	Deep Diversity, Garden City.
Giant Musselburgh *Musselburgh, Scotch Flag*	Very large thick tender stems up to 25 cm (10 in). Broad green leaves. Fine mild flavor.	Mar. inside. Apr. outside.	135 days.	Popular and very hardy. First introduced in 1834.	DeGiorgi, Vesey's.
Hivor	Firm white stems. Green leaves with purple shading which intensifies in cold weather. Pungent flavor.	Spring, summer.	112 days.	Very hardy.	Pinetree.
Kajak	Very long white stems. Dark green foliage.	Spring.	Fall, winter.	A late cultivar. Some resistance to virus and leaf spot.	Deep Diversity.
King Richard	Long stems up to 30 cm (12 in). Upright blue-green leaves. Delicate mild flavor.	Late winter inside. Early spring outside.	Summer and fall. 75–100 days.	Fast growing. Early, high yields. Will stand medium to heavy frosts but will not over-winter in cold regions.	Garden City, Gourmet Gardener, Johnny's, Pinetree, Seeds Trust.
Large American Flag *American Flag, Broad London*	Medium stems 18–30 cm (7–12 in) long, 2½–4 cm (1–1½ in) thick. Semi-upright medium blue-green leaves. Sweet distinct flavor.	Early spring.	140 days.	Hardy and vigorous. Needs a long growing season.	Jung's, Lockhart, Pinetree, Southern Exposure.

Cultivar Name (other names in italics)	Description	When to Plant	Harvest and Storage	Comments	Suppliers (see also Appendix 4)
Laura	White medium shank with little bulbing. Upright deep blue-green leaves.	Spring, summer and fall.	Late fall, winter and spring. 115 days.	Very hardy. Good late-harvest leek.	Johnny's.
Lungo d'Inverno	Long slender stalks. 2½ cm (1 in) diam., 25 cm (10 in) long.	Spring.	Late fall, winter and spring.	Winter hardy. Popular Italian variety.	Redwood City.
Lyon *The Lyon, Prizetaker*	Pure white medium thick stems. Mild flavor.	Spring.	Fall to winter. 130–140 days.	Cold hardy. An old English cultivar, introduced 1886.	Deep Diversity.
Otina	Long thick creamy fine-textured stems. Blue-green foliage. Mild delicate flavor.	Spring.	Late summer, fall. 120 days.	French cultivar. Harvest as 'baby' leeks or leave to fully develop. Use raw or cooked.	Shepherd's.
Pancho	Heavy thick white stems to about 25 cm (10 in). No bulbing. Blue-green leaves.	Spring.	Summer and fall. 80 days.	Combines early maturing with frost tolerance. Also tolerant to foliage diseases.	Johnny's.
St. Victor	Tender thick stems. Deep blue-green leaves which develop violet tints after frost. Crisp sweet and mildly pungent flavor.	Spring to summer.	Fall and winter.	Strain of old French cultivar 'Bleu Solaise'. High yielding. Thrives in cold conditions.	Deep Diversity, Shepherd's.
Splendid	Tender slim white stems to 25 cm (10 in). Medium fresh green leaves. More tender than other over-wintering cultivars.	Sow Feb. and Mar. Transplant May.	Fall to early winter. About 105 days.	Grows rapidly and vigorously but will only grow over winter in very mild climates. Heavy yields. Good for dehydration.	PSR, Stokes, Territorial.
Titan	Medium slim white stems to 15 cm (6 in), slightly bulbous base. Dark green leaves.	Sow Feb. and Mar. inside, Apr. and June outside.	Summer to fall. 70 days.	An early type. Vigorous growth. Not winter hardy.	Stokes.
Unique	Thick long white stem to 20 cm (8 in). Dark blue-green leaves.	Feb. and Mar. inside, Apr. and June outside.	Fall to winter. 100 days.	Will tolerate extreme cold and stores well.	Stokes.
Varna	Long slender white stems to average 36 cm (14 in). Light green leaves.	Direct seed in spring.	Summer to fall. 60–75 days.	Very fast growing and productive. Will not survive cold winters. Excellent for early harvesting of slender leeks.	Johnny's, Territorial.
Winter Giant *Winter-reuzen*	Thick long white stems. Dark green leaves. Tender mild flavor.	Spring.	Oct. to Jan.	Over-wintering type. Very cold hardy.	Deep Diversity.

Appendix 3.3   Onion Cultivars

Cultivar Name (other names in italics)	Description	When to Plant	When to Harvest	Keeping Qualities	**Day length	Other Comments	Suppliers (see also Appendix 4) S = seed St = sets P = plants
Ailsa Craig *Ailsa Craig Exhibition*	Huge teardrop-shaped bulbs. Straw-yellow skins. White flesh. Juicy sweet very mild flavor.	Sow inside in Jan. or Feb. and transplant in early spring to achieve really large bulbs. Otherwise sow in early spring. Can also be sown in fall.	Fall. 105–110 days.	Medium.	Intermediate to long.	Open pollinated. High yielding. Originally from England. Bulbs can be heavier than 1½ kg (3lbs). Excellent sliced raw. Good for northern and eastern growers because it doesn't require as long a season as other large sweet types.	Johnny's (S), PSR (S, P), Pinetree (S).
Bingo	Bronze skins. Thin necks. Very hard flesh.	Early spring.	100 days.	Very good.	Long.	Hybrid. High yielding.	Stokes (S).
Blanco Duro	Large high globe. Ivory-white thin skin. White flesh. Tangy but sweet flavor.	Early spring.	Late summer or fall. About 110–130 days.	Medium to good.	Long.	Open pollinated. Uniform. Good yields. Very tolerant to pink root.	Lockhart (S), Pinetree (S), Territorial (S).
Bermuda Yellow	Medium, flat bulbs. Light straw skin. White flesh. Juicy sweet mild flavor.	Early spring.	92 days.	Poor.	Short.	Popular in the south-west. Tolerant to pink root. Resistant to splitting and bolting.	DeGiorgi (S).
Blizzard	Very large globes. Thin white skin. White flesh.	Early spring.	Late summer or fall. 130 days.	Poor.	Long.	Hybrid. Uniform. Use fresh.	Lockhart (S).
Brahma F1	Medium to large globes. Light brown skins. Mild sweet juicy flavor.	Early spring.	Late summer or fall. 110 days.	Good.	Long.	Hybrid. Uniform. High yields.	Territorial (S).
Buffalo F1	Large flattened globes. Yellow skin.	1. Aug. to Sept. 2. Spring (where winter temps get below −10°F).	1. Early June. 2. Late Aug. About 90 days.	Short to medium	Intermediate to long.	Hybrid. Good dual-purpose onion. Matures well ahead of other early varieties.	Territorial (S), Johnny's (S).
Burrell's Yellow Valencia	Large globe. Deep bronze skins. Fine sweet flavor.	Early spring.	Fall. 120 days.	Good.		Open pollinated. Vigorous foliage. Resistant to thrip.	PSR (S,P).
Canada Maple	Round, very hard bulbs. Small necks.	Early spring.	98 days.	Good.	Long.	Hybrid. Good yields.	Stokes (S).
Candy	Very large, flat globe. Golden yellow skin. White flesh. Sweet flavor.	Fall.	Late spring to early summer. 98–105 days.	Poor.	Intermediate.	Hybrid. Transplants well.	Lockhart (S).
Cannon	Medium globe. Bronze skins. Firm flesh.	Early spring.	Fall. 90–95 days.	Medium.	Long.	Hybrid. High yielding.	Vesey's (S).
Capable	High globe shape. Firm flesh.	Early spring.	98 days.	Good.	Long.	Hybrid. Recommended for Quebec, New York and northern Michigan.	Stokes (S).

Variety	Description	Sowing time	Maturity	Storage	Day length	Notes	Supplier
Celebrity	Medium globe. Coppery brown skins.	Inside Jan. to Feb. Transplant early spring.	September. 108 days.	Medium to good.	Long.	Hybrid. High yielding.	Stokes (S).
Cimmaron	Large full globe. Thin yellow skin. White flesh. Mildly pungent flavor.	Fall.	Late spring to early summer. 195 days.	Medium.	Intermediate.	Hybrid. Good resistance to pink root. Uniform size.	Lockhart (S).
Copper King	Very large globes. Dark copper skins.	Apr. to early May.	95 days.	Good.	Long.	Hybrid. Early type with good tolerance to pink root.	Stokes (S).
Copra F1	Medium blocky round bulb. Very hard, thin neck. Dark copper-yellow skin. White flesh. Mildly pungent flavor.	Apr. to early May.	Fall. 104–112 days.	Very good.	Long.	Hybrid. Bolt resistant in cool weather conditions. One of the longest storage types. High yields.	Johnny's (S), Stokes (S), Territorial (S).
Crystal White Wax *Bermuda White*	Medium flat bulb. Waxy white skin. White flesh. Juicy, mild flavor.	Early spring.	90 days.	Medium.	Short.	Good for sandwiches and salads. Can be used for early bunching onions in the tropics and pickling in cooler climates.	DeGiorgi (S).
Duration	Blocky globe. Coppery bronze hard skins.	Early spring.	110 days.	Very good.	Long.	Hybrid. Tolerance to fusarium and pink root. High yielding.	Stokes (S).
Early Pak	Medium globe. Tan skin. Mild flavor.	As early in spring as possible.	Fall. 95–100 days.	Good.	Long.	Hybrid. Ideal for short-season regions. The earlier they can be planted, the larger the bulbs.	Vesey's (S).
Early Red Burger	Medium to large thick flat bulb. Deep red skin. White flesh with red tinges. Mildly pungent flavor.	Fall.	Late spring to early summer. 172 days.	Medium.	Intermediate.	Open pollinated. Early widely adapted cultivar. Non-bolting and good tolerance to pink root.	Lockhart (S).
Early Supreme	Large firm globe. Small necks. Thin white skin. Chalk-white flesh. Mild flavor.	Fall.	Early spring, 150 days.	Poor.	Short.	Hybrid. Pink root resistant.	Lockhart (S).
Early Yellow Globe	Medium to large globe to flattened globe. Tough, light bronze-yellow skin. Firm white flesh. Mildly pungent flavor.	Apr. to early May.	Mid-summer onwards. 100–110 days.	Medium.	Long.	Open pollinated. High yielding. Introduced about 1930.	DeGiorgi, Jung's, Pinetree, Southern Exposure, Stokes, Territorial (All S).
Eskimo	Medium globe. Firm flesh.	Inside late winter. Outside Apr. to early May.	80 days.	Medium to good.	Long.	Hybrid.	Stokes (S).
Experimental 6404 *Condor*	Uniform globe shape.	Early spring.	98 days	Good.	Long.	Hybrid. Tolerant to fusarium basal rot and leaf spot.	Stokes (S).
Fiesta	Large globes. Yellow-copper skins. Moderate pungency.	Early spring.	Late summer or fall. 110 days.	Medium to good.	Long.	Hybrid. Sweet Spanish type, fairly tolerant to purple blotch.	Lockhart (S).
First Edition *Sleeping onion*	Medium round globe. Brown skins. Creamy yellow flesh. Pungent flavor.	Inside in late winter. Outside Apr. to early May.	105 days.	Very good.	Long.	Hybrid. Tolerates a wide range of storage temps. Developed for mid-west and northern USA and into Canada. Good tolerance to pink root.	Dixondale Farms (P*), Jung's (S, P), Territorial (P*), Thompson & Morgan (S).

Appendix 3.3   Onion Cultivars continued

Cultivar Name (other names in italics)	Description	When to Plant	When to Harvest	Keeping Qualities	**Day length	Other Comments	Suppliers (see also Appendix 4) S = seed St = sets P = plants
Fresno White	Large thick flattened bulb. Thin White skin. White flesh. Moderate pungency.	Fall.	Late spring to early summer. 194 days.	Poor.	Intermediate.	Open pollinated. Non-bolting. Good tolerance to pink root.	Lockhart (S, P—bulk).
Gringo	Medium to large, deep globes. Thin necks. Thick copper-colored skins.	Inside Jan. to Feb. Transplant early spring.	September. 105 days.	Medium.	Long.	Hybrid. Early Sweet Spanish type.	Stokes (S).
Hi-Ball F1	Deep globe. Thin necks. Yellow-tan skin. Yellow-white flesh. Crisp, juicy. Mildly pungent flavor.	Late summer or fall.	Spring.	Medium.	Long.	Hybrid. Good all-purpose onion. Use fresh or cooked.	Territorial (S).
Italian Red Torpedo	Large torpedo-shaped bulb. Thin light reddish-purple skin. Pale red flesh. Sweet.	Fall.	Late spring to summer. 200 days after planting.	Poor.	Short to intermediate.	Open pollinated. Very productive, non-bolting. Good tolerance to pink root.	Lockhart (S, P).
James Longkeeper	Small to medium pear-shaped bulb. Coppery red skin.	Early spring.	Late summer to fall.	Good.	Long.	Open pollinated. Introduced about 1834.	Deep Diversity (S).
Jet Set Hybrid	Large globe. Straw-colored skin. Pale yellow flesh.	Seeds in spring. Sets the following spring.	Sets in fall. Fully grown bulbs following spring.	Good.	Short to intermediate.	Hybrid. Grow sets from seed. Replant sets the following spring. Good bolt resistance. High yield.	Thompson & Morgan (S), Vesey's (St—early spring).
Joint Venture	Deep globe shape.	Early spring.	100 days.	Very good.	Long.	Hybrid. Fusarium tolerant.	Stokes (S).
Kelsae Sweet Spanish	Gigantic top-shaped bulbs. Straw-yellow skins. Mild sweet flavor.	Inside Jan. to Feb. Transplant early spring.	110 days.	Poor.	Long.	Open pollinated. World-record onions.	Stokes (S).
Lancastrian *Football onion*	Very large. Pale gold skin. White flesh. Very sweet and crisp flavor.	Inside Jan. to Feb. Transplant early spring.	95 days.	Medium.	Long.	Open pollinated. A contender for the world's largest onion.	Thompson & Morgan (S).
Legacy	Large hard deep blocky globe.	Early spring.	108 days.	Very good.	Long.	Hybrid. Good tolerance to fusarium and pink root.	Stokes (S).
Lisbon White *White Lisbon*	Round flattened small bulbs. White skin. White flesh. Mild flavor.	Spring.	60–110 days.	Poor.	Long.	Open pollinated. Very quick growing.	DeGiorgi (S).
Lucifer	Large. Blood-red skins.	Inside Jan. to Feb. Transplant early spring.	Sept. 106 days.	Medium.	Long.	Early hybrid red.	Stokes (S).
Mambo F1	Large blocky round bulb. Reddish purple skin. White flesh with red rings. Moderate pungency, sweet.	Inside Jan. to Feb. Transplant or direct seed early spring.	Late summer onwards. 112 days.	Medium.	Long.	Hybrid. Good combination of size, color and storability.	Johnny's (S).

Variety	Description	Sowing/Planting	Maturity	Storage	Day length	Comments	Suppliers
Mars	Large very firm globes. Bright red skins. Red and white flesh.	Inside Jan. to Feb. Transplant or direct seed early spring.	Sept. 108 days.	Medium.	Long.	Hybrid.	Stokes (S).
New York Early	Medium, large, high globe shape. Very hard. Brown yellow skin. Tender mild flavor.	Inside Jan. to Feb. Direct seed Apr. to early May.	Mid-summer onwards. 98 days.	Medium to good.	Long.	Open pollinated. Early productive strain of Early Yellow Globe. Selected and maintained by NY growers.	Garden City (S), Johnny's (S), Stokes (S).
Nordic	Brown-yellow skin.	Inside late winter. Outside early spring.	97 days.	Good.	Long.	Hybrid of New York Early. Some tolerance to pink root.	Stokes (S).
Norstar	Medium globe. Light brown skin. White flesh. Mild flavor.	Inside late winter. Outside early spring.	Late summer to fall. 78–90 days.	Medium to good.	Long.	Hybrid. Bred for cooler northern regions. Some resistance to botrytis and white rot.	Stokes (S), Vesey's (S).
Northern Oak	Hard bulbs. Small necks. Rich oak-colored skins.	Inside late winter. Outside early spring.	108 days.	Good.	Long.	Hybrid. Tolerance to fusarium and some pink root.	Stokes (S).
Prince F1	Large blocky globes. Thin necks. Satiny yellow skins.	Inside late winter. Outside early spring.	106 days.	Good.	Long.	Hybrid. Big onions for long storage.	Johnny's (S).
Red Baron	Globe to semi-globe. Dark red skin. White flesh with pink rings. Pungent flavor.	Early spring.	115 days.	Good.	Long.	Southport Red Globe hybrid. Good yields.	Thompson & Morgan (S).
Red Burgermaster F1	Large globe. Bright purpley red skin. Red flesh. Sweet and tangy flavor.	Early spring.	Late summer or fall. 100–112 days.	Good.	Long.	A Southport Red Globe hybrid. Does best if seed sown in containers and seedlings transplanted. Good in salad, sandwiches and hamburgers.	Jung's (S), Pinetree (S), Territorial (S).
Red Creole	Thick flat small to medium bulb. Thick red skin. Red hard flesh. Pungent flavor.	Fall.	Early spring. 187 days.	Good.	Short.	Open pollinated. Very hardy, good in tropical regions.	Lockhart (S).
Red Granex	Large thick flat globe. Thin dark red skin. Red flesh. Mild flavor.	Fall.	Early spring. 162 days.	Poor to medium.	Short.	Hybrid. Protect from strong sunlight. Very productive.	Lockhart (S).
Redman	Medium to large globe. Burgundy-red skins. Red flesh after storing.	Mid-Apr. to early May.	Early maturing, by mid-Sept.	Medium.	Long.	Open pollinated. Moderate pungency.	Johnny's (S), Territorial (S).
Red Sets	Medium globe. Bright purplish-red skin. Firm, white, crunchy, sweet and mild.	Spring.	Summer and fall.	Medium.	Long.	Good for northern gardens. Unnamed cultivar.	Jung's (St).
Red Simiane	Long cylindrical bulb. Purplish-red skin. Pink flesh, white in centre. Mild sweet flavor.	Inside in early Feb.	105 days.	Poor.	Long.	Open pollinated. Popular in south France. Can be harvested and eaten before mature.	Gourmet Gardener (S), Pinetree (S).
Red Wethersfield	Large flat bulbs. Deep red skins. Purplish-white flesh. Mild good flavor.	Early spring.	103 days.	Good.	Long.	Good for home gardeners and growing onion sets. Plant sets immediately.	Deep Diversity (S), DeGiorgi (S), Pinetree (St*).
Ringmaker		Inside Jan. to Feb. Transplant early spring.	Sept. 108 days.	Good.	Long.	New early Spanish Hybrid.	Stokes (S).

Appendix 3.3 Onion Cultivars continued

Cultivar Name (other names in italics)	Description	When to Plant	When to Harvest	Keeping Qualities	**Day length	Other Comments	Suppliers (see also Appendix 4 S=seed St=sets P=plants)
Riverside Sweet Spanish	Very large bulb. Thin neck. Thick skin. Mild flavor.	Inside Jan. to Feb. Transplant early spring. Or direct seed in early spring.	Sept. 115 days.	Medium to good.	Long.	Open pollinated.	Stokes (S).
Ruby *Ruby Red Globe*	Medium to large globe to deep globe. Deep red skin. Pink flesh. Pungent flavor.	Early spring.	Late summer or fall. 105 days.	Medium.	Long.	Open pollinated. A selection of Southport Red Globe.	Deep Diversity (S), Lockhart (S).
Simcoe F1	Medium globe. Narrow necks. Yellow skin. Pungent flavor.	Apr. to early May.	120 days.	Good.	Long.	Similar to Early Yellow Globe.	Territorial (S).
Southport Red Globe	Medium to deep globe. Thick deep purplish-red skin. Red flesh. Pungent strong flavor.	Early spring.	Late summer or fall. 100–110 days.	Medium to good.	Long.	Open pollinated. Start indoors a few weeks before last frost. The standard red variety. Used chiefly as a dried onion. High yields.	DeGiorgi (S), Garden City (S, St—Apr), Jung's (S), Lockhart (S), Pinetree (S).
Southport White Globe	Large perfect globe. Thin pure white skin. White firm flesh. Pungent flavor.	Early spring.	112 days.	Good.	Long.	One of the best for storing over winter.	Deep Diversity (S), DeGiorgi (S).
Spanish	Large, slightly elongated bulb. Light brown skin. Mild sweet flavor.	Early spring.	Late summer to fall.	Medium.	Long.		Vesey's (St).
Spano	Large full globe. Thin yellow skin. Clear white flesh. Mildly pungent.	Fall.	Late spring to early summer. 205 days.	Medium.	Intermediate.	Hybrid. Transplants well, good tolerance to pink root.	Lockhart (S).
Stockton Early Red	Large thick flat bulb. Thin dark red skin. White flesh with pink rings. Mildly pungent.	Late summer to fall. Transplant late fall.	Late spring to early summer. 180 days.	Poor.	Intermediate to long.	Open pollinated. Very productive, non-bolting, pink root tolerant. About 10 days earlier than Stockton Red.	Lockhart (S, P—bulk), PSR (S, P), Territorial (S).
Stockton Early Yellow	Medium to large flattened globe. Light brown to yellow skin. White flesh. Mildly pungent.	Fall.	Spring to early summer. 184 days.	Poor.	Intermediate.	Open pollinated. Very productive. Non-bolting. Pink root tolerant.	Lockhart (S, P—bulk).
Stockton Red	Medium to large flattened globe. Thin burgundy-red skin. White flesh with pink rings. Mildly pungent.	Fall. Transplants in spring.	Spring to early summer. 188 days.	Medium.	Intermediate.	Open-pollinated. Excellent in salads, sandwiches, hamburgers.	Lockhart (S), Shepherd's (P*), Territorial (P*).
Stockton Yellow	Large flattened globe. Light yellow brown skin. White flesh. Mildly pungent.	Fall.	Spring to early summer. 194 days.	Poor.	Intermediate.	Open-pollinated. Very productive. Non-bolting. Pink root tolerant.	Lockhart (S).

Variety	Description	Planting	Maturity	Storage	Day length	Notes	Sources
Stuttgarter *Yellow Stuttgarter*	Large flattened globe. Glossy pale brown skin. Crisp, tasty, pungent flavor.	Sets late winter to spring.	120 days.	Good.	Long.	Very resistant to running to seed in unfavourable weather. Good yields. Good for bunching.	Jung's (St), Pinetree (St*), Thompson & Morgan (St), Vesey's (St*).
Sweet Flat Red	Large flattened globe. Red skin. White and red flesh. Sweet flavor.	Plants late winter to spring.	Summer.	Poor.	Short.	Good for southern and mid-west gardens.	Dixondale Farms (P*), Jung's (P).
Sweet Sandwich Hybrid	Very large, slightly flattened globe. Pale brown skin. Creamy white flesh. Pungent when harvested, very mild after storage.	Plant inside in late winter or outside in early spring.	112 days.	Good.	Long.	Hybrid. Very sweet and crisp after 6–8 weeks storage. Can eat raw like an apple.	Garden City (S), Jung's (S), Pinetree (S), Thompson & Morgan (S).
Tarmagon	Globe with squarish shoulders. Golden brown skins.	Plant inside late winter. Direct seed Apr. to May.	76 days.	Poor to medium.	Long.	Hybrid. Early maturing.	Stokes (S).
Texas 1015Y Supersweet	Very large tall globes. Yellow skins. Pearly white flesh. Very mild sweet flavor.	Plants in spring.	Fall.	Medium.	Short.	Can get as big as softballs. Good for southern and mid-west gardens. Disease resistant.	Dixondale Farms (P*), Jung's (P).
Texas Grano 502 PRR	Large, top shaped. Straw-yellow thin dry skin. White, soft, mildly pungent flavor.	Fall.	Early spring. 168 days.	Poor.	Short.	Open pollinated. Pink root resistant.	Lockhart (S).
Torque	Globe shape. Copper skins. Firm flesh.	Sow Mar. Transplant mid-May.	Mid-Aug. and later. 95 days.	Good.	Long.	Hybrid. Matures quickly. Some disease tolerance. Good for heavier soils. Uniform, good yield.	Pinetree (S).
Valiant	Huge globe.	Inside in Jan. to Feb. Transplant early spring. Outdoors by mid-Apr.	Oct.	Good.	Long.	Hybrid. Fusarium tolerant.	Stokes (S).
Vaquero	Very large globe. Dark yellow skin. White flesh. Crisp, mild flavor.	Early spring.	Late summer or fall. 122 days.	Medium.	Long.	Hybrid. High-yielding Spanish type. Very tolerant to pink root and fusarium.	Lockhart (S).
Vega	Very large globe. Light brown skin. Mildly pungent.	Early spring.	Late summer or fall. 120 days.	Medium to good.	Long.	Hybrid. Performs well under adverse weather conditions.	Lockhart (S).
Vidalia Sweet *Sweet Apple onions*	Thick fat bulbs. Yellow skin. Very sweet and juicy flesh.	Fall.	Spring, summer.	Poor.	Short.	Early maturing. Good for southern growers.	Shepherd's (P*).

Appendix 3.3　Onion Cultivars continued

Cultivar Name (other names in italics)	Description	When to Plant	When to Harvest	Keeping Qualities	**Day length	Other Comments	Suppliers (see also Appendix 4) S = seed St = sets P = plants
Walla Walla Sweet / *Giant Walla Walla*	Large flattened globe. Yellow skin. Yellowy white flesh. Very mild flavor.	Fall or early spring. Plants early spring.	Fall: 300 days. Spring: 125 days. From seedlings: 75–80 days.	Poor.	Intermediate to long.	Open pollinated. Exceptionally mild. Delicious fresh or baked. Bulbs tend to be more pungent from spring sowing.	Deep Diversity (S), Dixondale Farms (P*), Garden City (S), Gourmet Gardener (S), Johnny's (S), Jung's (S, P), Lockhart (S), PSR (S, P), Pinetree (S), Shepherds (P*), Territorial (S, P*), Thompson & Morgan (S).
White Bermuda / *Crystal Wax*	Thick flattened globe. Thin white skin. White flesh. Very mild flavor.	Plants in spring.	Fall. 90 days.	Poor.	Short.	An old favorite. Grows best in southern regions.	Dixondale Farms (P*).
White Ebenezer	White skin. White flesh. Mild and sweet flavor.	Sets in early spring.	Fall.	Medium.	Long.	Excellent for cooking.	Garden City (St*), Pinetree (St*).
White Granex / *Miss Society, White Vidalia*	Thick flattened globe. White skin. White mild flesh.	Plants early spring.	Fall.	Poor.	Short.	Hybrid. The same as Yellow Granex except for the color.	Dixondale Farms (P—Jan.–May).
White Keeper	Round globe. Pale white skin. White firm flesh.	Early spring.	Fall. 105 days.	Medium.	Long.	Hybrid. Bred from Sweet Spanish and Southport White Globe.	Pinetree (S).
White Sweet Spanish / *White Spanish*	Large globe, up to 3 lbs. Pure white skin. White flesh. Mildly pungent flavor.	Inside in Jan. to Feb. Transplant early spring.	Sept. 110 to 120 days.	Good.	Long.	Open pollinated. Identical to Sweet Spanish except white. Good for northern gardens. Excellent for fried onion rings.	DeGiorgi (S), Dixondale Farms (P*), Pinetree (S), Stokes (S).
White Sweet Spanish Jumbo / *Giant White Sweet Spanish*	Very large globe to deep globe. White flesh. Crisp, mildly pungent.	Early spring.	Late summer or fall. 130 days.	Medium to good.	Long.	Open pollinated. Adapted to western U.S. High yielding. Tolerant to thrips.	Jung's (P), Lockhart (S).
Yellow Ebenezer / *Ebenezer*	Medium to large flattened globe. Yellow brown skin. Yellowy white flesh. Medium pungency.	Late winter to spring (sets).	Mid-summer onwards. About 110 days.	Good.	Long.	Open-pollinated. Introduced in 1906 from Japan. Good cultivar for sets.	Southern Exposure (S), Thompson & Morgan (St).
Yellow Globe / *Golden Globe*	Medium globular bulb. Brownish-yellow skin. Firm and pungent.	Early spring.	Mid-season. 114 days.	Medium.	Long.	Very productive. No thick necks. Good for green onions.	DeGiorgi (S), Pinetree (St*).

Cultivar Name	Description	When to Plant	When to Harvest	Keeping Qualities		Other Comments	Suppliers
Granex, Maui, Noonday	Thin yellow skin. White flesh. Crunchy, mild and sweet flavor.	to Mar.	days.	medium.		to bolting and pink root. Eat raw in salads and sandwiches.	(P*), Lockhart (S), Southern Exposure (S).
Yellow Rock	Light tan skin.			Good.		Open pollinated. Low tendency to neck rot.	Garden City (St*).
Yellow Spanish Hybrid	Large globe. Straw-yellow skin. Pure white flesh. Tender, sweet and mild.	Early spring.	100 days.	Medium to good.	Long.	Big Mac hybrid strain. Easy to grow. Good pink root tolerance.	Jung's (S).
Yellow Sweet Spanish *Yellow Spanish*	Large globe. Dark yellow skin. Creamy white flesh. Mildly pungent flavor.	Early spring.	110 days.	Medium to good.	Long.	Open pollinated. Withstands unfavorable growing conditions better than many varieties. Good for northern gardens. Good for fried onion rings. Can be used for bunching when young.	DeGiorgi (S), Dixondale Farms (P*), Southern Exposure (S).
Yellow Sweet Spanish Utah Jumbo	Large globe to deep globe. Dark yellow skin. White flesh. Mildly pungent flavor.	Early spring.	Late summer or fall. 130 days.	Medium to good.	Long.	Open pollinated. Late maturing. High yielding. Tolerant to thrips and mildew.	Lockhart (S).
Yellow Sweet Spanish Hybrid	Large globe. Creamy white flesh. Tender mild and sweet.	Plants in spring.	Summer to fall.	Medium.	Long.	Hybrid. Often reach over 1 lb in weight.	Jung's (P).
Yula	Large flattened globe. Thin neck. Golden straw skin. White flesh. Mildly pungent flavor.	Fall.	Late spring to early summer. 200 days.	Good.	Intermediate to long.	Hybrid. Early, high yields of uniform bulbs. Good tolerance to pink root.	Lockhart (S).

**Short day cultivars are suited to regions south of 32°N. Intermediate day cultivars to regions between 32° and 40°N. Long day cultivars should be planted in regions north of 36°N.

Pickling, Pearl or Baby Onion Cultivars

Cultivar Name (other names in italics)	Description	When to Plant	When to Harvest	Keeping Qualities	Other Comments	Suppliers
Early Aviv	Flattened globe up to 5 cm (2 in) diam. Bulb silvery white with thin green markings.	Spring and summer.	Summer and fall. Up to 78 days after harvesting.	Poor.	Very early. Developed by Israeli breeders. Eat baked, boiled, fried.	Shepherd's (S).
Borettana Italian Cipollini *Cipollini*	Flat bulb resembles a button. 2 in diam, 1 in thick. Satiny rose-bronze skin. White, firm, fine-grained flesh. Good flavor.	Early spring.	120 days.	Good.	Long day heirloom cultivar. Traditionally served whole and braised or pickled.	Shepherd's (S).
Pompeii *Pompeii Perla Prima*	Round miniature bulb. Thin necked. Skinless, pure white flesh. Mild flavor.	Early to mid-spring.	Young as scallions or 75 days once rounded out.	Poor.	Gourmet. Excellent cocktail onions.	Seeds Trust (S), Stokes (S).
Purplette	Glossy rich burgundy skin. Pink when cooked. Delicate flavor.	Spring.	Young as purple scallions or 60 days as small golf balls.	Poor.	Tasty, versatile and easy to grow.	Johnny's (S), Seeds Trust (S).

Pickling, Pearl or Baby Onion Cultivars continued

Cultivar Name (other names in italics)	Description	When to Plant	When to Harvest	Keeping Qualities	Other Comments	Suppliers
Snow Baby	Round mini-onion. Waxy white appearance.	Spring.	Late spring, mid-summer. 57 days.	Poor.	Good for freezing, canning and pickling.	Johnny's (S).
White Barletta *Barletta*	Globe shape. Slightly flattened top and bottom. Narrow neck. Pure white skins. Crisp, mild flavor.	Early to mid-spring.	70–90 days after planting.	Poor.	Perfect for pickling, freezing and cooking.	Stokes (S), Vesey's (S).

Spring (or Bunching) Onion Cultivars

See Appendix 3.5 for more bunching onions.

Cultivar Name	Description	When to Plant	When to Harvest	Other Comments	Suppliers
Beltsville Bunching	Long stems. Slight bulbing. Tender, crisp and mild flavor.	Spring, summer and fall in warmer regions.	Start about 60 days after planting.	A *cepa-fistulosum* cultivar. Tolerates hot dry conditions.	Stokes (S), Vesey's (S).
Long White Summer Bunching	Long white stems to 18 cm (7 in). Non-bulbing. Upright dark green leaves.	Spring, summer.	About 60 days.	Improved Nebuka type. Tolerant to pink root and fusarium.	Stokes (S).
Southport White (green bunching strain)	Mild sweet flavor.	Spring.	65 days.	A *cepa* cultivar. Used only to produce green bunching onions.	Stokes (S).
Southport White Globe		Spring.	65 days.	A *cepa* cultivar. May be used for green bunching, or left to develop globes.	Stokes (S).
White Knight	Long white stems. Small bulbs. Medium–tall dark green tops.	Spring, summer.	60 days. Harvest before the bulbs swell too much.	Widely adapted. Good tolerance to some strains of pink root.	Lockhart (S), Stokes (S).
White Lisbon	Long white stems. Tender juicy green tops. Mild sweet flavor. Crisp texture.		50–65 days.	A *cepa* cultivar. Very fast growing and grows well in a variety of soils and conditions.	Shepherd's (S), Territorial (S), Thompson & Morgan (S).
White Sweet Spanish	White stems. Dark green foliage.	Spring.	75 days after planting, or leave to mature for white globe onion.	A *cepa* cultivar. Uniform stems. Sow thickly for bunching onions.	Stokes (S).
White Sweet Spanish Valencia	Long white stems. Dark green foliage.			A *cepa* cultivar. Doesn't tend to bulb.	Lockhart (S).
Winter White Bunching	Medium white stems. Slightly bulbier than some others.	Late Aug. or spring to summer.	Late May or summer to fall. About 60 days.	A *cepa* cultivar. Excellent for overwintering.	Thompson & Morgan (S).

Some seed companies sell bunching or spring onions under descriptive names which are not cultivar names; for example, scallion, spring onion, salad slim and spring salad. They are all good sources of spring onions and can be planted and harvested most of the year.

Appendix 3.4   Shallot Cultivars

Cultivar Name	Description	When to Plant (S = seed, B = bulb)	Harvest	Keeping Qualities	Comments	Supplier*
Atlas	Browny red skin. Pinkish-red flesh.	Direct seed in winter in mild regions. Early spring where winters are cold. S	Late spring to late summer.	Medium.	Early maturity. Widely adapted.	Johnny's.
Creation Hybrid	Yellowy brown skin. White mild flesh.	Sow direct outside from Feb. to late Apr. S	Matures a month later than shallots grown from bulbs.	Good.	Less prone to virus. Rarely bolts. Use thinnings in salad. Does best in more northern regions.	Johnny's, Thompson & Morgan.
De Jersey	Long tapered bulb up to 10 cm (4 in) long. Rose blush tan skin. Mild but slightly pungent flavor.	Sow direct outside from Feb. to late Apr. S	Aug. and Sept. 110–140 days.	Poor.	Very old French variety. Only produces 1 bulb per plant.	Pinetree.
French	Copper-colored skin. Sweet flavor.	Spring or fall in mild climates. B	About 80 days.	Good.		Shepherd's, Territorial.
French Red Shallot	Bulbs 2½–5 cm (1–2 in) diam. Each bulb produces 6–8. Reddish-pink skin. Purpley pink flesh. Sweet flavor.	Late winter to early spring. B	About 90 days.	Medium.	Also harvested as green 'scallions'. Widely adapted.	Southern Exposure.
Golden Gourmet	Round. Golden brown skins. Each bulb produces 5–6. Firm, crisp and crunchy.	Late winter to early spring. B	Early. 77 days.	Very good.	High yields.	Thompson & Morgan.
Odetta's White Shallot	Rounded bulbs up to 3 cm (1.25 in) diam. Pure white skin. Mild delicate flavor.	Late winter, spring. B	Mid to late summer.	Medium.	Pre-1900 heirloom from Kansas. Grown for 'scallions', green tops, pickling. Widely adapted.	Southern Exposure.
Red	Round with dark red skins. Each bulb divides into many. White flesh with pink rings. Good flavor.	Late winter to early spring. B	Early. 70 days after planting.	Very good.	High yields.	Thompson & Morgan.

*Jung's, Pinetree and Redwood City supply bulbs of unnamed shallot cultivars, while Gourmet Garden supplies seed of an unnamed French cultivar.

Appendix 3.5   Welsh (or Bunching) Onion Cultivars

See *Allium cepa*, Bunching onions, for more bunching onions.

Cultivar Name (other names in italics)	Description and Shape	When to Plant	When to Harvest	Other Comments	Suppliers (see also Appendix 4)
Asagi Bunching	Tender soft short stems. 1 plant will produce about 6 stems. Crisp, mild flavor.	Spring and summer.	Fall. Yellows in winter.	Very high yielding. Used in salads and soups.	DeGiorgi.
Beltsville Bunching	Long smooth white stems. Slight bulbing. Tender flesh. Crisp mild flavor.	Spring, summer and fall in warmer regions.	Start about 60 days after planting.	A *cepa-fistulosum* hybrid. Tolerates hot dry conditions better than many. Resistant to pink root, smut, and thrips. Widely adapted.	Stokes, Vesey's.
Bunching Evergreen Hardy *Evergreen Bunching Nebuka*, *Evergreen Hardy*, *Evergreen Hardy White*, *Hardy White Bunching*.	Long slender crisp white stems. Non-bulbing. Long greens. 1 plant produces up to 10 stems. Tender flesh. Mild flavor	Spring or fall.	About 65 days.	An improved strain of He Shi Ko. Exceptionally hardy. Leave in ground all year. Resistant to thrips, smut and pink root.	Degiorgi, Garden City, Johnny's, Seeds Trust, Southern Exposure, Stokes.
Bunching Select	Long white stems. Dark green leaves. Tender flesh.	Spring and summer.	About 60.	Good uniformity. Good tolerance to pink root.	Lockhart.
Common Bunching	Plants about 60 cm (2 ft) tall. White stems to 20 cm (8 in). Mild flavor.	Spring.	About 65 days.	Use at any stage, good in salads or soups.	DeGiorgi.
Emerald Isle	Long white bulbless stems. Medium green strong straight tops. Tender flesh. Mild flavor.	Spring and summer.	64 days.	Heat tolerant.	Stokes.
He Shi Ko *Evergreen Bunching*	Long silver-white stem to 25 cm (10 in). Bulbless. Tender and mildly pungent.	Spring or fall.	Fall or spring.	Divides into a clump so can be perennial. Heat and cold tolerant.	Pinetree.
Ishikura *Ishikura Bunching*	Long thick white stems. Can reach 2½ cm (1 in) diam. Single stem type. Upright pale blue-green leaves. Tender distinctive flavor.	Spring and summer.	About 65 days.	Does not form bulbs, harvest from pencil size to carrot size. Not winter hardy.	Deep Diversity, Stokes, Thompson & Morgan.
Kincho	Long slim uniform white stems. Single stem type. Tender flesh. Mildly pungent.	Spring, summer, autumn.	Late summer, fall or over winter. 75 days.	Winter hardy in Southern Ontario, New York, Ohio, New Jersey. Good uniformity.	Stokes.
Long White Summer Bunching	Long white stems to 18 cm (7 in). Non-bulbing. Upright dark green leaves.	Spring and summer.	About 60 days.	Improved nebuka* type. Tolerant to pink root and fusarium.	Stokes.

Appendix 3.5   Welsh (or Bunching) Onion Cultivars continued

Cultivar Name (other names in italics)	Description and Shape	When to Plant	When to Harvest	Other Comments	Suppliers (see also Appendix 4)
Long White Tokyo *Tokyo Long White*	Long upright single stems to 46 cm (18 in) with almost no bulb. Dark blue-green leaves. Tender and tasty.	Spring and summer.	About 75 days.	Well suited to summer or fall bunching. Not very winter hardy. Resistant to thrip, pink root and smut.	Stokes, Vesey's.
Red Beard	46 cm (18 in) red stems with small white bases. Non-bulbing. Dark green leaves. Mild, crisp, very tender.	Spring and summer.	60–75 days.	Fast germinating. Imported from France.	Gourmet Gardener, Stokes.
Santa Clause	Rose red medium stems. Delicate distictive flavour.	Spring and summer.	6 weeks to 3 months after sowing.	Can be grilled to sweeten. Red color intensifies with cold.	Thompson & Morgan.
White Spear	Thick white cylindrical stems. 13–15 cm (5–6 in) long. Blue-green, tall, upright leaves.	Spring.	60 days.	Not as hardy as Bunching Evergreen Hardy. Stands up well to heat. Resistant to pink root.	Southern Exposure.

*The term 'nebuka' used in connection with welsh onions refers to the long white stem and is used to describe cultivars which have this characteristic. It should not be used as a cultivar name on its own.

Appendix 4 Stockists of Alliums

Most of the information in this chart and the charts in Appendix 3 has been compiled from suppliers' catalogs. The common and cultivar names of the plants listed are those used by the supplier. Bunching onions marked with * are probably *cepa-fistulosum* cultivars rather than *A. cepa* cultivars.

Supplier	*Allium ampeloprasum*	*Allium cepa*	*Allium sativum* Garlic	*Allium fistulosum* Welsh onion	Other alliums
Deep Diversity P.O. Box 15189, Santa Fe, New Mexico, 87506 5189. A planetary gene pool resource and service. Seed of rare and unusual herbs, vegetables, flowers, grasses and many others. Catalog available—send postage.	**Leek** Giant Carentan, Kajak, Lyon, St. Victor, Winter Giant, Mixed.	**Common onion** Seed—Grandpa Schneider's Red, James Longkeeper, Milanese Red, Red Wethersfield, Ruby, Southport White Globe, Walla Walla Sweet. **Spring (or Bunching) Onion** (See also *A. fistulosum*.)	Unnamed top-setting cultivar. Cloves and bulbils.	Ishikura.	Chives, Garlic chives, Mountain garlic (*A. senescens*)
DeGiorgi Seed Company 6011 'N' Street, Omaha, Nebraska, 68117 1634. Tel (800) 858 2580 (orders) or (402) 731 3901 (information), Fax (402) 731 8475. Seeds or flowers, herbs, vegetables. Books and garden supplies.	**Leek** Giant Musselburg.	**Common onion** Seed—Bermuda Yellow, Crystal White Wax, Early Yellow Globe, Lisbon White, Red Wethersfield, Southport Red Globe, Southport White Globe, White Sweet Spanish, Yellow Globe, Yellow Sweet Spanish. **Spring (or Bunching) onion** (See also *A. fistulosum*.) Common Bunching*.	German Red.	Asagi Bunching, Bunching Evergreen Hardy, Common Bunching.	Chives, Garlic chives.
Dixondale Farms P.O. Box 127, Carrizo Springs, Texas, 78834. Tel (210) 876 2430, Fax (210) 876 9640. Onion plants to U.S., Alaska and Hawaii. Free Catalog.		**Common onion** Plants—First Edition, Sweet Flat Red, Texas 1015Y Supersweet, Walla Walla Sweet, White Bermuda, White Granex, White Sweet Spanish, Yellow Granex, Yellow Sweet Spanish.			
Filaree Farm/Filaree Productions 182 Conconully Hwy, Okanogan, Washington, 98840. Tel. (509) 422 6940. Garlic bulbs, books.			The biggest range of garlic varieties in the U.S.A.		

Garden City Seeds
778 Hwy 93, North Hamilton, Montana, 59840.
Tel (406) 961 4837,
Fax (406) 961 4877.
E-mail: gdnctyds@cyberport.net
'Montana Hardy Seeds' of heirloom, organic vegetables, flowers and herbs. Also roots, bulbs and tubers, garden supplies, pest controls, books and much more.

Common onion Seed—Copra F1, New York Early, Southport Red Globe, Sweet Sandwich Hybrid, Walla Walla Sweet. Sets—Southport Red Globe, White Ebenezer, Yellow Rock.
Dixon Strain, Inchelium Red, Montana Roja, 'Roja' Spanish Red.
Spring (or Bunching) onion (See also *A. fistulosum.*)
Bunching Evergreen Hardy.
Chives, Garlic chives.
Leeks Giant Carentan, King Richard.

The Gourmet Gardener
8650 College Blvd, Overland Park, Kansas, 66210-1806.
Tel (913) 345 0490,
Fax (913) 451 2443.
Internet address:
http://metroux.metrobbs.com/tgg/
Over 150 hard-to-find herbs, vegetables, and edible flower seeds from world-wide sources to U.S. and Canada. Also gifts and books.

Common onion Red Simiane, Walla Walla Sweet.
Inchelium Red (not outside U.S.A.)
Spring (or Bunching) onion Red beard*.
Red Beard.
Other French Shallots (seed).
Chives, Garlic chives.
Leeks Alaska, King Richard.

Johnny's Selected Seed
Foss Hill Rd, Albion, Maine, 04910.
Tel (207) 437 4301,
Fax (207) 437 2165.
Seed breeders, growers and merchants of vegetables, herbs and flowers. Also farm and specialty seed, books, tools and equipment.

Common onion Ailsa Craig, Buffalo F1, Copra F1, Mambo F1, New York Early, Prince F1, Redman, Walla Walla Sweet.
German Extra Hardy, New York White.
Spring (or Bunching) onion (See also *A. fistulosum.*) White Spear*.
Bunching Evergreen Hardy, New York White.
Pearl onion Purplette, Snow Baby.
Other Atlas and Creation Shallots (seed), French Shallots (bulb).
Chives, Garlic chives.
Leeks King Richard, Laura, Pancho, Varna.
Other Elephant garlic.

Appendix 4   Stockists of Alliums continued

Supplier	*Allium ampeloprasum*	*Allium cepa*	*Allium sativum* Garlic	*Allium fistulosum* Welsh onion	Other alliums
J.W. Jung Seed Co. 335 S. High St, Randolph, Wisconsin, 53957. Tel (414) 326 3121, Fax (414) 326 5769. Quality seeds, plants, garden gifts and bulbs. Spring, and Summer and Fall catalogs free.	**Leeks** American Flag. **Other** Elephant garlic.	**Common onion** Seed—Early Yellow Globe, First Edition Hybrid, Red Burgermaster F1, Southport Red Globe, Sweet Sandwich Hybrid, Walla Walla, Yellow Spanish Hybrid. Sets—Red Sets, Stuttgarter. Plants—First Edition Hybrid, Giant White Sweet Spanish Jumbo, Hybrid Yellow, Sweet Flat Red, Sweet Spanish Hybrid, Texas 1015Y Supersweet, Walla Walla Sweet. **Spring (or Bunching) onion** (See also *A. fistulosum*.) **Other** Shallots, Multiplier onion (Tree onion).	California White.	Evergreen Bunching.	Chives, Garlic chives, *Allium giganteum, Allium sphaerocephalum.*
Lockhart Seeds Inc. P.O. Box 1361, 3 North Wilson Way, Stockton, California, 95205. Tel (209) 466 4401 Vegetables for commercial and home growers, latest hybrids, old favorites, oriental, highest quality.	**Leeks** Large American Flag. **Other** Elephant garlic (California only).	**Common onion** Seed—Blanco Duro, Blizzard, Candy, Cimmaron, Early Red Burger, Early Supreme, Fiesta, Fresno White, Italian Red Torpedo, Red Creole, Red Granex, Ruby, Southport Red Globe, Spano, Stockton Early Red, Stockton Early Yellow, Stockton Red, Stockton Yellow, Texas Grano 502 PRR, Vaquero, Vega, Walla Walla Sweet, White Sweet Spanish Jumbo, Yellow Granex, Yellow Sweet Spanish Utah Jumbo, Yula. Sets—Red, Yellow and White (California only). Plants—Fresno White, Italian Red Torpedo, Stockton Early Red, Stockton Early Yellow (California only). **Spring (or Bunching) onion** (See also *A. fistulosum*.) Bunching Select, White Knight, White Spanish Valencia. **Other** Shallot bulbs (California only).	Italian Red, Pink (late), White (early)—all to California only.	Bunching Select.	Chives.

Supplier	Allium species	Chives	Welsh onion	Garlic	Common onion	Spring (or Bunching) onion	Pearl onion	Leeks
McClure & Zimmerman — Quality Flowerbulb Brokers, 108 W. Winnebago St, P.O. Box 368, Friesland, Wisconsin, 53935. Tel (414) 326 4220, Fax—toll free (800) 692 5864. Bulbs, corms, tubers, rootstocks, books.	A. cernuum, A. chinense, A. giganteum, A. neopolitanum, A. roseum, A. sphaerocephalum, A. triquetrum.							
Pinetree Garden Seeds — Box 300, New Gloucester, Maine, 04260. Tel 207 926 3400, Fax 207 926 3886. Specialises in a large variety, over 750 vegetable, herb, flower and everlasting seeds. Also bulbs, tubers, plants, gardening supplies and books. Catalog, USA free, overseas $1.50.		Chives, Garlic chives.	He Ski Ko.	Garlic—unnamed cultivar.	**Common Onion** Seed—Ailsa Craig, Blanco Duro, Early Yellow Globe, Red Burgermaster F1, Red Simiane, Southport Red Globe, Sweet Sandwich Hybrid, Torque, Walla Walla Sweet, White Keeper, White Sweet Spanish. Sets—Yellow Globe, Red Wethersfield, Stuttgarter, White Ebenezer. **Other** Shallot: De Jersey, unnamed cultivar; Tree onion.			Furor, Hivor, King Richard, Large American Flag.
PSR—Peters Seed Research — 407 Maranatha Le, Myrtle Creek, Oregon, 97457. Non-hybrid seed of unusual varieties of vegetables and some flowers. Books.					**Common onion** Ailsa Craig, Burrell's Yellow Valencia, Stockton Early Red, Walla Walla. (All also available as transplants).			Bulgarian Triumph, Durabel, Splendid. (All also available as transplants).
The Redwood City Seed Company — P.O. Box 361, Redwood City, California, 94064. Tel (415) 325 7333. Endangered cultivated plants, vegetables, herbs, wildflowers. Also books. To USA, Canada and Mexico.		Chives, Garlic chives.	Welsh onion.	California White, Purple.		**Spring (or Bunching) onion** (See also A. fistulosum.) Lungo d'Inverno. **Other** Shallots.		
Seeds Trust: High Altitude Gardening — P.O. Box 1048, Hailey, Idaho, 83333. Tel (208) 788 4363, Fax (208) 788 3452. Organic, classic and heirloom seeds of vegetables, flowers, herbs. Also books, tools, etc.		Chives, Garlic chives.	Bunching Evergreen Hardy.			**Spring (or Bunching) onion** (See also A. fistulosum.)	**Pearl onion** Pompeii, Purplette.	King Richard.

Appendix 4   Stockists of Alliums continued

Supplier	Allium ampeloprasum	Allium cepa	Allium sativum Garlic	Allium fistulosum Welsh onion	Other alliums
Shepherd's Garden Seeds Shipping Office, 30 Irene St, Torrington, Connecticut, 06790-6627. Tel (203) 482 3638, Fax (203) 482 0532. Unusual selection of quality seeds for home gardeners. Free catalog.	**Leeks** Otina, St. Victor.	**Common onion** Seed—Borettana Italian Cipollini, White Lisbon. Plants—Stockton Red, Vidalia Sweet (for southern gardeners), Walla Walla Sweet. Also southern and northern Rainbow Onion collections. **Pearl onion** Early Aviv, Borettana Italian Cipollini. **Other** French Shallot.	Gilroy, Italian Purple Skin.		Chives, Garlic chives.
Southern Exposure Seed Exchange P.O. Box 170, Earlysville, Virginia, 22936. Tel (804) 973 4703, Fax (804) 973 8717. Over 450 varieties of open-pollinated, heirloom and traditional varieties of vegetables, sunflowers, flowers and herbs. Also books, gardening supplies, seed saving supplies and information. Catalog—send postage.	**Leeks** Large American Flag. **Other** Elephant Garlic.	**Common onion** Early Yellow Globe, Yellow Ebenezer, Yellow Granex, Yellow Sweet Spanish. **Spring (or Bunching) onion** (See also *A. fistulosum.*) White Spear*. **Other** Potato onion (yellow); French Red Shallot, Odetta's White Shallot; Tree onions: Abermarle Egyptian, Moritz Egyptian, Norris Egyptian.	Brown Tempest, Chesnock Red, Chet's Italian Purple, German Red, Inchelium Red, Lorz Italian, Machashi, Mild French Silverskin, Red Toch, Romanian Red, Spanish Roja, Yugoslavian.	Bunching Evergreen Hardy White, White Spear.	Chives, Garlic chives.
Stokes P.O. Box 10, St Catharines, Ontario, L2R 6R6 Order toll free 1 800 263 7233, Customer service (905) 688 4300, Fax (905) 684 8411. Quality flower and vegetable seed. Free catalog. Canadian and American edition in English, Canadian edition in French.	**Leeks** Alaska, Arcona, Arkansas, Splendid, Titan, Unique.	**Common onions** Bingo, Canada Maple, Capable, Celebrity, Copper King, Copra F1, Duration, Early Yellow Globe, Eskimo, Experimental 6404, Gringo, Joint Venture, Kelsae Sweet Spanish, Legacy, Lucifer, Mars, New York Early, Nordic, Norstar, Northern Oak, Ringmaker, Riverside Sweet Spanish, Tarmagon, Valiant, White Sweet Spanish. **Spring (or Bunching) onion** (See also *A. fistulosum.*) Beltsville Bunching, Long White Summer Bunching*, Red Beard*, Southport White, Southport White Globe, White Knight, White Lisbon, White Sweet Spanish. **Pearl Onion** Pompeii Perla Prima, White Barletta.		Beltsville Bunching, Bunching Evergreen Hardy, Emerald Isle, Hardy White Bunching, Ishikura, Kincho, Long White Summer Bunching, Long White Tokyo, Red Beard.	Chives, Garlic chives.

Supplier	Common onion / Leeks / Other		Chives
Territorial Seed Company P.O. Box 157, 20 Palmer Avenue, Cottage Grove, Oregon, 97424. Tel (541) 942 9547 Fax (541) 942 9881. Vegetables, flowers, herbs, accessories for year round gardening. Free winter and spring catalogs.	**Common onion** Seed—Blanco Duro, Brahma F1, Buffalo F1, Copra F1, Early Yellow Globe, Hi-Ball F1, Red Burgermaster F1, Redman, Simcoe F1, Stockton Early Red, Walla Walla Sweet. Plants—First Edition, Stockton Red, Walla Walla. **Spring (or Bunching) onion** White Lisbon. **Other** French Shallot. **Leeks** Durabel, Splendid, Varna. **Other** Elephant garlic.	Italian Late, Korean Red, Romanian Red, Silver Rose, Spanish Roja.	Chives, Garlic chives.
Thompson & Morgan Inc. P.O. Box 1308, Jackson, New Jersey, O8527-0308 Tel (908) 363 2225, Fax (908) 363 9356. Order Toll Free: (800) 274 7333, 24 hours a day, 7 days a week.	**Common onion** Seed—First Edition (Sleeping Onion), Giant Walla Walla Sweet, Lancastrian, Red Baron, Sweet Sandwich Hybrid. Sets—Yellow Ebenezer, Stuttgarter. Sets from seed—Jet Set Hybrid. **Spring (or Bunching) onion** (See also *A. fistulosum*.) White Lisbon, Winter White Bunching. **Other** Seed—Creation Hybrid Shallot. Bulbs—Golden Gourmet Shallot, Red Shallot. **Leeks** Autumn Giant 2-Argenta, King Richard, Toledo. **Other** Elephant Garlic.	Ishikura, Santa Clause, Winter White Bunching.	Chives, Garlic chives.
Vesey's Seeds Ltd. York, P.O. Box 9000, Charlottetown, Prince Edward Island, Canada, C1A 8K6. Tel (902) 368 7333, Toll-free 1 (800) 363 7333, Fax (902) 566 1620. Seeds for short seasons. Vegetables, herbs and flowers. Gardening Aids. Free catalog to USA and Canada.	**Common onion** Seeds—Cannon, Early Pak, Norstar. Sets—Jet Set Hybrid, Stuttgarter, Spanish. **Spring (or Bunching) onion** (See also *A. fistulosum*.) Beltsville Bunching. **Pearl onion** White Barletta. **Leeks** Giant Musselburgh.	Beltsville Bunching, Long White Tokyo.	Chives, Garlic chives.

Every effort was made to contact as many seed suppliers as possible. All those who responded have been included in this listing. Any supplier who was not included but would like to be in future editions should contact the author c/o Hyland House Publishing.

Recipe Index

Index

To

....

HAPPY EASTER

Love

....

THE EASTER BUNNY
is coming to
OREGON

Written by Eric James   Illustrated by Mari Lobo

 sourcebooks
wonderland

The sweet Easter Bunny
is skipping along,
heading through Oregon
singing this song:

OREGON TRAIL TOYS

OPEN

Beaver
State
Easter
Parade
TODAY!

"The eggs are delivered.
My Easter job's done.
And now it is time
that I joined in the fun!"

She jumps down a tunnel
that runs underground,
and pops up again
in each city and town.

Hillsboro, Corvallis,
Pendleton, too.
I bet there's a tunnel
that's very near you!

HAPPY

In Portland young children
have smiles on their faces,
and eggs decorated
like people and places!

WESTERN
MEADOWLARK
PARK

But one little boy
drops the egg from his hands.
A loud **CRACKING** sound
can be heard as it lands.

"Oh dear!" says the bunny,
and dabs at a tear.
"You need cheering up
so thank goodness I'm here!"

She wiggles her ears,
she hops on the spot,
she waggles her tail,
and he giggles a lot!

In Salem, there is
an Easter parade.
Most children are clapping
but one looks afraid.

That clapping is noisy.
These legs are so TALL!
It's crowded and loud,
and she's ever so small!

"Gee whiz, what a din!
I know just what to do.
Come here little one
and I'll hold hands with you!"

She wiggles her ears,
and spins her around.
The little girl laughs
as her feet leave the ground!

Down in Eugene
while having a quick rest,
the bunny eats sweet Blackberry Pie.
(It's the best!)

Across in the park
there's an egg-rolling race.
A small boy falls down
and he's now lost his place!

The bunny trips up
as she's going to help.
She falls down the hill
with an OUCH and a YELP!

YELP!

OUCH!

She's just a big blur
as she tumbles on past.
The boy runs to help her.
He's going so FAST!

FINISH

She wiggles her ears,
he can't (but he tries!).
They hop up and down
for they've just won first prize!

In Beaverton, a girl's lost
her favorite stuffed bear.
Where could she have left him?
She's looked everywhere!

Oregon
Grape
Blossoms
just in!

"When I'm feeling sad
do you know what I do?
I hop up and down!
Do you want to try too?"

This day's been so busy
but also such fun.
The bunny daydreams
in the warm setting sun.

The twilight is coming,
the three chicks are lazing,
and tweeting about
how this day's been #AMAZING!

"Oregon's great
and we love being here.
We'll make lots more eggs
and we'll be back
next year!"

She wrinkles her nose,
she wiggles her ears,
she blows you a kiss,
and she just...disappears!

Written by Eric James
Illustrated by Mari Lobo
Additional artwork by Philip McIvor
Designed by Nicky Scott

Published by Sourcebooks Wonderland,
an imprint of Sourcebooks Kids
P.O. Box 4410, Naperville, Illinois 60567-4410
(630) 961-3900
sourcebookskids.com

Date of Production: August 2019
Run Number: 5015369
Printed and bound in China (1010)
10 9 8 7 6 5 4 3 2 1